Second Edition

Lines Lofting and Half Models

by

Walter J. Simmons

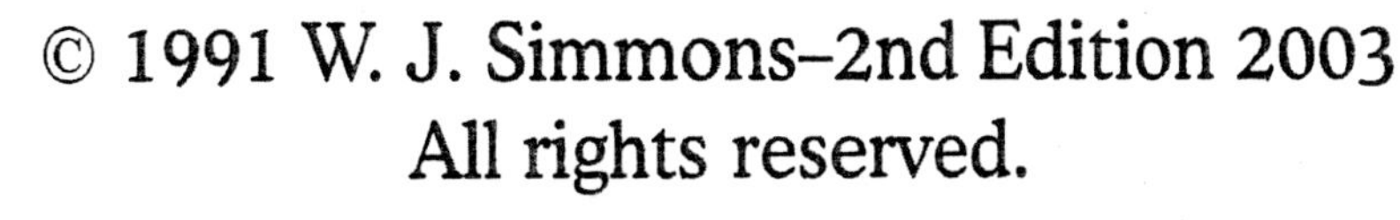

Duck Trap Press Lincolnville Beach, Maine

ISBN 0-924947-06-3

Table of Contents

Illustrations

Lines, Lofting, & Half Models
ISBN 0-924947-06-3
Second Edition 2003

Published by Duck Trap Press
P.O. Box 88 (Ducktrap Rd.)
Lincolnville Beach, Maine 04849

www.duck-trap.com

Introduction

Lines, lofting, and half models are so interrelated that I find it difficult to consider one without the others. They are all facets of boatbuilding, and all contribute to the understanding that keeps boatbuilding from being a hit or miss proposition. Together they make it possible for successive designers and builders to avail themselves of the work of their predecessors and verify their current work, so it in turn can be passed along to their successors.

There has probably been more written about the subject of lofting than any other aspect of boatbuilding. The most thorough discussions available to date have been found in Boatbuilding by Howard I. Chapelle and in Lofting by Alan Vaitses. What I have written here should not be construed as a detraction from their work, because what they wrote was well done. This book is intended to stand alone and should be considered an addition to their work as well as my own. I've read and worked from their books (as have many of those I taught), so I know from firsthand experience that further explanations are valuable to the point of necessity.

Until now, the connection between half models and lines and lofting has seldom been emphasized in print, and that connection is central to understanding what is otherwise a largely abstract concept. Learning is a cumulative discipline. Explaining lines and lofting without mentioning half models is working out of context and therefore becomes unnecessarily difficult if not impossible–frustrating in the very least.

The purpose of this book is to introduce you to half models so that the concept of lines and lofting can be viewed in context. Only in that way can you fully appreciate that lines, rather than being abstract, have a tangible basis in the form of half models. Unlike the lines of a plan, half models (like the boats built from them) are three-dimensional and so can be picked up, viewed from any angle, and measured. In the first section of this book, you can expect to learn their derivation and function, how to work with them, and even how to make half models of your own.

This book is arranged chronologically, as nearly as possible, so the second section deals with lines. Building plans are explained at length. You will learn what to look for as well as what to look out for, and how to interpret the information they provide. Explanations relate back to the half models and ahead to the lofting process. This section isn't wholly abstract either, and to that end, I have included a description of how to go about taking the lines off an existing boat so that you can draw your own plans.

The third section, and the longest, deals with lofting and its ramifications. If you consult the Table of Contents, you will see that it is broken down into individual operations. That makes for a little overlap here and there, but is offset by making it easier for the reader to turn right to a problem area for an immediate answer to a question. It begins with setting up your first lofting board and a preview of the entire operation. It continues all the way through to the expansion of a raking curved transom, and even discusses lofting the construction details you'll need.

At the end of the book you will find a glossary of over a hundred terms that you will encounter in your reading here and elsewhere, followed by a complete and detailed index. If you encounter an unfamiliar term, look it up then and there. Plenty of white space is included for your own notations, and it is comb bound so it will lie flat on your bench or lofting board within arm's reach. Those are the finishing touches to a book that has been designed more as a tool than a text.

"An expert", it is said, "is someone more than twenty miles from your home". Living here in the State of Maine, I guess I qualify as an expert on that score alone. But I learned this business in boatshops rather than in classrooms and by now have built and rebuilt well over 150 boats. (I've lost track of the actual number.) Some of them were in excess of 50', but most have been under 20' in length--the size of most boats being built today. During the course of those 22 years, I have also produced hundreds of half models and designed a dozen or more small craft, working day in and day out with the information needed most by beginning boatbuilders.

I have been sharing that information for years in print through books and articles as well as personally in our boatbuilding workshops. Since nearly every one of the hundreds who attended our workshops returned home to build their own boats, we were apparently doing something right. This book is written in the same manner in which I have taught for years; though here without time constraints, I have had the luxury of being able to explain in much greater detail. Those who use the information between these covers can become as adept as my apprentices in working with half models, plans, and lofting.

Walter J. Simmons
Lincolnville Beach, Maine
February 1991

Part 1: Half Models

THE BASICS

A discussion of half models is included here because they predate by centuries what we know today as “lines”. That in itself should serve to spark your interest, but even more important, the operations involved in making a half model–layout, carving, fairing, and measuring–are fundamental to both boat design and boatbuilding. Bear in mind that what was successful on the water years ago will be every bit as successful today. CAD (computer aided design) programs notwithstanding, all boat designs are based on something earlier. Today, sadly, half models are glossed over nearly everywhere outside of museums. Even in museums, with their vast array of models, both full-rigged and half-hull, visitors can become rapidly overwhelmed without a basic understanding of their application and importance.

First, why a “half” model when a full hull model would show you the entire hull? In a few instances a full model is helpful–mostly for advertizing and tank testing. Other than that, a half model is quite adequate for our purposes. Boatbuilders work with half models simply because the port and starboard halves of the boat are intended to be identical. There are some hulls that are intentionally asymmetrical, such as Venetian Gondolas and certain racing canoes. Those, of course, would require a full model or a mating pair of half models representing the port and starboard sides. Ultimately, the shape of the boat hull will depart slightly from this precise bilateral symmetry, but that is due to differing bending characteristics of hull members.

A half model, or more accurately, a half-hull model, is a deceptively simple looking tool. Long before the advent of the lines plan, the model was the final embodiment of a master builder’s new design. Under his planes and chisels and gouges his idea took form. Not only did the model provide verification of his idea, but when completed it would enable the prospective client to see the ultimate appearance of his boat. Further, that same model provided all pertinent information to the loftsman, who would then be able to work independently of the master in readying templates for the backbone and frames. Other members of the crew would use the model too: the cruiser, for determining how much timber he would have to locate for construction; the rigger for spar layout; the sparmakers, for location of mast steps and partners; and the planking boss, for the initial plank layout while the backbone was being readied.

All of this, of course, originated in the days when large wooden vessels were built, but the use of half models is by no means limited to large wooden craft nor to days gone by. Today, the construction of large steel vessels is usually accompanied by a whole series of

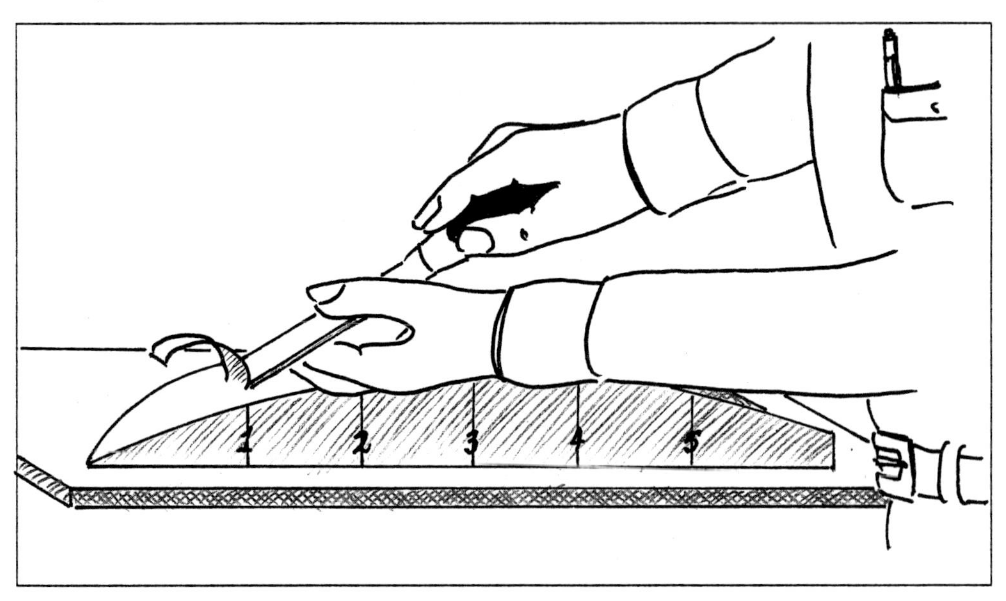

Carving a Half Model

models; what I would call a half model would be used as a plating model, and others would assist in interior layouts. But whatever its use, the model continues to serve its time-honored function: it provides a three-dimensional, scaled representation of the hull to be built. Once the concept is grasped, it tells even the beginning boatbuilder things that two-dimensional plans can never convey directly. It shows the overall fairness of the hull form. From that, a builder can determine whether indeed the hull can be planked and, if so, in what arrangement.

The best way to learn is by doing, so whether you intend to build a boat or not, the surest way is to make yourself a half model. As Pete Culler once observed, "Experience starts when you begin."

For your first attempt, the flow of the lines is really more important than absolute accuracy by measurement. In my estimation, model making becomes easier once you are accustomed to the carving operations involved. In subsequent models you should focus more on accuracy. For now, focus on tool handling and fair curves. That isn't to say that a neophyte is incapable of carving a fine half model on the very first attempt. I am simply suggesting this as a logical progression in learning how to carve a half model.

Whenever you decide to carve for accuracy of measurement as well as overall fairness, bear in mind that accuracy has three prerequisites: good clear wood for carving (white pine, basswood, or poplar, to name three), razor-sharp cutting tools, and probably most vital, the patience to see the job through to its proper completion. To be useful, a model should not only be accurate but also of a scale sufficiently large to be measured accurately–because as the scale decreases, your margin for error will increase. On models for boats of up to 20 feet in length, my preferred scale is 1-1/2" to 1 foot. That scale will yield a model large enough to be handled easily. It will also help later when you derive measurements from it, because you will be able to use any accurate ruler, not just a scale rule (1/8" on the model will be the equivalent of 1" on the lofting and the hull.).

When you come right down to it, the scale chosen for your model is really little more than a matter of preference. For example, a scale of 3/4" to 1' is just as readily measured with a standard rule, because every 1/16" on the model will be an inch on the lofting. I have a rather limited collection of folding two-foot rules, and most of them are calibrated not only in sixteenths, but also in twelfths (for reading 1" scale) and twenty-fourths (for reading 1/2" scale). The mere fact that they are calibrated for a variety of scales indicates that the 1-1/2" scale, though handy, is hardly universal.

Regardless of the scale you choose, remember this: the larger the scale, the smaller your chances for error. A 1/32" error on a 1-1/2" scale model amounts to a 1/4" error on the hull, while a 1/32" error on a model carved to 1/4" scale amounts to a 1-1/2" error on the hull–an error six times as great. That's a pretty good argument in favor of using the larger scale, in my opinion.

It is helpful to start with an old half model if possible–not that being old necessarily makes them preferable to new ones. They aren't really all that difficult to come by with the profusion of antique shops about. A local museum might even be willing to lend you one from storage. Lacking that, the museum staff might allow you to work with one on the premises. In either instance, select one whose looks appeal to you, that always helps.

A marine antiques dealer stopped by my shop one afternoon with a box full of old half models that he wanted me to identify (Identified half models are worth more than others.). Among the collection was a particularly fine looking one that I kept as my fee for identifying and explaining the others. That one is my oldest half model and is of a Newfoundland Trap Skiff. That is the largest of the wherries, with lines quite similar to our Lincolnville model. She has since proved to be a real beauty in every sense of the term.

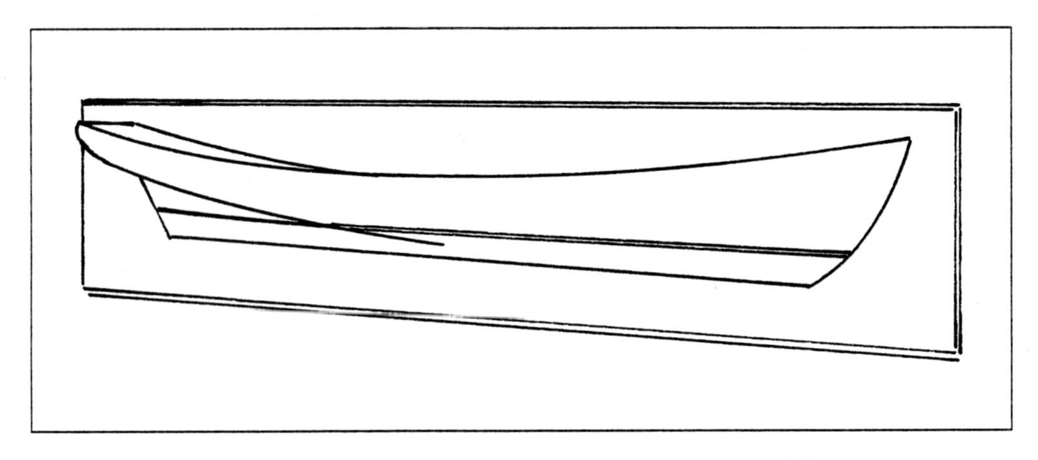

Half Model of a Newfoundland Trap Skiff

Much closer examination of the model later on revealed that not only had my model been carved to 3/4" scale (it said so faintly in pencil on the back), but that it had also been built on three moulds with the halfbreadths noted for each station, inside, on each lift. I have since learned that Newfoundland builders call those stations "fore hook", "aft hook", and "midship bend". Any lift model is handy to work from because the periphery of each lift traces one of the hull waterlines; that in conjunction with the view of the run, deadrise, and point of entry, help determine the suitability of the design for eventual construction.

All of this lends credibility to a half model, but in order to build a boat from it, you must take off its dimensions for transferal. In the old days, once the model was completed (and I'm talking here specifically about small boat construction), the measurements were used directly without the intermediate step of lofting. Direct measurements at each station from each lift would provide the points necessary for the construction of the moulds. Profile measurements would provide the shape of the stem, rake of the transom, sheer line, and keel rocker or profile depending on the model. It was assumed that a fair model would yield an equally fair hull, with the builder's skill accounting for any slight modifications indicated by his fairing batten.

Before I go any further, I want to make it clear that I am not recommending that you make a half model or use an existing model to avoid lofting. I was taught to build from half models, but the builder never failed to stress the importance of a properly executed lofting. Building from a half model assumes that you are conversant with hull construction methods, while a lofting can show you individual construction details along with the fair curves.

To make certain I understood the lesson, that old master builder had me take the lines off every one of the models nailed to the shop wall–I still have those lines after all these years. We didn't loft every one of them, but enough that I gained an understanding of half models and lofting that I could not have acquired by working with either system to the exclusion of the other. Because it worked for me, it is my hope that it can and will do the same for you. Using the methods detailed here, you should be able to draw the lines for any half model. There are, however, some observations I would like to pass along before we get on with the business of taking off lines.

First, old models usually are nicked and dinged about the edges, and some will even have missing parts. Unless the damage is extensive–in which case you should consult a professional–you can effect repairs, fairing the new pieces in with the old. Bear in mind that wood shrinks as it dries out, and an old model may have lifts that, though scaled to one measurement when carved, now scale somewhat less. Here you must assume that the original carver wasn't fool enough to space his waterlines, say, 2-15/16", but rather 3"; and you must assume 3" when you draw the plan. By the same token, the lifts will be somewhat narrower than they were originally. Making allowances for the width of a lift, however, is subject to conjecture, because there is no reliable way to determine the original dimension. Unless there is a notation somewhere on the model, it is probably best to make no halfbreadth allowances.

Second, you must determine whether your model shows a vertical or a plank keel. It makes a difference. Plank keel models are less common, but you must know which you are dealing with in order to begin drafting. The reason is that the back surface of the model denotes the centerline of the hull only in a plank keel model. If the model is of a hull with a vertical keel, its back surface denotes the depth of the rabbet. A local boat shop wanted to build a lobster boat and used one of the half models carved by that old builder that I told you about before. That had a vertical keel, obviously, but the shop builders figured the back of the model was the hull centerline. It amused Merrill no end to see their boat with 6" less beam than intended.

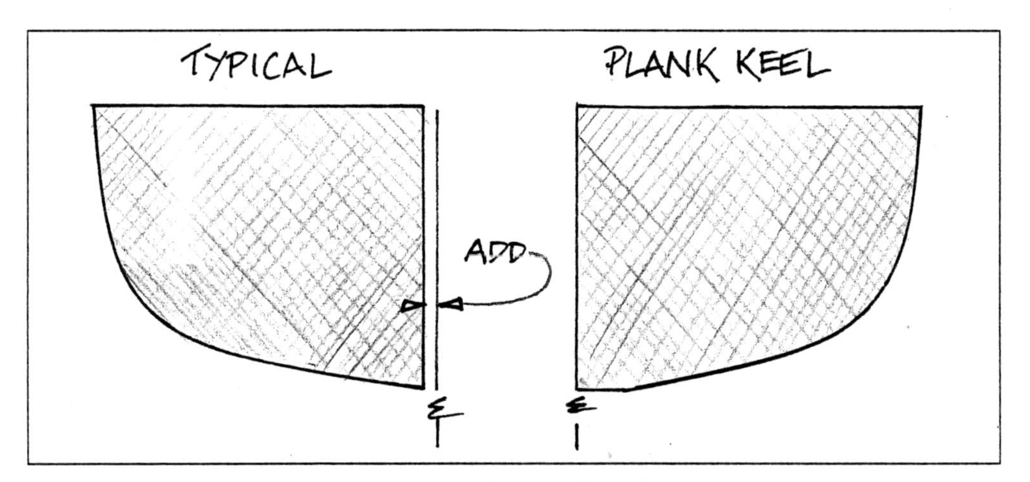

Half Model Cross Sections

Plank keeled models are easy to spot. They are the only ones that have a tapering flat area along the lower edge–that corresponds to the outboard surface of the plank keel. By convention, models are carved to the inside of the planking unless otherwise specified, but a vertical keeled model gives dimensions to the rabbet only. If the plan, lofting, and hull are to represent the half model faithfully, you have to add one-half the thickness of the keel to all halfbreadth measurements. That is readily done while drawing by adding a line parallel to the centerline, separated from it by the half-siding of the keel, and working from there. Note that even when a rudder, keel, or stem are attached to a half model, it does not mean that it was carved to represent the boat to the outside of the planking. More likely, they were added to give the prospective boat owner a better feel for the appearance of the completed boat.

Some, I realize are more comfortable looking at a full model. For them, and anyone else who happens to be curious, hold the half model against a polished metal surface, so that with the reflection you will see the full-bodied model. A mirror could be used, but it reflects light from its back surface, so using one results in twice the thickness of the glass appearing between the halves of the model. Carried to the extreme, you could hold the model against a mirror with a thickness matching the halfsiding of the keel to see a true portrayal of the whole hull. Polished metal, in contrast, is front reflective.

TAKING LINES FROM A LIFT MODEL

Taking off lines starts with tracing the model, so begin by removing the model from its backing. On your drawing board, establish a profile "waterline". (A hull actually has many waterlines, but this one is the LWL or load waterline, the level at which the boat is designed to float. Place the model on the drawing surface so that its LWL and the drawn line coincide; trace the profile of the model, and at the same time tick off the positions of all the other lifts fore and aft. If stations are indicated on the model (a rarity on a lift model), their location should be marked before it is set aside.

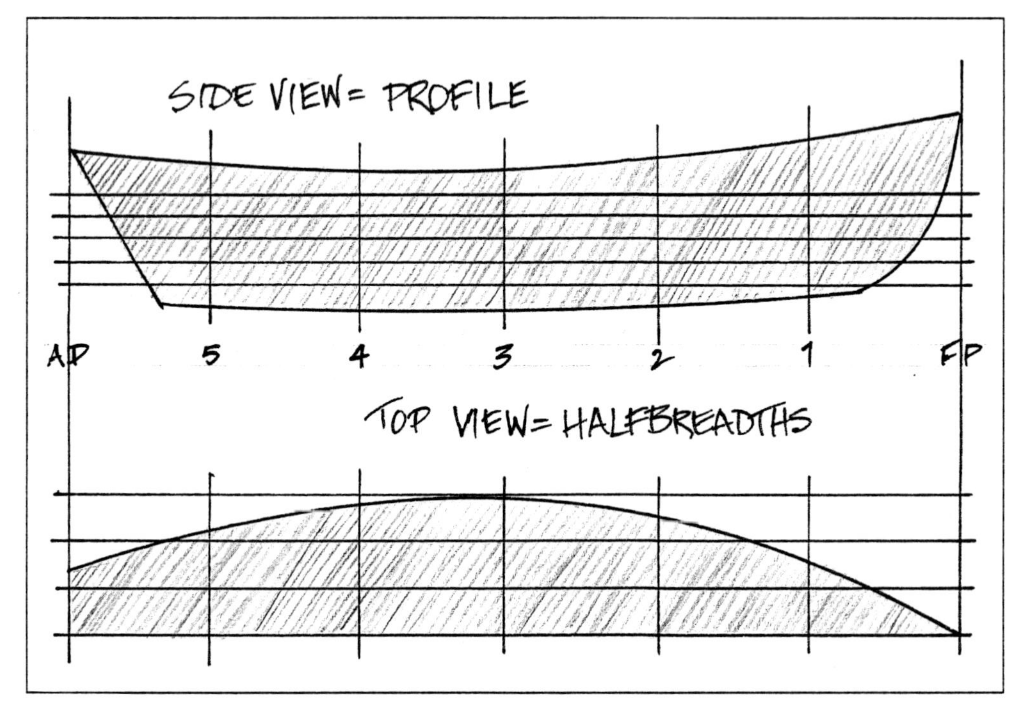

Gridwork for Tracing a Model

The next step is to carefully fair in the traced lines with a straightedge and ship's curves, French curves, a flexible batten, or a combination of means. When I say "carefully", I mean that you should not deviate from the traced lines other than to fair in over nicks, dings, and gaps. If the model were in mint condition, there would be no need for fairing at all.

Next add reference lines to your drawing. Erect perpendiculars at both ends of the faired profile. As the name implies, they should be at 90° to the load waterline, and should just touch the ends of the profile. In boatbuilder's parlance, they are known as forward and aft perpendiculars, and are abbreviated FP and AP respectively. With the perpendiculars in place, draw in all of the straight profile waterlines. Viewed broadside, the "waterline" of a boat is straight–and so are these. They are located equidistant above and below the LWL, and correspond to the top of the individual lifts that you marked when you traced the profile. If you want, you can add a baseline to your plan, though it isn't absolutely necessary. If you find that comforting, it should be located a multiple of the waterline spacing below the LWL, parallel to the LWL, and clear of the profile with a little to spare.

Stations, if any, should be added. They are erected perpendicular to the LWL unless otherwise specified on the model. For examples of non-perpendicular stations, refer to Howard I. Chapelle's American Small Sailing Craft. You will find there that the stations of 18th and 19th century boats were frequently perpendicular to the keel.

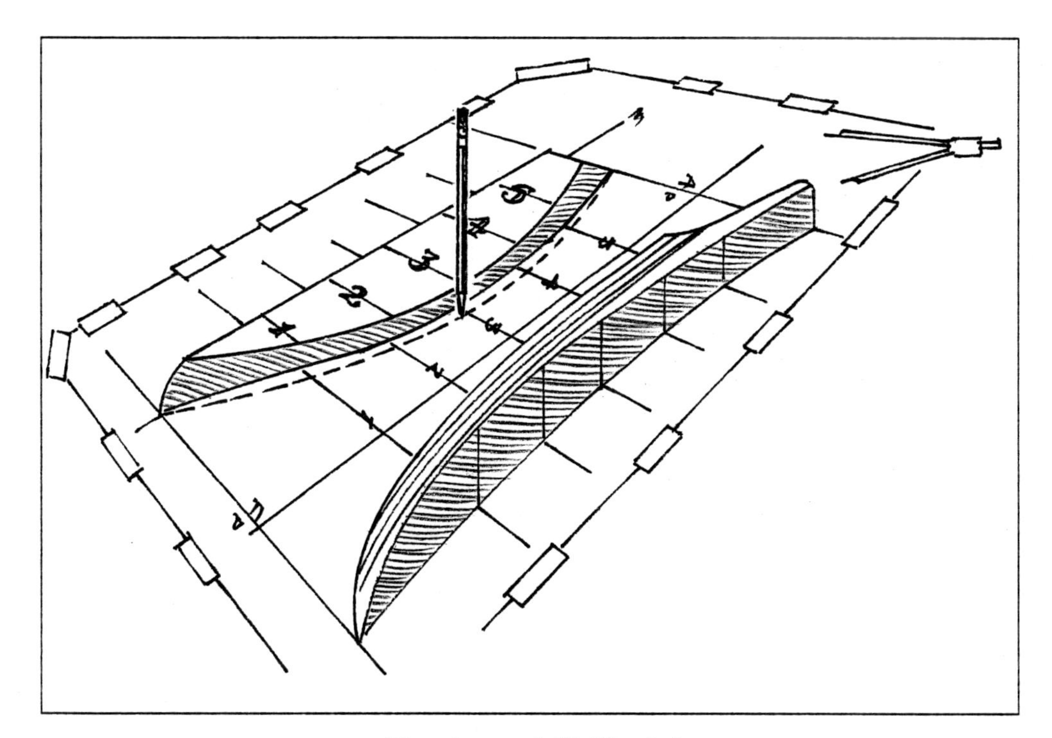

Tracing a Lift Model

The halfbreadth or top view of the model is drawn next. You will need reference lines for this too, but you can make use of all the perpendiculars that have already been drawn. Simply extend them upward from the profile far enough that the halfbreadth view of the model can be drawn apart from the profile. With the perpendiculars in place, draw a line parallel to the LWL to serve as the centerline of the top view. Remembering our earlier discussion concerning plank keel verses vertical keel models, if yours does have a vertical keel, add another reference line parallel to the centerline, spaced half the keel dimension away. This second line will help position the individual lifts.

In a nutshell, the waterline curves of a lift model are derived by separating the lifts, aligning each with the centerline (or keel line, depending on type), and tracing. All tracing is done along the wider edge of each lift. The hitch is positioning the lifts correctly fore and aft. The traced profile view provides the solution. Using a drafting triangle, t-square, rafter square, or similar tool, project the intersections of the straight waterlines with the profile stem and stern from the profile view into the halfbreadths. Simply align the square with a waterline or the baseline, and draw lines from the intersection points to the centerline of the halfbreadth view. Those projected lines fix the fore and aft position of every lift.

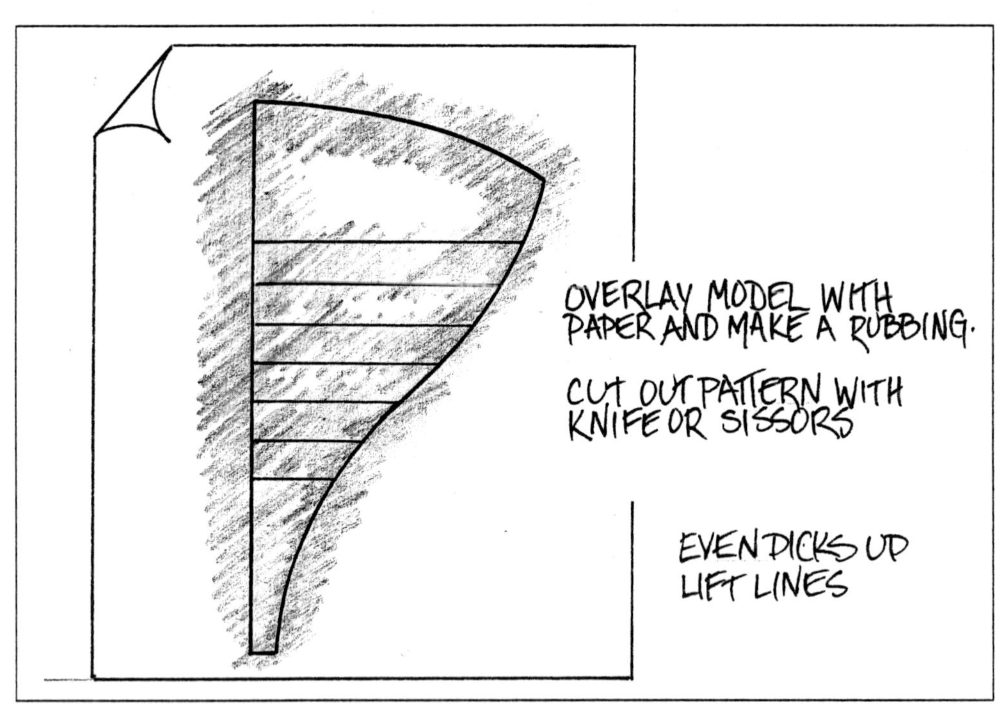

Taking Off Transom Shape

The only three places where direct tracing is difficult is the sheer, the transom, and the plank keel (assuming there is one). At the moment we are not concerned with picking off dimensions–that follows–here we are interested in direct transferal of lines information from the model. To trace the sheer, lay it on your drawing, aligning it with the fore and aft projections (in this case

FP and AP) and the centerline, shim the middle portion so that its flat surface is held parallel to the paper, and trace by sighting down past the edge. If your lift exhibits tumblehome, do the best you canthere are checks that we can apply to the tracing.

Transom shape is copied by tracing. This time, use the traced profile of the transom as the hull centerline, and holding the transom end of the model there against the paper, trace its outline. If it happens to be a curved transom, do a rubbing of the transom, cut it out, and trace that in the same place. Drawn in, it looks like nothing quite so much as an inverted rudder attached to a boat. Similarly, plank keel shape is picked off by rubbing, cutting out, and tracing on the drawing.

There is really only one rule when it comes to taking a lift model apart so that it can be used: do it carefully so that the lifts and pegs aren't damaged. The safest approach is to slide a putty knife between the lifts from the backside and pry them apart gently. Start with the top lift, prying and working back and forth until it separates from the others sufficiently to grip–then carefully pull it off over the pegs. Those pegs are usually hand made and tapered, and driven from the underside. Sometimes the pegs can be tapped loose using a softwood drive pin of somewhat lesser diameter than the pegs.

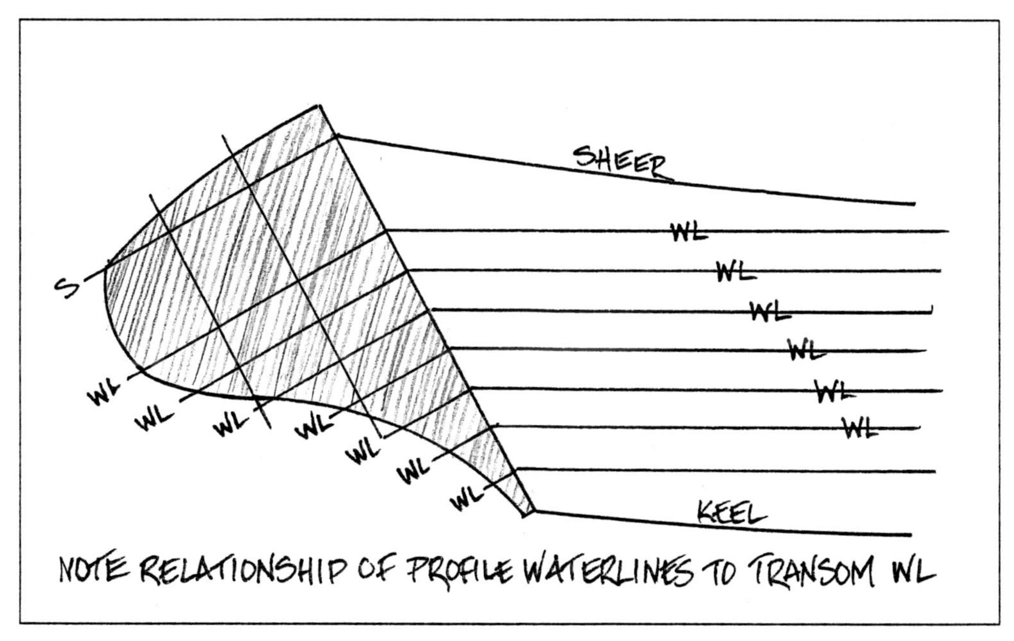

Transom Expansion

Station lines should be extended from the profile into the halfbreadth view, and even buttock lines can be added. The important point is that the contours of the model are now on paper, and with reference lines in place, can be measured, recorded, and duplicated full size. The drafting doesn't have to be pretty, just accurate. The lofting will help you iron out any slight discrepancies here and there.

TAKING LINES FROM A SOLID MODEL

Taking lines from a lift model is a bit easier than doing the same thing with a solid model–but not much. Solid models, obviously, cannot be taken apart without being damaged. They can, however, be removed from their backing, and that is the first step.

If the model is old, its stations may be indicated on the reverse side (previously obscured by the backing). If they are, you have an obvious starting point. If no evidence of stations exists, you must establish some of your own. They will want to be equally spaced. A time-honored way has been to erect the end stations where profile and LWL intersect, and then divide the space between into equal segments. If your solid model has a contrasting "waterline", by the way, its lower edge is the actual LWL that you want. It is mostly there for decorative purposes with the different colored wood approximating the boottop on the hull.

For drafting, lofting, and building small craft I use a total of five stations–10 for larger boats. After the divisions have been made, extend the stations across the back of the model with a square, making certain to keep them perpendicular to the run of the load waterline. With a soft pencil, make small marks along the keel and on the deck of the model so that when it is placed flat against the drawing surface, the station locations can be easily seen.

As with the lift model, start by drawing a profile LWL, and position the model on that so that its profile can be traced. This time too, erect perpendiculars at both ends of the profile. Be sure to tick off the locations of the stations above and below the model, before it moves.

With a lift model, you trace the waterlines in order to derive the stations. This time, we will be taking off the contours of the stations so that we can derive the run of the waterlines. We will arrive at the same destination via different routes.

There are several ways to pick off those station shapes. Back when I was learning this, I was taught to shape templates out of thin pieces of pine. Making them is simply a matter of scribing and fitting. Even on the larger models where a single piece wouldn't work, sections were glued together with a backing piece in order to span the curve between keel and sheer. Regardless of the size of the template required, bear in mind that to be right, when it is in its final position against the side of the model, that its face must align with the station marks and be perpendicular to the back surface of the model. Lead and copper strips can be bent to the shape of the stations too, and they are faster, but they tend to mar finely finished models, and make a smudgy mess of a drawing to boot.

Carved Station Templates

If you happen to share my fondness for gadgetry, perhaps you will be intrigued by a machine that takes the station shapes directly from a half model. I built mine while taking lines off a series of half models for the Penobscot Marine Museum in Searsport, Maine, and have been using it for my own work ever since.

First you will need a smooth drawing surface, sufficiently large to encompass the stations–a piece of 1/2" plywood is fine. Fix the board above the model so that the plane of the drawing surface is in line with the station being copied. The legs that support the board, of course, will have to be equipped with feet to hold the works upright. Two more things are needed: a pointer and a sliding mechanism in which to mount it. The slide I used is nearly identical to the runner on a slide rule (for those readers who still recognize the term), the only difference being that while the slide moves horizontally on the rails of the board, its pointer moves vertically. The reason is one of necessity–in order to follow the contour of the half model, the pointer must traverse the station from keel to sheer while the model halfbreadths are increasing on the way to the sheer.

Tape a sheet of paper to the board and let the pointer rest on the backing of the model. Mark the paper and the pointer for the transferred model centerline. At that spot, put a notch in the side of the pointer above the point, just large enough to allow a sharp pencil point to reach the drawing paper. Before you start, you need to know where the plane of the drawing surface is in regard to the base of the lines machine. Trace down each leg, and mark the plane's location on each foot.

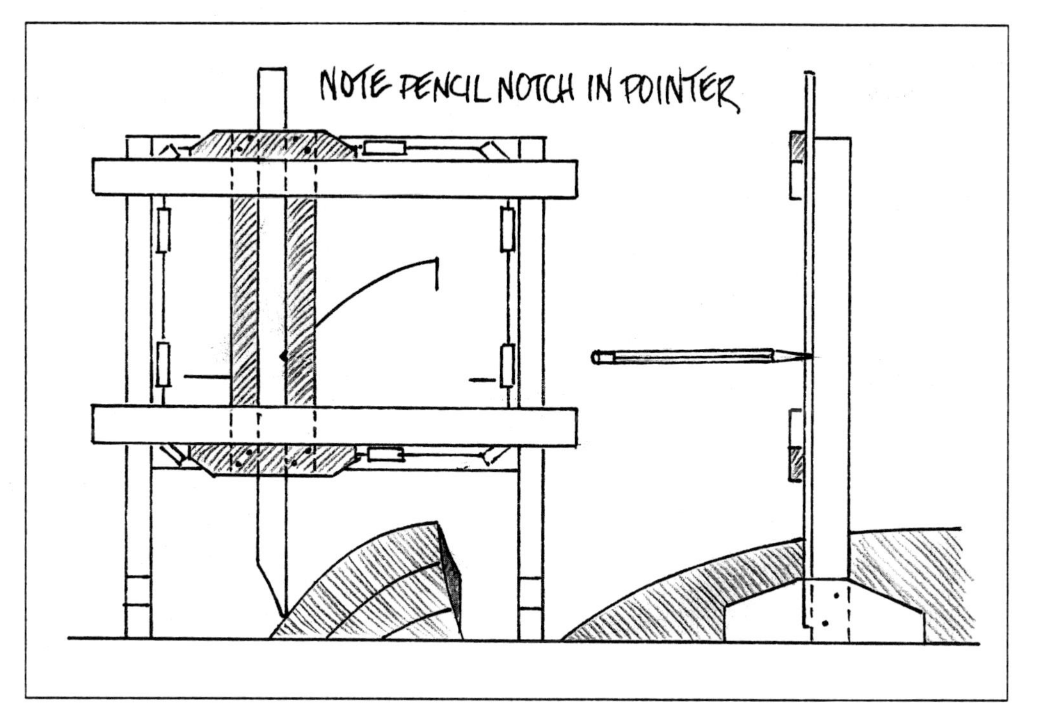

Half Model Tracing Machine

To start, draw a straight line on the surface that will be supporting the half model. The witness marks on each foot of the lines machine must align with that line, and each of the model's stations will align with it in turn. Don't try to put all of the stations on the same piece of paper; it's difficult to arrange them correctly with respect to each other, and there really is no need. It is easier to take off the contours a station at a time, and then trace them later to your complete lines drawing.

With the whole assembly and the model held so that neither will move, run the pointer over each station. One hand guides the pointer, while the other holds the pencil square to the surface of the paper and eases the runner along. It takes a bit of practice to get synchronized, but once you become used to the process, tracing each station is only a few seconds' work. Once your coordination improves, you can take off waterlines and even buttock lines (though of course you will need a longer drawing board than you used for the stations).

Now that I have told you all of the methods that involve work, and those traditionally used, I can relate the easier methods. The first involves a nifty little device known as a copycat gauge. They are found in hardware stores all over. Their intended function is to copy the contours of intricate moldings. It consists of a handle about 4" long through which pass 40 or more 18 gauge wires, about 4" long. The wires are held in place by a friction fit in the handle. To use this clever tool, hold it against the model at a station, and push the wires against the curve until you have a copy. Like the templates made earlier, take the gauge to your drawing and there trace the shape of the station onto the body plan. Use the LWL for vertical alignment, and the width of the sheer at that station for horizontal alignment.

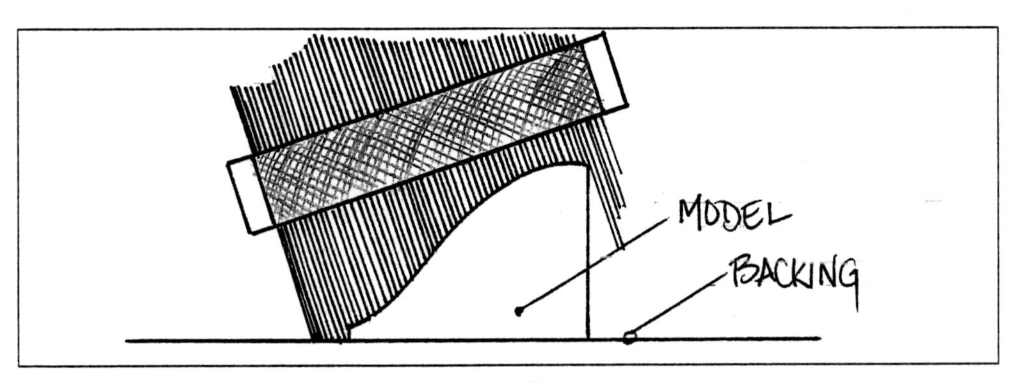

Copycat Gauge

Some years ago, under the press of a construction deadline, I resorted to the fastest method of all. That involves laying out the stations on the surface of the half model and then sawing the model apart on those lines. Taking off the shapes of the stations after that, was just a matter of tracing–fast, to be sure, but a little hard on the model.

The balance of the operation is drafting. Refer to an existing plan for the typical arrangement of a lines drawing, and set up your profile, halfbreadths, and body plan accordingly. At that point, the only things separating your drafting from a complete set of plans are the construction details and a verified table of offsets. We will be discussing both directly.

MAKING A LIFT MODEL

You can make your own lift model. It is a type infrequently made today because builders are accustomed to working from hull sections taken perpendicular to the load waterline. The reason is readily apparent: in order to build small craft, you first have to build the moulds, and they are outlined by the station curves of the body plan. In wooden ship construction, as practiced years ago, no moulds were used. Instead, nearly wall-to-wall sawn timbers provided the framework for the planking. To derive all those offset measurements, would have required a station corresponding to each timber. That method of construction made it far easier to use waterlines as their primary source of measurement, and hence the utility of the lift models.

To begin with, you are going to need well-seasoned wood–white pine and basswood are good, though standard kiln dried stock is too unstable. If you have had those pieces around long enough to air dry, they ought to be just fine. Lacking that, one of the mahoganies could be used. They are a bit tougher to carve, but stable. The reason stability is all-important, is that a proper lift model is held together with pegs. Sometimes blind screws are used inside, but to a traditional builder that's cheating. The intent is to use neither nails nor glue, just friction-fit pegs. Unless the model can be completely disassembled, its only value is aesthetic.

The procedure is much the same as that explained for laying out a solid model. The primary difference is that you must work with a greater number of pieces. The solid model required three pieces, the lift model calls for a separate piece for each waterline space shown on the plan. There are two exceptions: the deck and keel lifts. The deck lift (so-called whether the boat has a deck or not), should be continuous, meaning that it includes the lowest point of the sheer as well as the higher points at stem and transom. Its thickness is determined by measuring the plan from the last through (continuous) waterline to the top of the stem. The keel lift is a little different though the same rationale applies: it needs to be continuous and of sufficient width to hold the assembly pegs. In many cases it would be nothing but a sliver if it contained solely the lowermost waterline space. Usually it is sufficient for it to contain the two lowest waterline spaces.

You could assemble the lifts here and now, make yourself sectional templates, and carve this model as if it were a solid block. If you were working from someone else's plans that shouldn't be defaced in any way, a prudent intermediate step would be to trace their plan and make your model from the tracing. Once you have a working plan, the lifts can be positioned under it one at time so that you can prick through to transfer the waterline curves. Another approach is to use carbon paper between the plan and the lift, and overdraw the plan to transfer the curve. Regardless of the method, be sure to include at least one station for a check against the fore and aft alignment of the lifts.

The next step is to cut out the lifts. Saw just wide of the line and plane the edge to the curve. It's best to leave the pencil line intact. Edges should be square and the curves fair overall. As you finish each one, use the side of your pencil to darken the waterline edges–that indicates what is not to be removed until the final sanding.

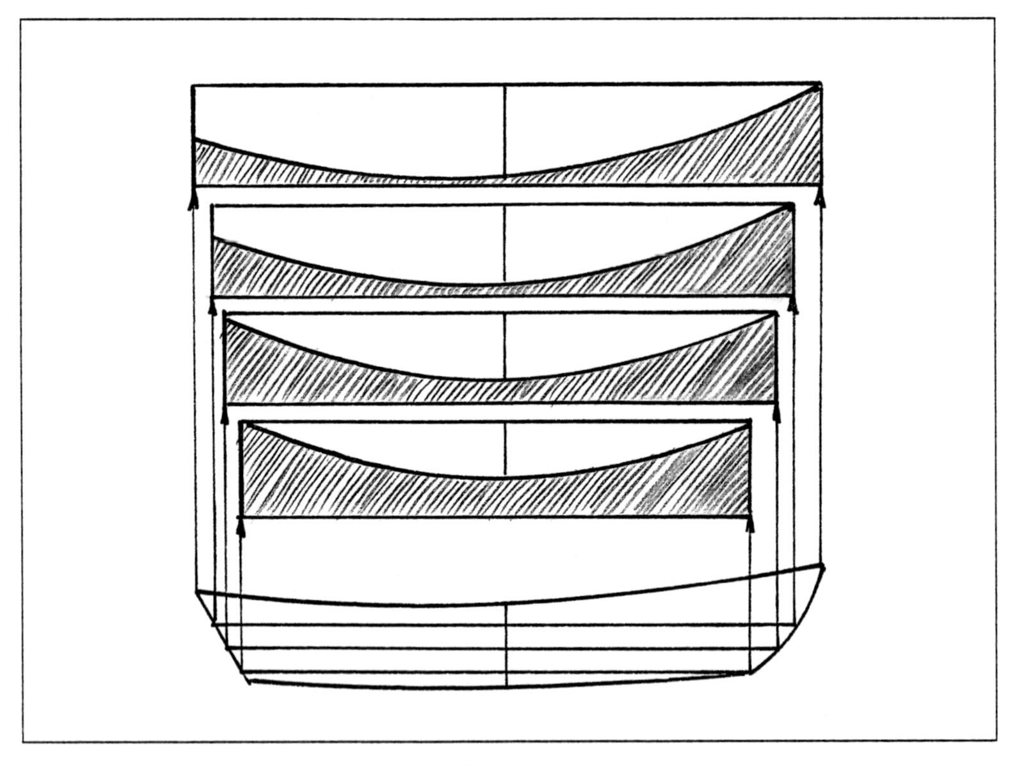

Individual Lifts

You must assemble the pieces before any further shaping. The assembly of a lift model is straightforward, but does require a bit of forethought. The first step is to align all lifts with each other (using the transferred station mark) and with the centerline plane (make the backs flush). Clamp the pieces together solidly, using clamp pads to avoid damaging the surfaces.

The easiest method of pinning the lifts together is to take the clamped assembly to a vise where it can be held securely, bore through with a 1/2" bit, and install snugly fitting dowels made of the same material as the lifts. I make lifts and pegs of the same wood because the pegs will then have the same expansion coefficient as the lifts, and hence will never be too tight to remove or too loose to hold the pieces together.

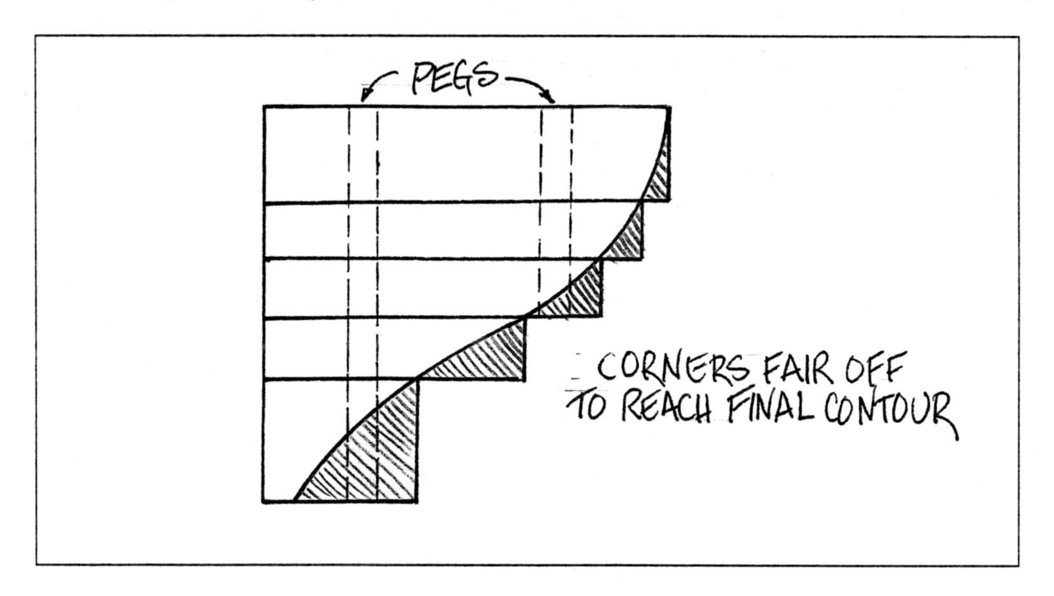

Sectional View of a Lift Model

The placement of pegs depends on the configuration of your particular model. For the model of a Whitehall, for example, I would likely use one each, fore and aft, about 3/4" from the back of the model, with another amidships about an inch back from the sheer line. The trick is to hold the pieces together, of course, so you will have to use your judgment. My original Newfoundland Trap Skiff model is held together with six 3/16" pegs. One old wherry model that I copied years ago, was held together with two rectangular pegs tapered so that they were wider at the bottom than at the top. They were cross-pinned at the deck to provide a very effective locking mechanism. The rectangular pegs are more work to fit, but they are certainly effective, and result in a classy-looking half model.

After all of this preparation, the final shaping of the half model seems nearly anticlimactic. My first step is to saw the model to the plan profile. The back of the model is flat, so transferring the profile, lining it up with the station and the ends of the lifts is not difficult. Because the face of the model is stepped at this point, bandsawing it to shape is going to require some care. Just block it up so that it doesn't wobble on its path through the saw, and keep your fingers out of harms way. I prefer to use the scrap from the lifts for the blocking, because they are already contoured and mate well with the assembled lifts.

Carving consists of fairing off the unwanted corners of the lifts. Be careful not to remove all of the darkened wood at the edge of the liftsthat disappears with the final sanding. If you are well equipped with carving tools, you will be happy to learn that you won't need more than a couple of them. Most of my model carving is accomplished with a 7/8" firmer chisel and a pair of gouges–one of shallow radius and one of about 1/4" radius for the really tight spots. I sand with 80-grit aluminum oxide paper to complete the fairing, followed with 120-grit and finally 220 to eliminate the scratches remaining.

Mounting is a matter of individual preference. Few of the old half models had mountings–hence the reason that most of their thin edges are damaged. If you use one, the model is held there with screws driven through the mounting into the back of the lifts, so that it can be removed without difficulty. My model with the rectangular pegs doesn't have a mounting; rather, it is hung from holes in the extension of the pegs above the sheer line.

MAKING A SOLID MODEL

If you would like to try your hand at model making, a solid model is a good place to start. You could work from the set of lines you have just taken off an existing half model, working to duplicate the original, or you could work directly from a lines plan. For your first attempt, 1-1/2" to 1'-0" is a good scale to work from, and you will need the profile, halfbreadths, and the stations. But don't make it hard on yourself–if your plan is drawn to another scale, use it the way it is rather than redrafting to 1-1/2" scale.

The selection of carving material is all-important. I favor what we call "Pumpkin Pine", a particular type of Maine white pine that is easy to carve, has a pleasing, mellow color, and is available in large, clear chunks. A second choice would be Basswood (called that despite the fact that it comes from Linden trees). Its carving characteristics are akin to that of the pumpkin pine, with the added advantage that it can be carved in nearly any direction. Good Basswood has a rather nondescript grain pattern that makes it what computer types would call "user friendly", and it too is available in large, clear chunks.

Either wood, or one with similar carving characteristics, is a good choice for your half model. That isn't to say that other alternatives aren't every bit as good. I have carved some to U.S. Navy specifications, and those are much fancier. They call for sugar pine topsides, black walnut boottop, and Honduras mahogany below the waterline. They are mounted on walnut.That combination makes for a striking combination of woods, though overall it is quite a bit more difficult to carve.

I use three separate pieces to glue up a block from which to carve the model: two pieces of pine–one for above and one for below the load waterline–and a piece of mahogany for contrast, to denote the position of the load waterline. Consult the plan for the size of the individual pieces. A very pleasing model will result if you can find a piece of pine sufficiently large to encompass the entire profile. Saw the block along the LWL and insert the contrasting "waterline" so that the grain, after assembly, will run interrupted through the model and approximate the run of the planking.

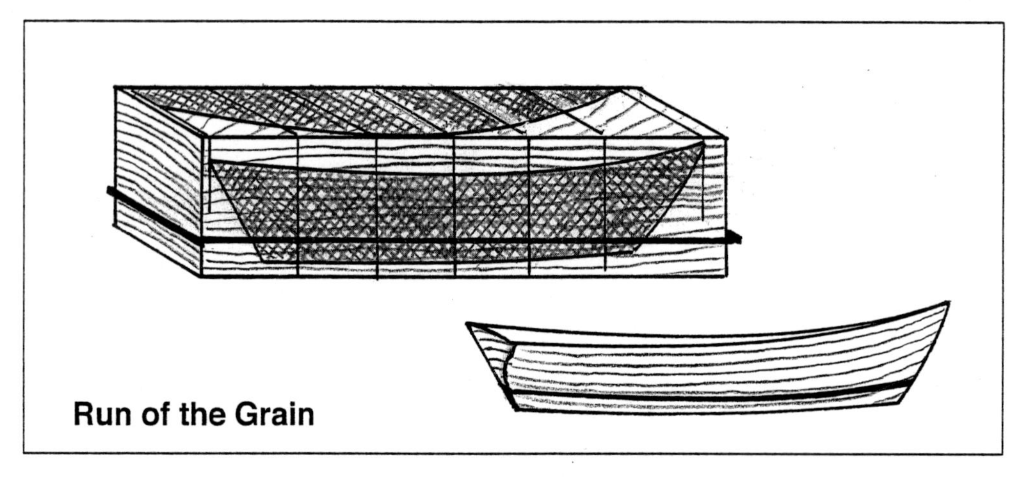

Run of the Grain

If you can't find a single piece large enough, you can laminate thinner pieces together to achieve the thickness needed. To make carving easier, be certain that the grains of the pieces run in the same direction, and, if possible, make certain the deck is unbroken by a glue joint. Glue joints are harder than the adjacent wood and therefore would make the deck more difficult to fair off accurately. I use mostly Weldwood Plastic Resin Glue because it is pretty much a staple in boatshops like mine, but Elmer's Carpenter's Glue will work too, as will Elmer's White Glue (which dries clear). My current glue of choice is Titebond II, though that is waterproof, and the original Titebond yellow glue works just fine. Regardless of your choice, once glue is applied, the trick is to tack the pieces together at a corners, to keep them from slipping under clamping pressure–and not clamping them so tightly that an excessive amount of glue is extruded and the joints become glue starved.

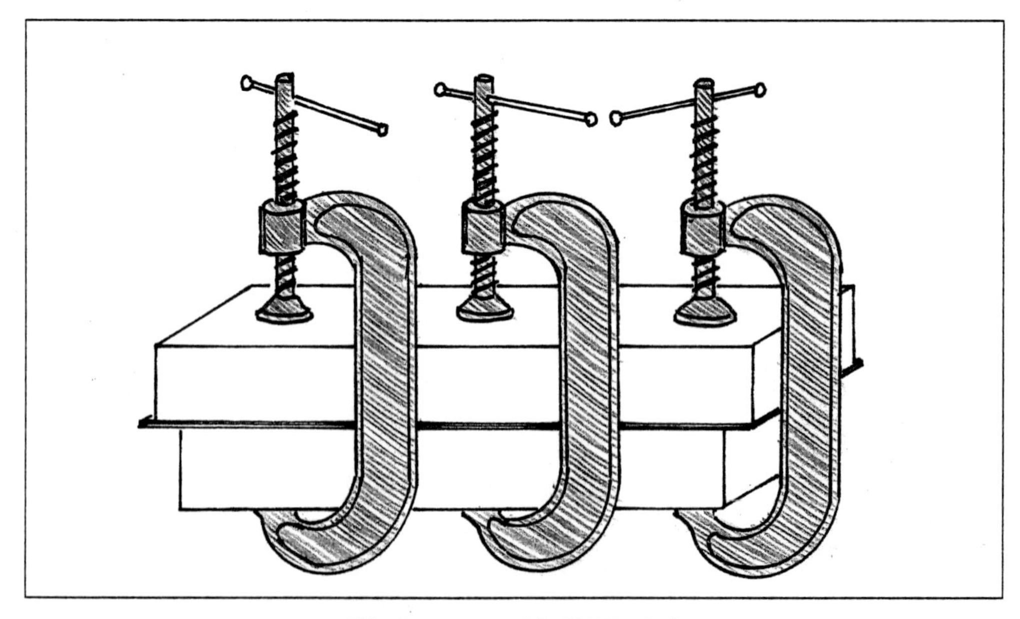

Gluing up a Half Model

After the glue cures, the next step is to plane the front and rear of the block so that they are flat and parallel to one another. The cured glue won't do a plane any good, so it is best to remove as much of it as possible with a Surform tool or chisel (it won't do the chisel's edge any good either, but it is easier to resharpen than a plane). An alternative is to grind or sand the glue away, but use safety goggles or a face shield and respiratory protection if you do, because Weldwood glue contains the carcinogen formaldehyde.

Now that the block has two smooth surfaces, you are ready to lay out the profile, either by striking in the perpendiculars and taking the heights directly from the plan using dividers, or by making a template from the plan and tracing that on the model. Most half models portray the starboard side of the hull ("sailing east", builders say), with the bow of the model to the right.

Next turn your attention to the stations. Use a square to extend station lines across the deck and keel. With a template made from your plan, overlay the top of the model, and trace the halfbreadth sheer line onto the top of the block. Lacking a template, dimensions can be transferred using dividers, but you will have to fair in the sheer line between the points with a flexible batten. That template, or those dimensions, by the way, should be from the maximum hull widths, not necessarily the sheer itself. If your boat exhibits tumblehome at the stern, the sheer in that area isn't the full beam of the boat. Draw the line to the widest dimension and we will carve away the excess at the sheer when the time comes.

Saw along the halfbreadth sheer line, and take both parts back to the bench. There, reassemble the pieces with brads placed in the scrap corners, or with double-sided tape. Go back to the bandsaw and saw out the profile. Having put the part you sawed away back on the model helps you to hold it steady during the sawing. Now you have a squared off version of your model.

In order to carve the stations, you will need a template for each. My first templates were made from 1/16" white pine (see page 14). I slid them under the lines drawing, pricked through to transfer the station curve and the location of the centerline, LWL, and sheer, and then carved away the excess. You could also make them out of poster board. Most of the ones I use now are Mylar (technology marches on). I transfer the body plan to Mylar drafting film, and then cut it down the centerline. I can pinch that between two sticks that are tacked together with wire nails, and simply cut away each station in turn. The age of disposable templates has arrived. You will also need a template for the transom, but unlike the others, this one only needs to be traced on the stern of the model.

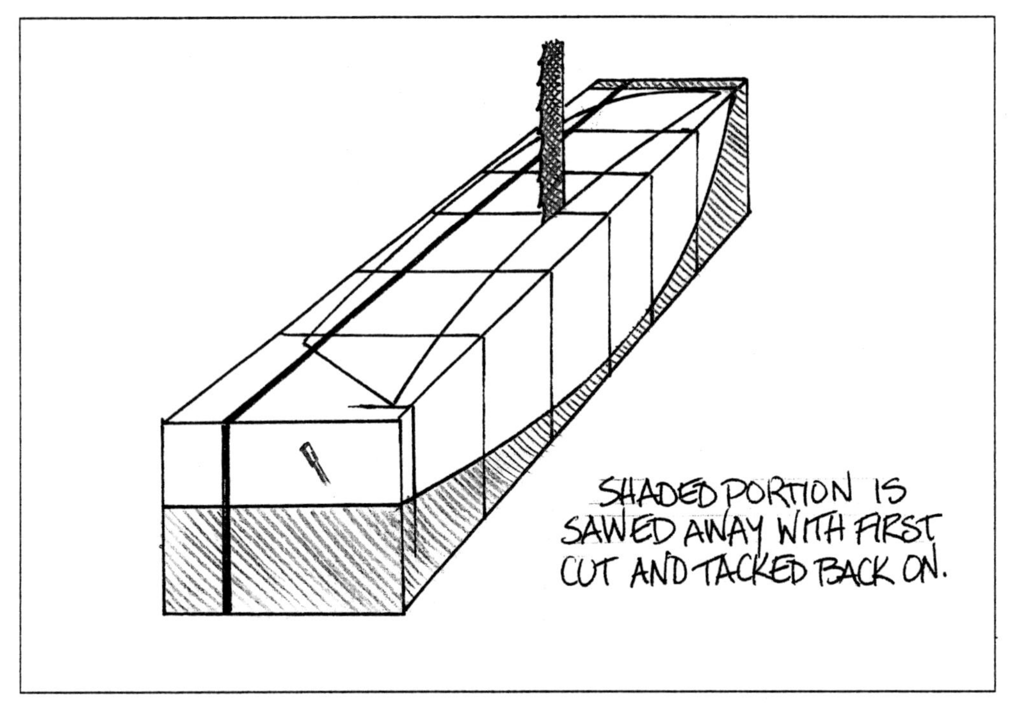

Making the Second Cut

You are almost ready to pick up a chisel, but first fasten your model to a backing. The board's purpose is threefold: it allows you to secure the model to bench top or in a vise, freeing both hands, it supports thin sections of the model to keep them from cracking under carving pressure, and it provides a place for indicating station positions along the keel where they would otherwise be impossibly small. I use backing boards of pine or even plywood, just make certain yours is large enough to support the entire model with enough to spare at the ends to prevent the chisel from going completely past the backing if you slip. Screw fasten the model to the board from the back, using 1-1/2" x 10 flat head screws. Two screws are usually enough for models up to 30" long. Drywall screws are currently popular, but aren't well suited to this job because their much smaller diameter gives them less bearing and therefore less resistance to the shearing pressures exerted during carving.

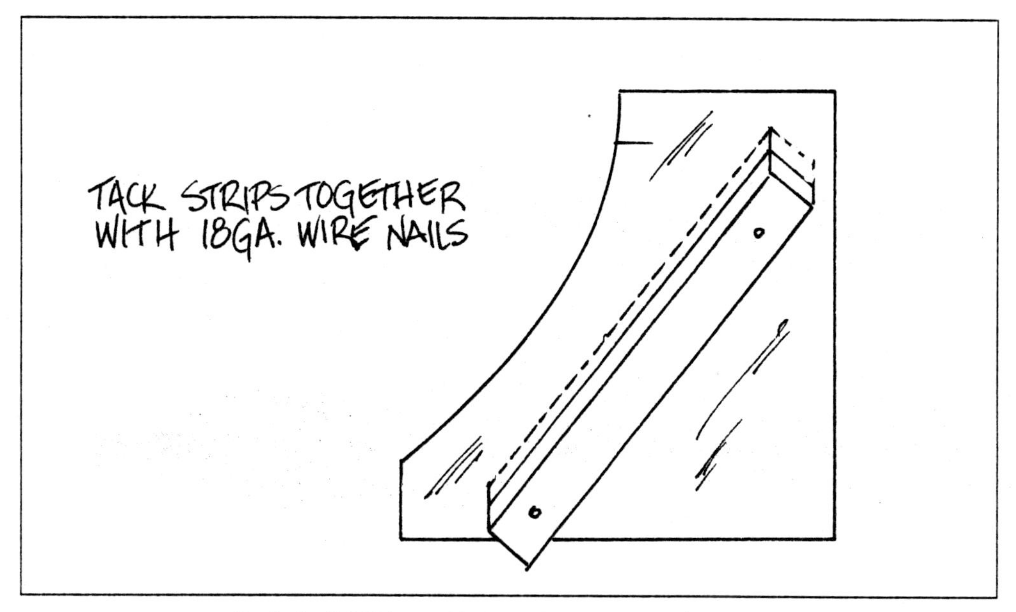

Quick 'N Dirty Mylar Carving Template

Carving begins at the first station and progresses back to the midship or to where the grain runs in the opposite direction. At that point, turn the model around and work from the transom back toward the midship station. The actual carving is easier to accomplish than to explain–I could have carved a half model in the time it has taken to write this section. Working a station at a time, alternate carving with checking with your template. As you near the curvature of the station, take smaller and smaller shavings, smoothing the surface with your chisel or gouge as best you can. As you finish each station, hold the template in place and trace it with a pencil.

Don't attempt to bring down all the adjacent wood to the final shape of the model until after all of the individual stations have been carved. When you do get to fairing it off, take pains not to cut into the profile or to remove any of the penciled in station marks on the face of the model. Marking the periphery of the model with the side of a pencil is a wise precaution. When each station is fully carved, the centerline edge of the template should rest flat against the backing board; the LWL and sheer marks should coincide with those places on the model; the top of the template should align with the station line on deck; and, the template should fit tightly to the curvature of the hull. Remember, I warned you the explanation was wordy.

When all of the stations and the transom have been carved, turn your attention to fairing off the model between stations using chisels and gouges, as required. On long models, battens covered with colored chalk are often employed at this stage; when rubbed across the model, they leave chalk on the high spots yet to be removed. As a matter of fact, the same approach is used during the final fairing on large, smooth-planked hulls. For a small model with relatively quick curves, however, the fairing off is done by eye and by feel. Frequently, you will be able to feel a high spot that is difficult to see.

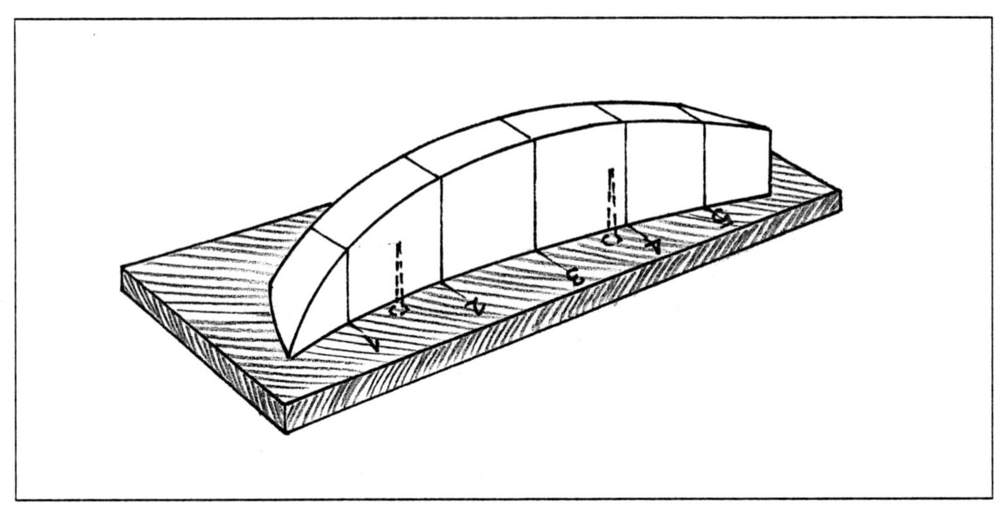

Backing Board

It is easiest to fair off the deck if you reposition the model so that the sheer line is clear of the top edge of the board. That way, when the board is held vertically in a vise, the deck is unobstructed. Comparatively speaking, deck curvature is so slight that often it can be faired using a block wrapped in 80-grit sandpaper. Once the deck fairing is finished, return the model to its original position on the board to protect the finished edges along the top of the sheer and transom.

To complete the fairing, use sandpaper: 80-grit aluminum oxide to start followed with 120-grit, and finally 220. Using too fine a grade to begin with tends to result in an unfair model, as many of the high spots will be merely rounded, rather than eliminated. On the other hand, overly coarse sandpaper results in unnecessarily deep scratches, and you stand a good chance of removing more wood than you intend.

Finishing and mounting are matters of individual preference.

Personally, I do not like models finished to a high gloss, so I do not use varnish. Instead I apply two coats of 3 pound cut white shellac. The second coat goes on as soon as the first is dry, and a day later, I rub it down with 0000 grade steel wool. The result is a very smooth low luster finish, though most of the time I will follow that with an application of Butcher's Paste Wax™. An alternative finish is Deft™ brand spray lacquer–that takes three or four coats depending on the porosity of the wood.

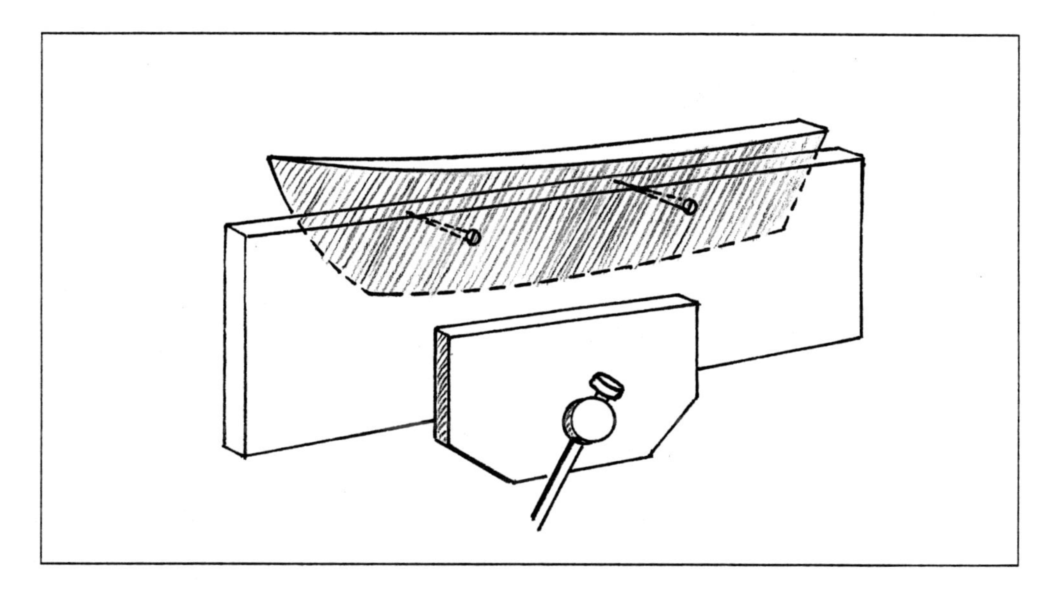

Carving the Deck

Just as you used a backing board to protect the edges of the model during carving, it is a good idea to mount your completed half model on a backing. The model fastens to the backing with screws, as before, and is usually fitted with a hanger or keyhole slots in the back for wall mounting. Your model should be identified with type, scale, and stations, as well as the completion date and your name. All that information should be written on the backing board, if not on the back of the model itself, using a pencil or a burning pen for permanence. Even the so-called permanent ink degrades in time. I've worked on a number of models more than a century old, and the pencil markings on them are still legible.

WORKING FROM PHOTOS

Should you become adept at carving models, you may eventually be asked to carve one of a boat for which lines are impossible to attain. Actually, with a little experience, that doesn't present much of a problem. If you have worked your way through the earlier sections, you already have some idea of the shapes involvedhulls of a given type being remarkably similar in regard to their sections and the run of their load waterline. That may sound like a rather indefinite bit of information, but it will prove helpful when you are faced with a job for which actual measurements are virtually nonexistent.

By far the greatest single help is photographs. Even though a boat owner may not have the lines of his craft, he almost certainly has pictures. Unfortunately, though, pictures of the boat out of the water–the ones most valuable to a carver–are scarce at best. If you have to take the photos yourself, the preferred views will be: the profile; from forward and aft, looking right down the centerline of the hull; a view of the starboard quarter above the sheer; and a view from the same angle, but looking upward from below the LWL. Most of these are easy to take when the boat is being put overboard in the spring or when she is being hauled out at the end of the season. Obviously, while you are at it you should also photograph any special details that you might want to portray in the model.

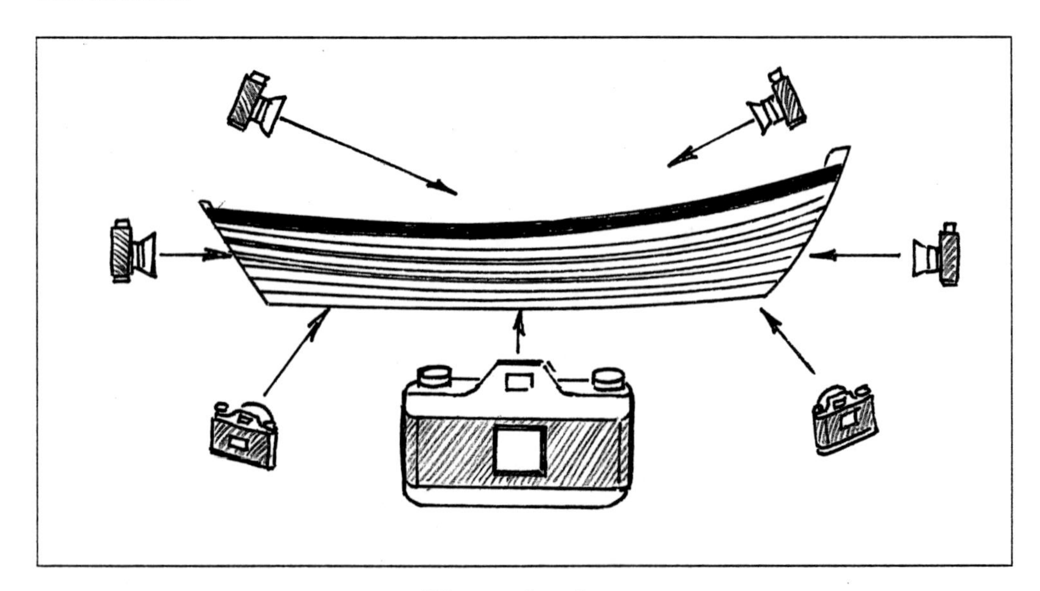

Photo Angles

The carving procedure using photos as your guide is simplicity itself, though I will admit that it takes some practice to carve what you see. It is actually the three-dimensional equivalent of viewing a scene and then trying to render a likeness in a pencil sketch–you know what you want, the difficulty is getting it.

The judgment required to carve a half model solely from photos is based in part on past observation of similar hulls along with continual comparison of your emerging model with the photos in front of you. Invariably, I lay out and saw the profile first, then lay off what I consider to be a suitable sheer (viewed from above). Your photos will indicate whether she is long and sleek or more blunt. In each instance, lay out and then make careful comparison with the photos, working as much by trial and error as by instinct. Ask yourself; do they look the same? If not, why not, and how do I correct it?

Unlike carving half models where I am working from a lines plan, I start carving these at the midship station. It is a safe place to begin because it requires removal of the least amount of wood. Bear in mind from here on that the wood remaining on the model forward of the midship station, and from there aft to the transom, must be faired off. The run of the planking on the hull runs cleanly along her entire length, so your model must do likewise. Here, it would definitely be helpful to have a photo taken from directly beneath the keel, showing the run of the load waterline. Since that is an impossibility you must resort to the fore and aft views you could take, and interpolate. If the hull has a sharp point of entry and a hollow in the LWL, it will be evident in the photos and can be duplicated. The same reasoning applies to removal of wood from a tuck. Verify your carving, a section at a time, and then remove of the remaining wood to result in final hull fairness.

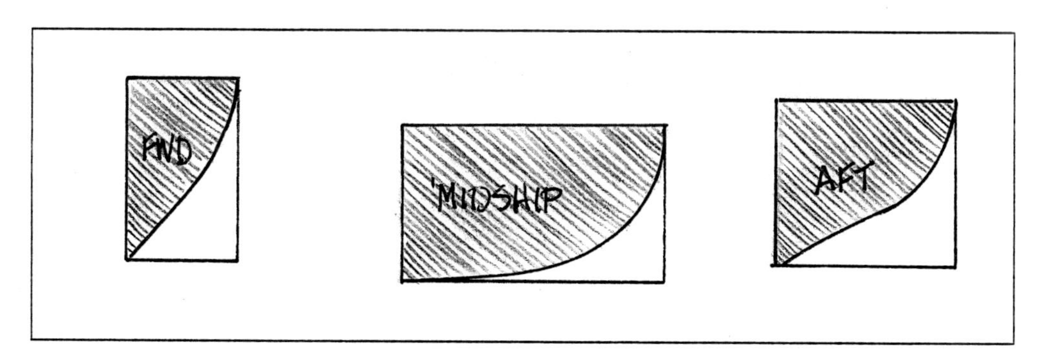

Model Sections

Those new to model carving tend to be overly cautious, and as a result tend to leave too much wood on the model. Be cautious, by all means, but don't hesitate to remove additional wood if your model doesn't compare favorably with the photos. It is not of life and death importance if you should carve away too much–my shop stove has fed on such fare–you could start over, as much as that might hurt.

These are decorative half models, as opposed to builder's models, of course. And because aesthetics is at least as important as getting a likeness, you must occasionally fudge the model a bit. A case in point is the model of a schooner I carved some years ago. The boat had been employed in the pilot service, so in addition to being fully rigged (two-masted, bald-headed), she had been equipped with diesel power. In order to arrive at a proper angle for her propeller shafts, the builders found it necessary to build a "bunch" into her tuck, port and starboard. That obviously would not be found on a schooner that was only intended to be sailed. I had the lines to work from, and I carved a model that was technically accurate. To make a long story short, the owner hated it. I took the model back to my shop, carved out the bunch I spoke of earlier, and took it back to him. "There", he said, "you finally got it right".

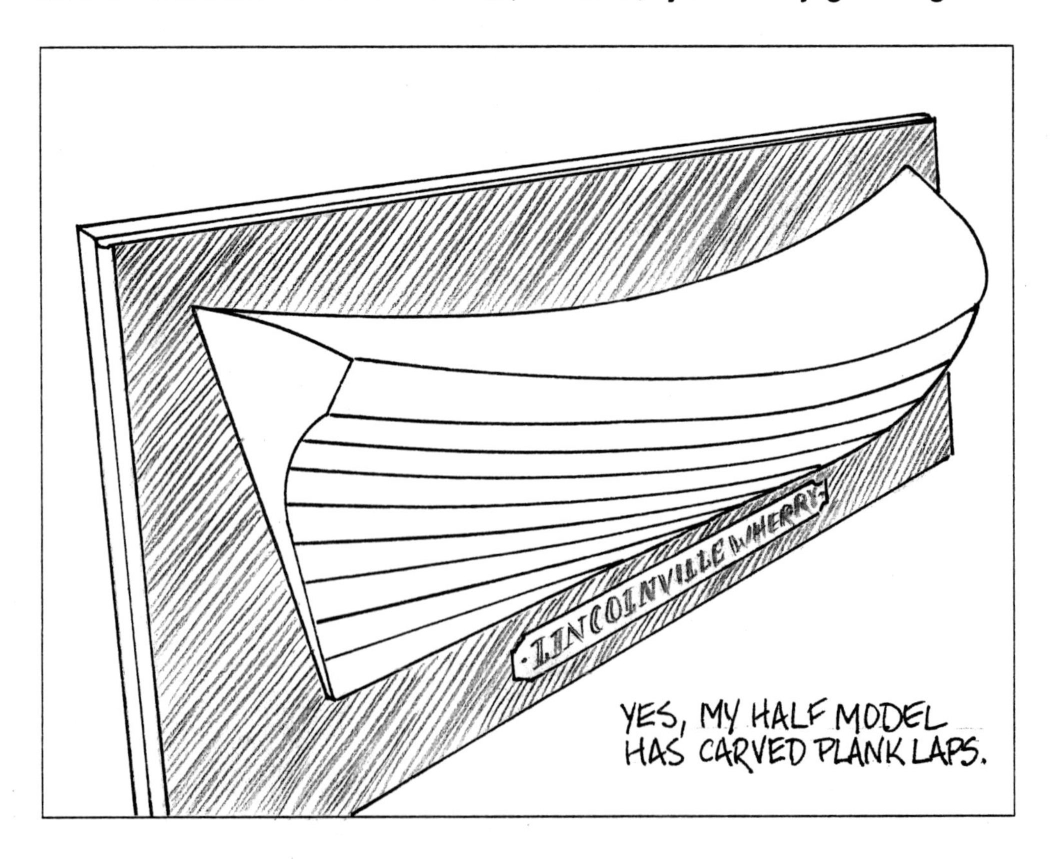

The moral of the story is that decorative models, to be warmly received, had best fulfill the skipper's mental picture of his boat. Nobody wants an ugly model, particularly one of his own boat. When aesthetics are the primary concern, I can't see that it does any harm to flatter the boat and through it, her owner.

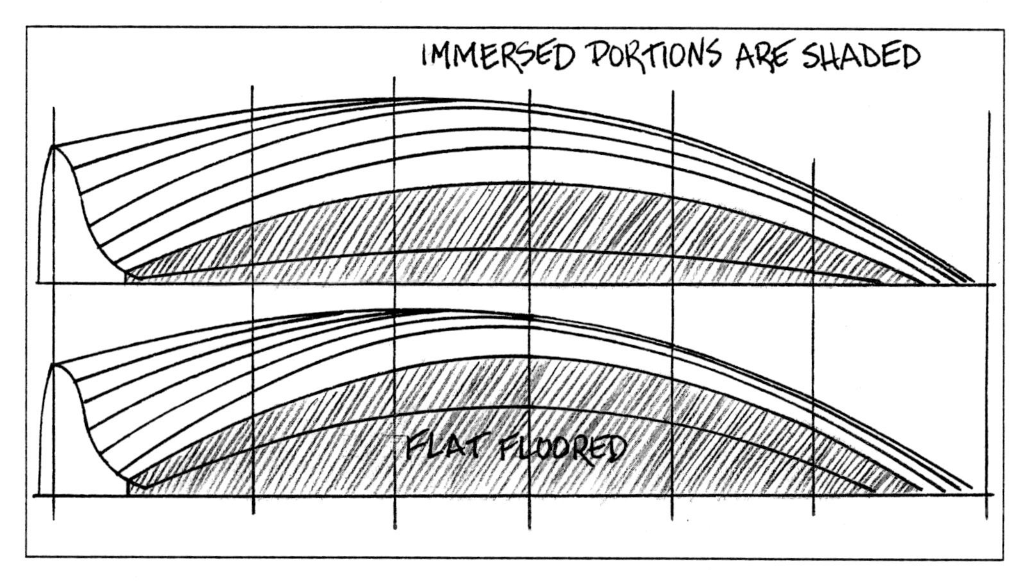

Comparing Waterlines

Part 2: Lines

PLANS

A natural outgrowth of lines technology has been the market for boatbuilding plans. It seems that there has a been a profusion of plans offered for sale, just in the last ten years. Perhaps that has been the case right along, and I simply was unaware of it. In either case, with more plans available for sale than ever before, you should approach the purchase of a set of plans with caution and not a little skepticism.

I am certain that the explosion of the boat plan market is in direct response to the number of recreational boatbuilders. If that is the case, not only are "beginners" responsible for the majority of new small craft being built, their success–or lack of it–will depend largely on the quality of plans being offered.

Advertizements seem to favor lavishly illustrated plans, but they are only responding to the public's proclivity for them. They may well be excellent plans, but they aren't necessarily the best available. "Cute" designs are the bane of beginning and professional builder alike. Utility is the essence of small craft design, and they are intended to be simple and straightforward, not cluttery. Good designs aren't enhanced by superfluous construction details, that in fact, make construction needlessly difficult and costly. On the other hand, aesthetics are a viable concern, and there is an important distinction to be made between cute (what Maine builders call West Coast Fancy) and aesthetically pleasing.

If you want to enjoy building as well as using your new boat, the best advice I can offer is to keep it simple. That begins with a good set of plans. Begin your appraisal with study sets or photos of completed boats built from the plans. A study set is a simplified and miniaturized rendition of the actual plans of the boat. Enough information is included to whet your appetite, and to give you a general feeling for the lines, but little more. You could hardly expect otherwise. Folks in the business of selling plans can't be expected to furnish you with more than a taste. Study sets are certainly not something that you should consider building from.

There are those who think they can save themselves the cost of a set of plans by building directly from magazine articles. Be forewarned that what appears on the pages of a periodical may not be quite what you think. About fifteen years ago, I wrote a piece about one of the workboat types that I build regularly. The profile lines and a few other critical curves included in the article were intentionally altered. Turns out my paranoia wasn't groundless–about six months later a friend sent me photos of a boat built from that article. She was easy to spot with her stubby stern and exaggerated deadrise–not only a homely boat, but crank to boot. She was a far cry from what that professional shop could have built had they been forthright and ordered the building plans. Study plans, like magazine articles, are useful for purposes of comparison; they aren't suitable or for more than that.

Your eventual selection of plans should be based on the suitability of the model for your particular purposes, and the skill with which the plans explain her construction. Only the actual plans provide sufficient detail (hopefully), and to a scale that you can read without squinting. You could make yourself an approximate half model, but unless you are experienced in evaluating models–or have access to someone who is–it won't tell you much more than whether she appeals to your aesthetic sensibilities. Once you have the building plans in hand, evaluation is far easier. At that point, they can be inspected for clarity; you can carve an accurate half model, and even loft the boat. The first two will tell you whether sufficient details have been included, and the latter will verify or condemn their accuracy.

You should be aware that few offer plans for unlimited use, and many are protected by the copyright laws of the United States. What you are purchasing are the construction rights for one boat, and using my own as an example, are stamped like this:

Design_______Sheet_______Of________

Property of
DUCK TRAP WOODWORKING
****

This print sold to______________________________
for the construction of one boat only.

Even when you have the plans rolled out on the bench, most people are inclined to focus their attention on the profile plan, when in fact, other features provide more information. The body plan, for example, will tell you a great deal about the planking–and you will spend more of your hard earned cash there than anywhere else. In general terms, the flatter the floors, the more shapely the planks, and the greater the number of board feet you will have to buy. It is a relative term, of course, but Pete Culler's "Staten Island Skiff" and Chapelle's "Jonesport Peapod" are good examples of flat floored boats. It follows that models with more deadrise such as a Lincolnville Salmon Wherry or a Matinicus Double Ender, will have comparatively straighter planking. That translates into fewer dollars out of pocket as well as a less difficult planking job.

If the concept of "flatter floors" still seems a little nebulous, look at the halfbreadth portion of the plan. There, viewed from above, the waterline curves are concave to the hull centerline. The flatter the floors of a hull, the more concave those waterlines become. It's a matter of degree. Those that are less flat are said to exhibit more deadrise, and have waterlines that are still concave, but are much closer to the centerline–more flat, less deadrise, simple as that.

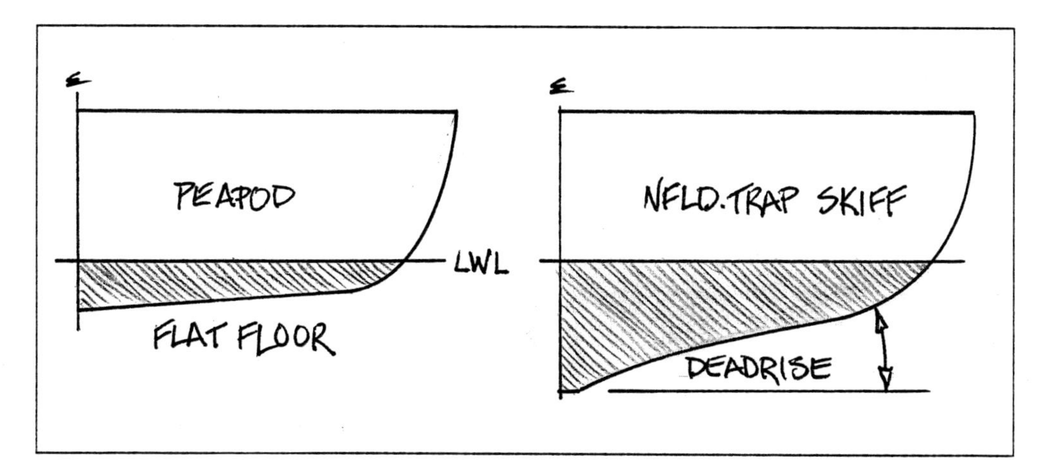

Floors and Deadrise

In the profile view, the buttock line curves are convex to the baseline, and tell you essentially the same thing–only in profile, the closer their midsections are to the baseline, the flatter floored the boat. It's much like reading the contour lines on a topographical map: the closer the contour lines, the steeper the slope.

The act of designing is a combination of art and alchemy, all of it based on the work of previous designers. The experienced designers and builders "have been there", as the saying goes, and all are best advised to gain some working experience before questioning their judgment. I am constantly amazed that those without experience–by their own admission–want to modify a proven design. Human nature being what it is, when the plans show a 16 footer, people invariably want to built the boat 6" longer or shorter. That's not usually more than a nuisance; what I am cautioning against here is major modifications such as repositioning centerboard cases, thwarts, mast partners, and even manipulation of hull sections.

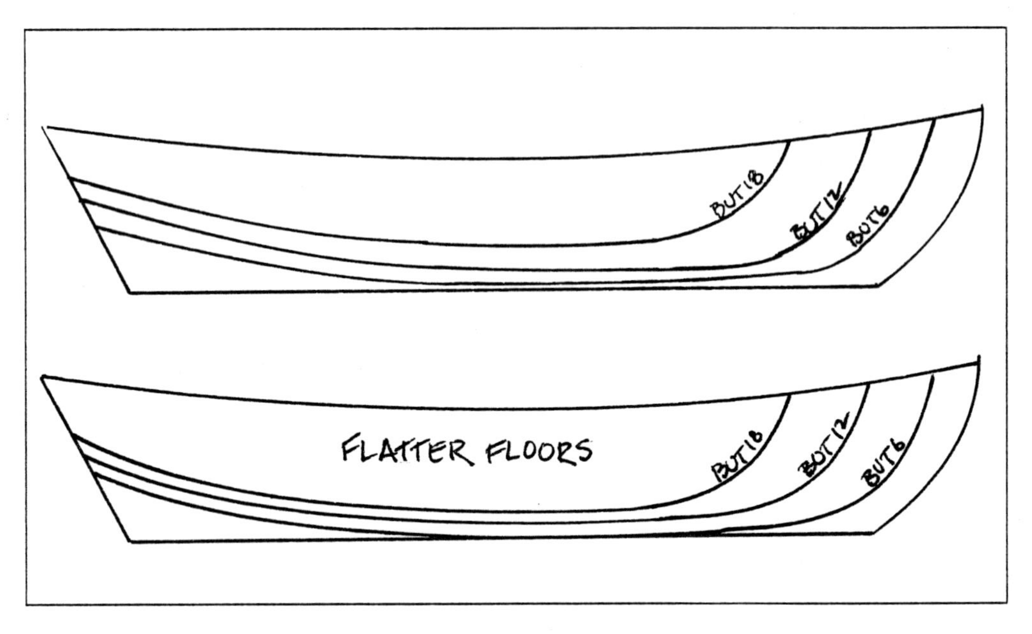

Buttock Line Curves

Whenever I get into such a discussion I remember Westy Farmer talking about a novice builder in the Midwest who purchased a set of his plans. Some time after building was completed, he received a letter from the builder saying that he had followed the plans implicitly, except that he had increased the amount of freeboard, moved the cabin and the engine forward, and the fuel tanks aft. And by the way, she was unhandy as the devil afloat, and just what the hell was wrong with the design?

While you are considering the purchase of a set of plans, bear in mind that small craft are not hydrodynamically proportional. A 17' Whitehall, for example, is a beautiful pulling boat in all respects, while abbreviating the same lines will yield a vastly different craft. Shortening any boat flattens her waterlines, and only an experienced builder or designer can hope to predict the modification's behaviour with any degree of certainty. In general terms, and this is by no means an absolute, the result of stretching lines is more favorable than shortening them, because it increases the bearing in the ends of the boat. If you have your heart set on a 15' Whitehall, and none that are available appeal to you, stretch the lines of an appealing 14 footer.

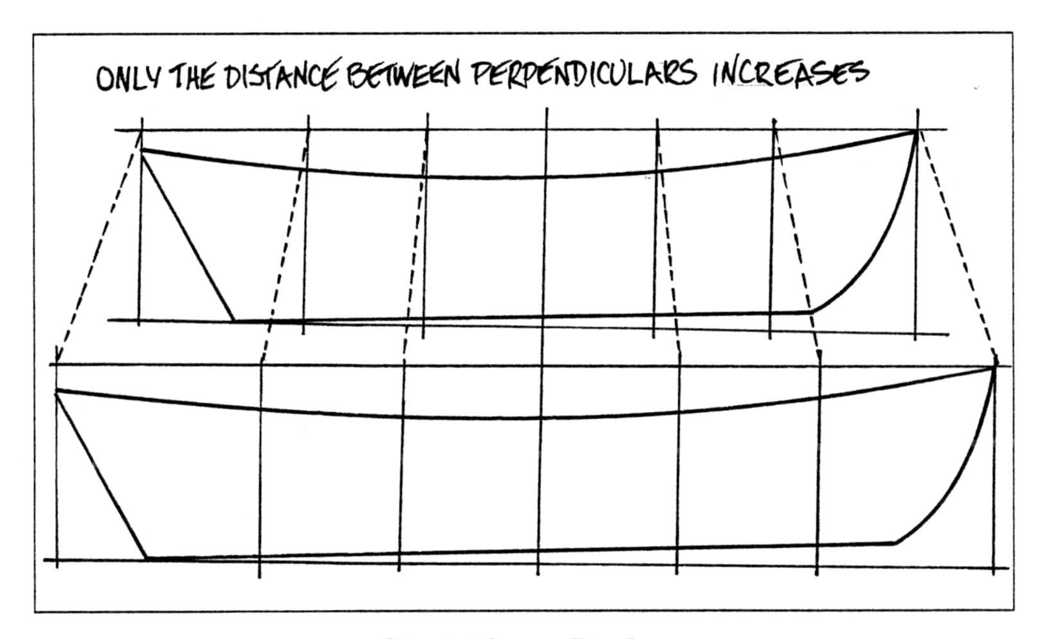

Stretching a Design

There really is a great deal more that goes into a design than is apparent at first glance at the blue lines of a diazo copy. From a builder's perspective, the best plans are the ones that have been proved, which is to say, proved by actual construction. There can be a big difference between theory and practice, and nothing verifies construction details like building the boat. That way, modifications, corrections, and details can be added to make subsequent use of the plans far easier. Be very wary of plans lacking in specific detail drawings.

As time goes on, you are apt to see more and more computer generated plans. Those can even be drawn on a modest-sized computer like mine with 640K RAM and a 20MB hard disc. CAD programs are available from a few hundred dollars up, and can readily draw curves through points you enter on the screen. The difficulty is that unless professionally done, it is all too easy to generate a faired plan that is difficult if not impossible to build from;

in fact, such plans may never have been built from at all.

Obviously, computers and CAD programs have undergone considerable improvement since those words were first written on '91. Today there is specialty software written specifically for marine use, and I have files on this Power Mac that are larger than my hard drive was then. And yet with all that capacity, there is still no substitute for a loftsman working with battens.

To complicate your life, not all details are as helpful as you might think. Plank dimensions on the plans of round-bottomed boats don't mean much. Do look for them on the plans of flat-bottomed skiffs, punts, and rowboats, and even on V-bottoms intended for plywood construction. Due to the complexities of the hull form, the validity of measurements for planking of round-bottom boats should be suspect. There are just too many variables in setting up, lining off, and spiling to allow exact duplication of plank shapes from one boat to the next. About all they would be good for would be to give you an approximation of the planking sizes required.

If no indication of plank shapes is made, the plans can still describe them in general terms. Lengths are easy to figure: the garboard plank is the shortest, and is usually about a foot shorter than the overall length of the boat. There is little curvature to it, so its length can be scaled from the profile view of the hull. For most pulling boats, the longest plank required, which of course is the sheer strake, will be about a foot greater than the overall length of the boat. The sheer strakes of lapstrake canoes are only about 6" longer, owing to their much finer lines, and resulting narrower beam.

Determining the widths of the pieces needed isn't quite so easy. Rules of thumb vary according to the model being built, though plank widths are remarkably similar regardless of the length of a given model. In basic terms, the garboard planks are nearly straight, meaning that a parallel edged piece an inch or so greater than the maximum width of the finished plank will suffice. That accounts for the bulge in the garboard amidships as well as the upsweep of the ends. The bilge plank, too, will be very nearly straight, and the same observations apply.

The difficult planks to assess are those between garboard and bilge strake, and between bilge and sheer. Each plank above the garboard becomes increasingly more shapely, with the ends turning downward. On a really flat floored model such as a Staten Island Skiff, the plank immediately below the turn of the bilge would have required a parallel edged plank 21" wide, or a live edge piece with sufficient curvature. Above the turn of the bilge the planks become increasingly more shapely with the ends pointing upward. The sheer strake requires the widest piece, and because it is nearly vertical from end to end, its width can be scaled right off the profile of the hull. Draw a straight line from stem to stern, connecting the sheer at the stem rabbet with the sheer at the edge of the transom, and scale the distance between the line and the lower edge of the sheer plank amidships.

A few plans will indicate the widths of planks required, but they are few and far between, even as helpful as that information would be to a builder. In practice, builders usually scarph together pieces of lesser width to yield the overall curvature and width needed while eliminating cross grain. But if you know the maximum widths needed, you can interpolate as the circumstances demand. For purposes of comparison, consult the chart of plank dimensions. The measurements derive from my having built each of these boats (many times) and recording the dimensions as planking progressed.

Comparison of Plank Widths

Plank	MDE	Canoe	Wherry	Peapod
Garboard	7	6	8.5	8
2	6.5	7	9	9
3	9	8	10	10
4	9	8	11.5	11
5	5.5	4.5	10	13
6	8.5	7	8.5	7.5
7	12.5	8	7	6.5
8	n/a	n/a	9.5	10
9	n/a	n/a	10	12

(See explanation on following page.)

Table above: Dimensions are in inches, and refer to widths of parallel edged stock required for each of these planks. “MDE” refers to a 16’ Matinicus Double Ender, “Canoe” refers to a 15’ lapstrake canoe, “Wherry” refers to a 14’ Lincolnville Salmon Wherry, and “Peapod” refers to a 16’ Jonesport Peapod.

You have a right to expect the plans you purchase to be accurate. *Caveat emptor.* Do your homework, and look over the pre-purchase materials with a wary eye. Pick a model that suits your purposes and abilities; concentrate on the basics, and then go looking for a set of plans that will guide you throughout the layout and building. There is certainly a profusion of plans in today’s market, and among them are some excellent designs, well documented in the plans package. Hopefully, now you will know what constitutes a good set of plans.

FIELD WORK

Having alluded earlier to the similarities between taking the lines off a half model and off a boat, I ought to follow up before going further. Assuming that you have read through the sections on half models and lines work, you have nearly all the information you need to go out and take the lines of an existing boat.

A model is convenient, for it can be easily moved around and is of manageable size. The very size of a boat is reason enough to expect additional work. Neither the processes involved nor their progression varies from what has already been explained, simply the scale. All you really need to know now are the "extras".

If you understand how to work with a boat located out-of-doors, it follows that you will have an easier time of it when you are able to move one into your garage or shop. Outside you seldom will find convenient points of attachment for holding measuring devices. You'll have to start from scratch. For taking the lines off a boat up to about 16' overall, the materials required are:

(1) A 5/4" x 4" or 6" board, boat length
(2) Two 6-8' long 2x4's
(3) Five station forms
(4) 60 to 100, pointers (cross battens) 8" long
(5) A level, rule, and 2' steel square
(6) Pencils and paper
(7) Bracing for the measuring frame
(8) Hammer and nails

I suppose that sounds like quite an assortment, but except for the three long members, it will fit into an average tool box.
Optional extras would include:

(1) Plumb bob and inclinometer
(2) Saw horses
(3) 35mm camera with a 50mm lens
(4) ASA 400 film
(5) Voice activated tape recorder
(6) A digital camera

The first two are additional measuring devices, of course. The plumb bob is useful for establishing end perpendiculars. The inclinometer measures angles (inclines and declines, actually), so is useful for recording alignment of stem and station forms. The camera and the recorder spare you having to write notes as you work. I have found both to be valuable additions, often saving a trip back outside while you are laying down the lines in the shop.

The intent of this discussion is simply to describe how to measure a hull accurately so that it may be duplicated in some form. It is not the usual practice of builders to try to duplicate every construction detail, because it is assumed that they already know how to assemble a boat.

On the other hand, if your primary concern is documentation of the boat for purposes of historical preservation, your work will necessarily be more detailed. In those instances, the 35mm camera is invaluable–just make certain there is a rule present in each photo because it will spare you from having to measure every individual hull member.

Another advantage of photography is that you will be recording the colors of the boat along with linear details. If you are going to be working in a dark spot, I would suggest that you invest in some faster ASA 1000 film so that you can work with available light and not have to lug auxiliary lighting. Kodak's Ektar™ is a good one. In recent years I have used a video camera and a digital still camera as well, but that is more to get a feel for the boat than for measurement of any kind because of the difference in lens quality from the tried-and-true 50mm.

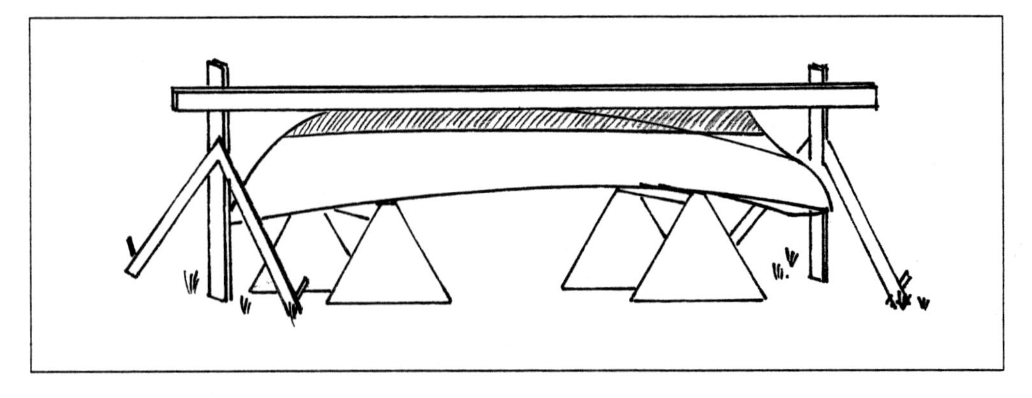

Getting Ready to Take Off Lines

Small craft are very accommodating because they can be moved into position with little difficulty. I find the whole measuring process easier when I invert the boat and support it on saw horses 24-30" above the ground. That is a convenient working height and saves crawling about on the ground–which, you understand, is often the rocks and wet sand of a beach–to take dimensions below the waterline.

A half model has a visible centerline plane. Since the boat does not, the first step in establishing that plane is to level the hull fore and aft and athwartships. To level side-to-side, use your carpenter's level across the midship station (lowest point on the sheer is close enough, usually). The first step to getting a level reading fore and aft is to make an informed estimate. Step back 20' or more from the boat, hold your level out horizontally at arm's reach, and sight by it to the side of the boat. It usually takes a few trips back and forth to adjust the hull, but it does work. Working right next to Penobscot Bay, I have often stepped back and sighted against the horizon. Why not? Horizontal and "level" mean parallel to the horizon. That approach can be used anywhere that the horizon is unobstructed: from a salt shore, to a large lake, to a Kansas wheat field. A water level is also a nifty little tool for the job, particularly advantageous if you happen to be working alone. A garden hose works just fine, though clear tubing is better.

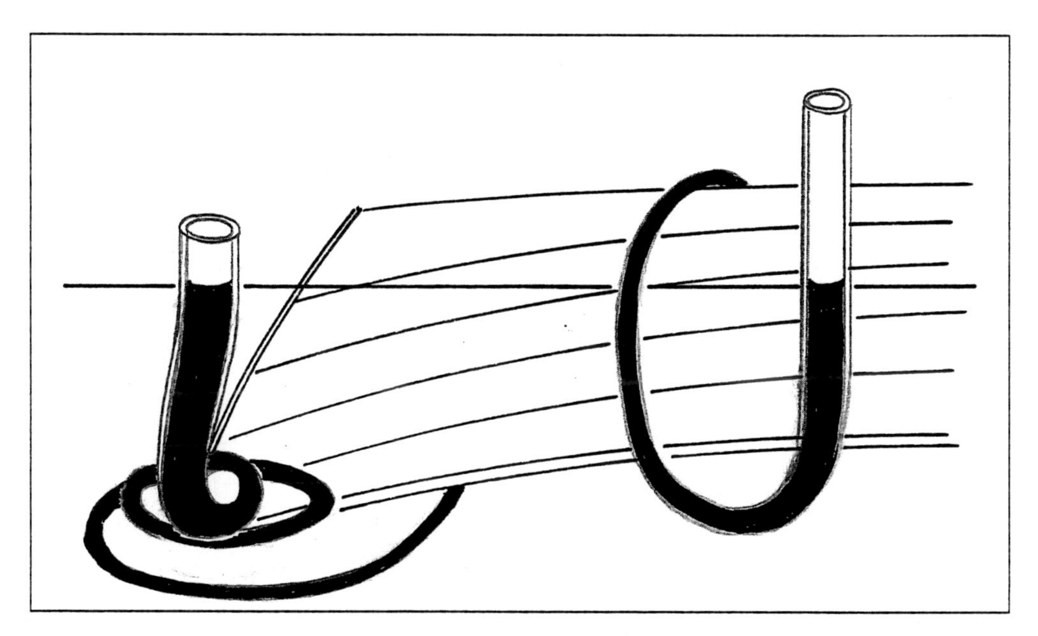

Using a Water Level

Athwartship measurement of the keel will tell you where its centerline is located. Using the two 2x4s as vertical supports, position the long member so that one wide face aligns with the centerline. The wide face thus becomes an extension of the hull's centerline plane, and its lower edge will become the baseline of the measurements yet to be taken. Brace the entire assembly so that it won't be disturbed by vibrations caused by nailing. Once firmly in place, layout station locations on the centerline board.

From this point onward, proceed as you would to take the lines from a solid model. The hull is too large to permit the carving of individual station templates, so use the station forms in conjunction with the 8" pointers. At each station, the sequence is the same. Position the station form square to the centerline plane; place the battens in position; and secure each in turn to the form. As each station is thus duplicated, set the form aside carefully and go on to the next. Don't neglect to add station numbers to the forms.

Station Forms and Pointers

The profile of the stem is taken in exactly the same way, or you can establish a forward perpendicular on the forward upright brace and measure from that to the stem at regular intervals–suit yourself. The outline of the transom is measured no differently. Should you be running short of time, however, you could stretch a sufficiently large piece of paper (newsprint, brown, or even red rosin building paper) across the transom and make a rubbing of its outline with a soft pencil or even chalk. Use any approach that works. The object is to derive an accurate representation of the portion being measured.

The halfbreadth and height of the sheer at each station are, of course, recorded along with the rest of the station dimensions. Since those dimensions are critical to the realignment of your templates back at the shop, record those same measurements again. This time, use just your level and ruler. Record the beam at each station and its distance from the base (extending the base outward from the center using your level, and measuring with your rule from there).

Unless you are interested in recording other such information as thwart, centerboard, and mast step locations, the sole remaining measurement needed is plank thickness. Why? Because you have just taken the hull dimensions to the outside of the planking, and it is the inside dimensions that are required if you plan to build moulds or a builder's model.

Anyone who is thinking to himself that he can simply deduct the plank thickness from the dimensions picked off the hull will be sadly mistaken. Such an approach is valid only where the planking lies square to the centerline plane (as do some sections of the sheer strake). At all other locations, the planking is at an angle to that centerline, so the angular dimension must be deducted.

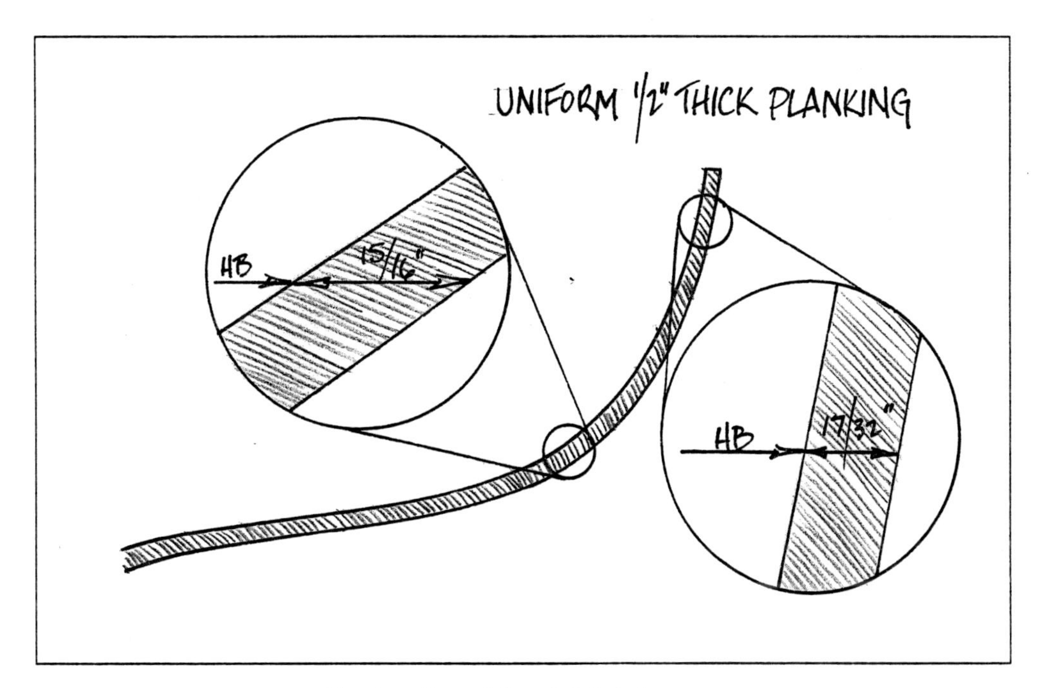

Deducting Plank Thickness

The final derivation of inside measurements is quite simple, if a bit tedious. Transfer your halfbreadths to the lofting board by springing a batten around the cross battens and drawing the curve indicated. Make a plank gauge the exact thickness of the boat's planking on the original hull, and use that to determine the precise inside dimensions. If you are working with a smooth-planked boat, align one edge with the curve you drew, and mark at each waterline intersection. For a lapstrake boat, use the plank gauge to "reconstruct" the appearance of the laps and take your new measurements from the inside thus derived.

If all this sounds like a great deal of needless work that could be avoided having used the station forms inside the hull, by all means try it that way. I'll assure you, though, that thwarts, thwart rails, and inwales can make removal of templates very difficult and frustrating. Certainly it can be done, but I only did it once.

Taking Off the Station Shape from Inboard

The information needed for taking the lines off a small boat is here. Use it to your advantage, but don't let my words dissuade you from being innovative. The accuracy of the end result is the only important consideration.

Patterns are easily made on the site, but the final measurements (or rather their interpretation) is much more easily handled in the shop. I use this particular approach because all the individual pieces can be taken back to the shop with me–not only the station forms, but also the centerline batten, which serves as a storey pole. On it are located both perpendiculars, the position of each station, and the information necessary to duplicate the rake of the transom. Taken together, these pieces comprise a full-dimension model of sorts, and as we've discussed, they can be treated in exactly the same manner.

All of this work of taking off the lines is a means to an end, of course. The next step involves taking your patterns, measurements, notes, and photos to a lofting board where they can be compiled. If you want to skip right to the lofting section now, go right ahead, but you need to know that the information in the next three sections can help the lofting go easier for you–especially if this is your first time.

DRAFTING

This section is not a general discussion of drafting, but rather a continuation of working with half models, describing the process of transferring the information the model has to offer to paper. It also applies to getting information picked off an existing hull down on paper, though that usually follows lofting and fairing.

Tools that fall into the "nice to have even if they aren't essential" category include an adjustable parallel, mechanical pencils with 0.5mm lead, and a flexible curve or ship's curves. The adjustable parallel can be the type that rides on cable guides, as on a professional drawing board, or a rolling ruler equipped with guide wheels, or the traditional T-square that works off the edge of the drawing board.

The only tools really needed, other than those ready discussed, are a 30-60-90 drafting triangle and some pencils with lead for drafting film (2H and 4H seem the most versatile). Regular pencils will work, but will smudge on the plastic surface. The triangle should be transparent, and will serve as a see-through straightedge as well as a square for projecting from one view into the other.

Set the model aside for now. On the paper you have drawn the profile, and above that the halfbreadth view complete with waterlines and sheer. The load waterline and hull centerline are already drawn. Now you must add stations and forward and after perpendiculars, and a base line. All these will serve as reference lines for future measurement. Some builders, notably Pete Culler, dispensed with the base line altogether, measuring heights from the load waterline and noting on the table of offsets whether measurements are above or below that line. My Duck Trap Wherry plan is done the same way because I began the design process with a half model. Currently, however, it is more common to measure all heights from the base.

Assuming that you have chosen the base line method, you must first establish one on your lines drawing. By convention, the base line is parallel to the profile waterlines and is located at some multiple of the waterline spacing beneath the lowest waterline–and in such a position (usually) that it does not intersect any portion of the keel or deadwood. The reason is simply that it is much easier to interpret lines with some white space between them than it is to differentiate between a series of overlapping lines. As long as you are the one doing the drafting, there is no sense making the operation unduly complicated.

Waterline Spacing–Profile View

I mentioned using a multiple of the waterline spacing. What I mean is that the lifts of the original model already dictate a particular distance between waterlines, commonly 3" for small craft. If the spacing is 3", and the lowest point on the tracing is 5" below that, locate the plan base line 6" below the LWL in order to clear all drawn lines.

Stations, where moulds will be placed during the actual building of the boat, should be placed realistically. If they are too close together, the inside of the hull will be needlessly cluttered and building will be difficult–too far apart, and they won't provide adequate support for the planking. You must think ahead a bit before you make your determination. Moulds spaced 30" apart are adequate for hulls with 7/16" planking; 5/16" planking, however, is more flexible and requires mould spacing of 24" or less. I've found that laying off five moulds with the midship mould at the point of greatest breadth works best for the types of boats I usually build, wherries and double enders. My canoes, with their 1/4" planking require 7 moulds.

If you are uncertain, go and ask a builder, consult the plans in one of Chapelle's books, or better yet, do both. The only standard for mould spacing is that imposed by the stiffness of the planking, at least for traditionally built small wooden boats. Bearing that in mind, lay out stations along the base line at equal intervals so that they are exactly perpendicular to the base and extend upward through the waterlines in the section of the plan above.

Now draw the straight profile waterlines (these show positions of the top of each lift that you marked on the plan when you were tracing), as well as the gridwork on which to draw the hull sections (body plan). In truth, this additional step could be eliminated and dimensions for building taken directly from the waterlines that have been traced and faired; but it is important to include them because the stations provide another check on the waterline curves. Often, it is only by drawing the body plan that you pick up an otherwise unforeseen discrepancy in the waterlines. The reason is that while long curves are relatively easy to fair in, shorter ones are far less forgiving. Hence, the stations are very important–much more so than would be expected by anyone who has never drawn plans or lofted a hull before.

In lofting, the stations are usually lofted directly on the profile at the midship station–that station serving as their centerline. Once you learn to differentiate the lines of the various overlapping plans, it is quite convenient. On the drawing board, however, you have the opportunity to separate the three plan parts because of the space available. The necessary gridwork consists of base line and centerline, waterlines and buttock lines, and is positioned wherever it happens to be convenient. Buttock lines trace fore and aft slices through the hull parallel to the centerline and perpendicular to the waterline planes. That makes them straight when seen from above in the halfbreadth view and convex with respect to the base in profile.

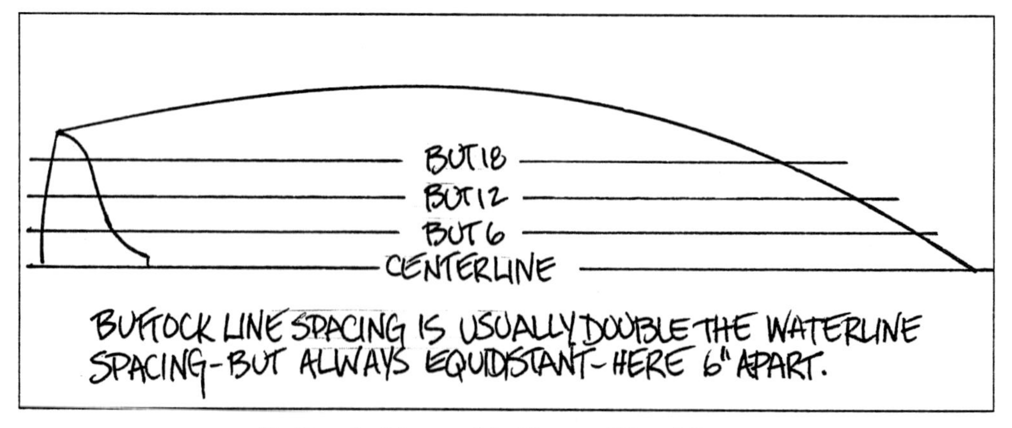

Buttock Lines–Halfbreadthg View

To complete the initial lines, lay out buttock lines on the halfbreadth view plan, and with your dividers pick off dimensions where they intersect waterlines and transfer them to the profile view. Heights for keel and sheer are derived from the profile plan and are also transferred for each station. After all halfbreadth dimensions are transferred, fair in the curve for each station. These curves are the shape of the moulds, to scale. Dimensions for the body plan are derived by picking off dimensions along each station between the centerline and the intersection of each curved waterline. Transfer them to the grid for the body plan working a station at a time and then fairing in the points. This part of the plan is finished off by connecting the sheer points and keel points with fair curves.

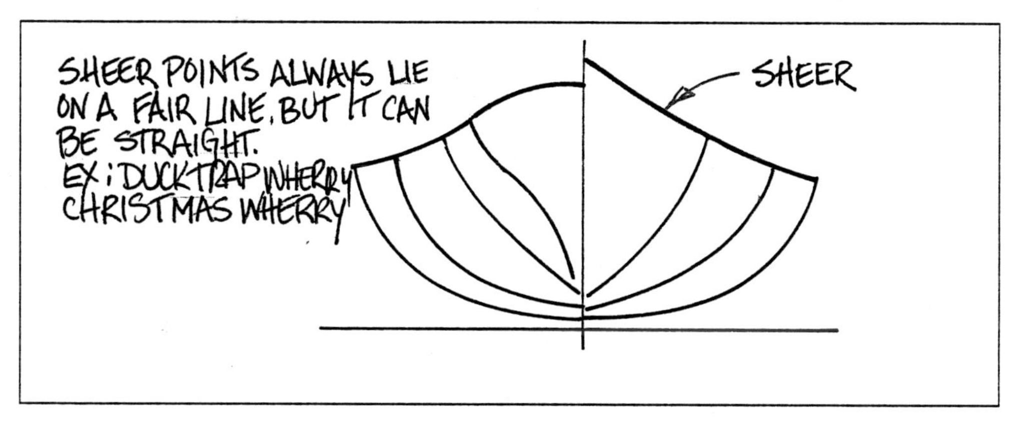

Body Plan Sheer Curves

In all cases, the points must fall along the fair curve; if they do not, go back and recheck the dimensions you picked off. Should that fail to reveal the error, take your dividers back to the model to determine whether, in fact, you originally picked off the dimension accurately. As a last resort, you will have to make a change somewhere in the plan. Remembering that the stations are the least forgiving, assume those dimensions to be correct and go back and refair the offending waterline. It's not a comforting thought, I know, but half models aren't infallible, errors are likely to be minor, to be sure, but enough to throw off the lines if undetected. That is one more reason that lofting would be the next logical step if you want to build this boat.

Unless you are considerably more accurate and meticulous than I, your plan at this point is a mass of erasures and corrections–hardly something you would wish to work from. It is a good idea therefore, to overlay your preliminary drafting with a good piece of Mylar™ or other drafting film and trace all the corrected lines up onto the new sheet. That makes for a much more professional looking job, and one that is considerably easier to read.

TABLE OF OFFSETS

Hulls are three dimensional objects consisting of several systems of curved lines. In order to measure, and thereby be able to duplicate those curves, a frame of reference is required. Elementary geometry deals with a two-dimensional system in which points are plotted by measuring from "X" and "Y" axes, one vertical, the other horizontal. In advanced geometry points in space are plotted, so the concept of depth, and with it a "Z" axis are introduced. If the location of a point can be measured from three axes perpendicularly arranged, its position in space can be ascertained. Straight lines can be defined by two points; curves require a minimum of three for definition. In boatbuilding, you will be dealing with both systems.

The table of offsets is unique to the construction of hulls, both floating and airborne. Its function is to allow the tablature of the measurements that locate points on the surface of the hull. It usually appears on the plans adjacent to the lines of the hull and are arranged in columns corresponding to stem, stations, and transom, with rows for each waterline, buttock line, and diagonal. The rows are grouped into sections for Heights Above Base, Halfbreadths, and Diagonals (if any). Abbreviations you will encounter there are: STA for station, WL for waterline, BUT for buttock line, and DIA for diagonal. Each is accompanied by a letter or number identifying its location on the plan, and subsequently on the lofting board as well.

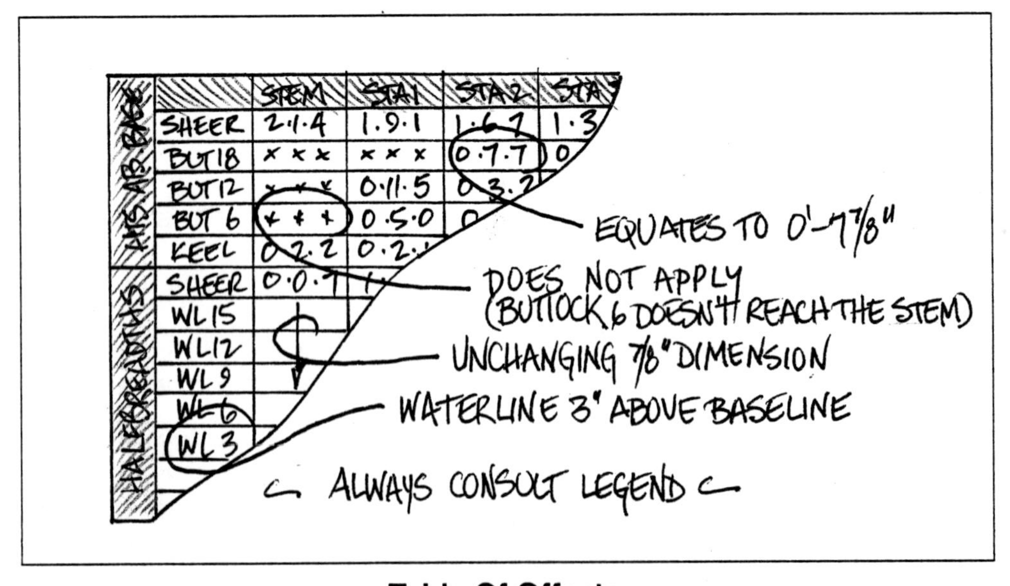

Table Of Offsets

Additionally, nearly all tables are accompanied by a legend–read the fine print, it's important. On my plans, it says something to the effect of "Lines given in feet, inches, and eighths, to the inside of the planking, outside of the transom and plank keel". It might say dimensions are in feet, inches, and sixteenths of an inch, or even that dimensions are to the outside of the planking. Either mention would change the way you would handle the numerical information contained in the table of offsets.

The "feet, inches, and eighths", is the traditional method of entering measurements in the table, and accounts for the unlikely appearance of the three-digit entries. Fractions are cluttery; these aren't. Neither are they bothersome to interpret: 3-2-5, for example, means 3'-2-5/8". On my plans and some others, pluses and minuses after the digits refer to sixteenths. Be sure to consult the legend accompanying the table to be certain, because every once in a while, the numbers will be feet, inches, and sixteenths.

The first time anyone works from a table of offsets, the natural tendency is to translate all of the offsets to familiar form. That makes it more difficult than it is. If you can make yourself say the offset aloud while reading it off a ruler, you will be using the offsets without translation in a short while. Reading a table of offsets is about as difficult as reading the mileage chart on a road map. To read the halfbreadth of waterline 6 at station 3, for example, find the column designated STA3, and run your finger down it until you reach the row labeled WL6. There you will find the offset which tells you the distance at which the waterline 6" above the baseline intersects station 3–on the plan and the lofting, that dimension is layed off in the body plan and in the halfbreadth view of the hull.

Despite the array of measurements in the table, it doesn't supply every one a builder would need to build the boat. If you look at the plan, you will see dimensions noted here and there that would not fit conveniently within the table of offsets. Such things as the height of the forefoot, or the precise juncture of the stem/keel joint are better entered right on the construction drawing.

A Table of Offsets is a tedious thing to compile due to the sheer number of measurements involved, yet without it you would have to scale every dimension from the lines or the half model in order to build a boat. I suppose this is hardly an encouraging note, but even the offsets given by Chapelle, Culler, and Pittaway contain errors here and there–I've found some in my own offsets, and the ones I didn't find were pointed out to me. Usually, though, you will discover that the erroneous entries are so far off that they are readily apparent. Transpositions are among the most frequent offenders.

Think you can compile a table of offsets flawlessly? Why don't you try? You have already learned how to take the lines off half hull models; the next step would be to tabulate the dimensions of those lines for future reference. Overcoming the tedium that engenders errors is your problem, but I can provide the mechanics if you are up to the challenge.

Begin layout on a separate sheet of 8-1/2 x 11" paper. All tables are essentially the same in that you must provide sufficient columns for all verticals, and enough rows for all horizontals. It is also helpful to provide lettering guidelines within the gridwork (those numbers so nicely lined up in each rectangle aren't there by happenstance). When the layout is complete, look to see where it fits best on the lines page, slide it underneath, and tape it down. From that position, trace up the table grid as needed, and make use of the lettering guidelines without ever having to add those lines to the finished copy. It is clean and neat, and can be set aside for reuse in the future.

		STEM	STA1	STA2	STA3	STA4	STA5	TRANS.
HEIGHTS	SHEER							
	BUT18							
	BUT12							
	BUT6							
	KEEL							
HALFBREADTHS	SHEER							
	WL18							
	WL15	← 1/4" GRAPH PAPER MAKES IT EASIER ←						
	WL12							
	WL9							
	WL6							
	WL3							
	KEEL							

Offset Table Layout

WHOLE MOULDING

Whole moulding is the missing link between half models and lofting. I mentioned that my original Newfoundland Trap Skiff model indicated three stations that the builders there call the fore hook, aft hook, and midship bend. "Moulds" is not quite accurate because this method of transferring measurements and shapes predates our contemporary lines system. The three stations, in fact, are indicative of the process known as whole moulding. My accounting of the method presented here comes from boatbuilder Stan Pisent of Gander Bay, Newfoundland, through the courtesy of folklorist David A. Taylor.

Stan Pisent builds his Trap Skiffs and Rodneys from half models that he has carved himself. His method differs from ours in one major respect–while I would measure a model in order to pick off the waterline and buttock dimensions, and fair in the lofted curves according to those measurements, he regards each of his three stations as a combination of sized arcs. While I pick off the individual points in order to draw the curve, he already has the curves in the form of "risings" that need only be positioned in the proper relationship to one another.

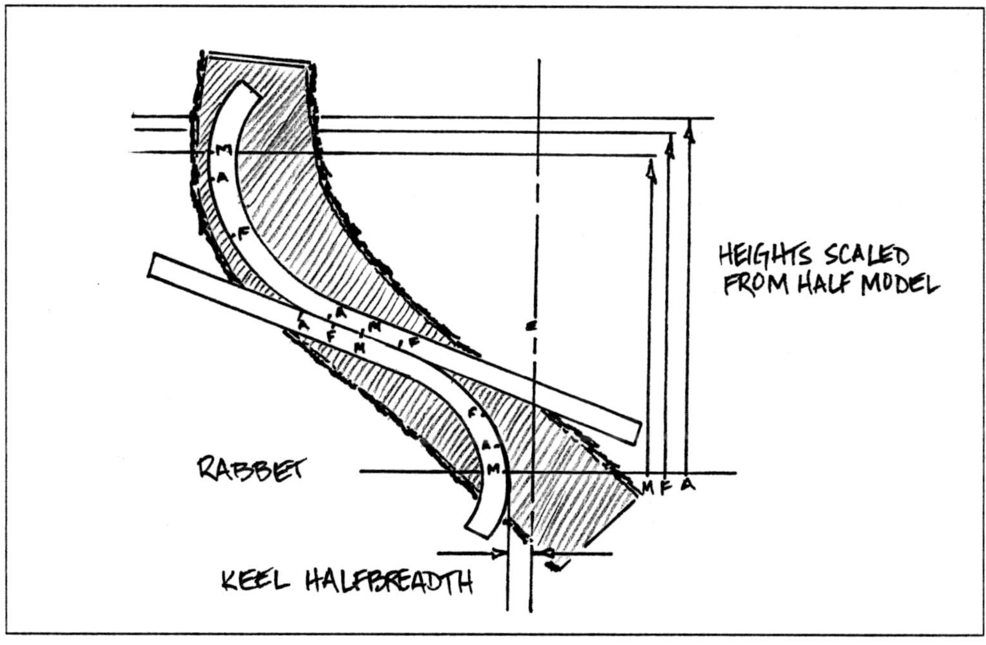

Using Rising Squares

Two rising squares are used, their exact locations determined by the half model. They differ from one another, but are used for all three stations by repositioning them to achieve the different station shapes. The accompanying illustration shows how the rising squares are set opposed to one another in order to yield the compound hull section at each station. Note also that each square contains a series of "sir" marks. The sir marks allow the squares to be repeatedly repositioned accurately.

A builder such as Mr. Pisent uses his rising squares to layout each of his three stations. Instead of a typical lofting board, he uses a large piece of brown paper. The paper is readily available , being the common wrapping for groceries at the local store, and it is easily cut with shears. We pick off lines and transfer them to our mould stock. Mr. Pisent cuts his paper pattern to the shape of the midship bend and traces the outline onto his mould stock. In turn, he cuts away the paper to the outline of the aft hook and eventually the fore hook and traces those as well. What could be more practical?

None of the builders who have learned to build in the old way ever stray very far from their builder's model; they cannot, for it is the final authority for all of their measurements. The rising squares by themselves would be insufficient, because they must be aligned with the hull centerline at keel and sheer–the squares are valid only between those two points. The half model, therefore, provides the measurements necessary for alignment, being picked off to scale and transferred full size to the brown paper.

The rising squares provide the outline to the inside of the planking for each station. They are then set aside until another boat is to be built. The remaining dimensions necessary to get out the backbone members are scaled directly from the half model. Stem profile, outline and rake of the transom, position of the keel, and profile of the sheer are thus derived without resort to lofting.

This whole moulding system does have one primary shortcoming–the ends of the hull cannot be closed without further work. For a professional boatbuilder, the amount of additional work required is negligible, but for a novice without guidance it could be disastrous. Our common method of lofting focuses on the waterline curves of the hull, which necessarily intersect the hull centerline fore and aft. The whole moulded setup provides the complete profile and exact measurement for each of the three moulds. That's all. In order to fair in the hull, (as you would have to do in order to install frames as they do in Newfoundland), the builders rely heavily on their lining battens. The battens will span each of the moulds, the stem, and the transom, and thereby verify whatever point they wish between them.

Actually, despite the way it may sound, it is not at all haphazard. The batten is used initially to give the approximate shape for the sawn frame. The frame is then "gotten out" as nearly as possible and secured to the keel and to the sheer batten. The rising squares or similar adjustable templates are used to pick off the intermediate frame shapes. After the frames are all in position, the lining or fairing batten is again sprung around the hull framework. Since the frames have some additional wood left on, the spare wood is carefully cut away until the batten lands fair on each and on the "hooks". Since the batten is employed to portray the run of the planking across each hull member, the sawn frames, moulds, transom, and stem rabbet are all faired in at the same time.

Sawn frames are as uncommon here now as whole moulding itself, but the battening procedure is otherwise identical to the one we use to fair off a new set of moulds prior to planking. In a lapstrake boat, the moulds are faired (beveled), and the planking follows immediately. In a smooth-planked boat, the operation would precede the installation of the ribbands to which the steamed frames would be temporarily fastened.

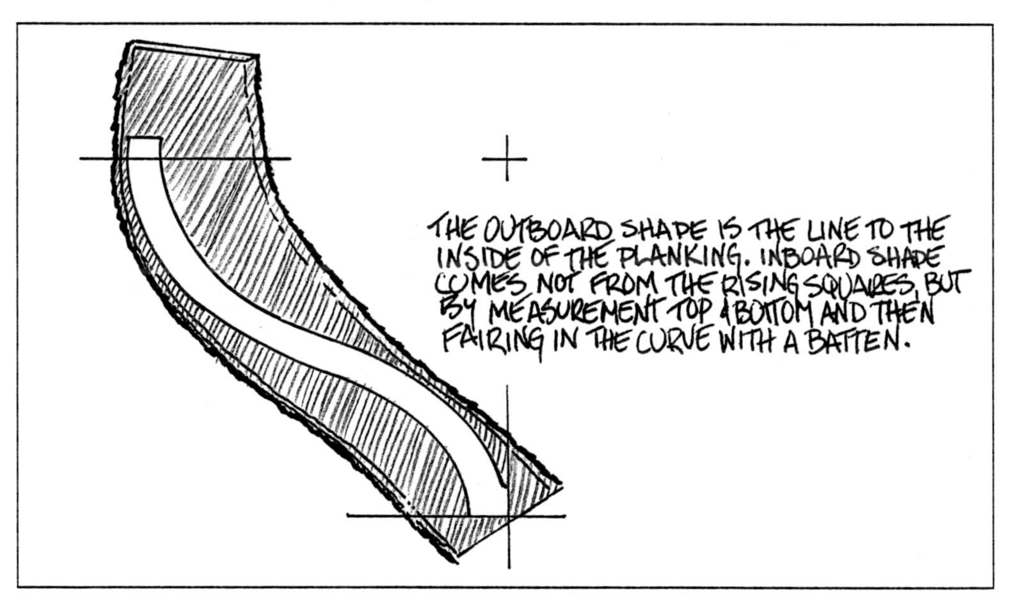

Sawn Frame

Methods vary according to the builder both here and in Newfoundland. With his rising squares, Mr. Pisent could construct many more than three moulds, or he could get out his sawn frames directly and use them rather than moulds in the manner of dory construction. Each builder uses the method most comfortable for him, and local tradition figures in prominently.

MAKING MODIFICATIONS

The subject of modifying lines should be approached with not a little trepidation. It can be an intriguing exercise, and one that can account for a considerable amount of your time, but be forewarned that it is all too easy to create a monster. Unless you are unconcerned about the time you will expend during the lofting and building, and as equally unconcerned about the cost of the materials, hull modifications below the load waterline should be kept to a minimum. Like a dictionary full of words of vastly different meaning, perhaps differing from the next by only a single letter, it doesn't take much of an alteration to effect a substantial change in a boat's seakeeping ability. When it comes right down to it, other than possibly satisfying your urge to tinker with a design, if it ain't broke, why fix it?

Most of the hull modifications I have been asked to incorporate over the years involved altering the length of the boat, though a few were requested for aesthetic reasons. In all cases, I prefer to preview the changes with a half model. If nothing else, it is a fast and inexpensive means of seeing your ideas in three-dimensional form prior to lofting; with more experience, it will help you evaluate the feasibility of the change.

We touched previously on the fact that insofar as handling characteristics are concerned, it is safer to lengthen an existing design to derive the overall length wanted than it is to shorten a design. Lengthening at least increases the bearing in the ends and the theoretical speed. Shortening has the opposite effect, plus stands a good chance of reducing the amount of secondary stability. A flat-bottomed skiff, for example, has high initial stability and low secondary–it has high resistance to heeling, but once she starts to go there is little secondary stability to keep her from turning turtle. By contrast, a double ender has moderate initial stability and high secondary–they will heel, but the farther over they go, the more they resist further heeling.

If you are working from lines to make a half model to evaluate an increase in overall length, start by increasing the station spacing proportionally. To do that, divide the new overall length by the old overall length, and multiply the station spacing by the resulting coefficient to derive the new station spacing. To increase from a 14' boat to a 16' boat, for example, the coefficient would be 16/14 = 1.143 (rounded off to three decimal places), station spacing would increase from 20" to 1.143(20)=22.86", or nearly 22-7/8" apart.

Please take note: There is no need to multiply the individual offsets by the coefficient. (Wouldn't that be a bear!) You need only stretch the hull, so heights and halfbreadths remain the same. Once you know the increased station spacing, it should be no problem for you to apply the plan offsets to make templates and carve an elongated half model.

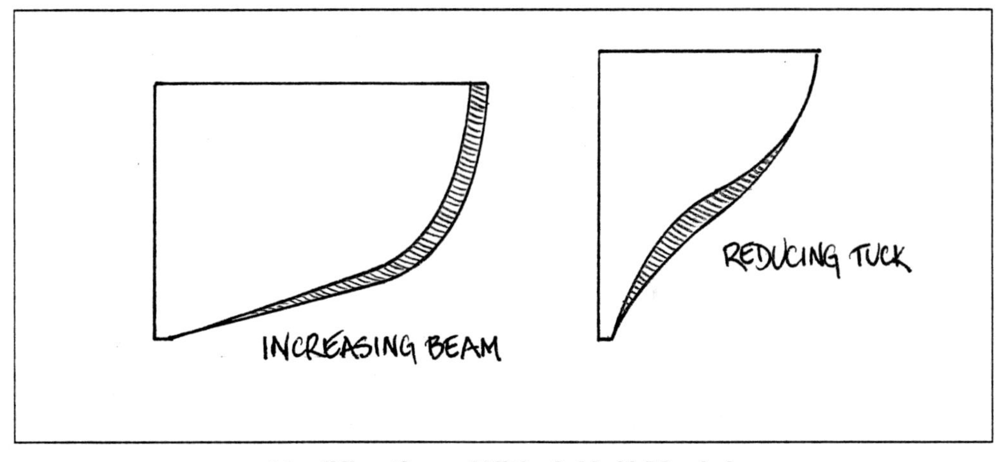

Modifications With A Half Model

Aesthetic changes benefit from the use of a half model too. Usually, these involve adding volume to the hull, so it isn't just a matter of recarving the existing model (though you could apply some modeling clay to preview the change before carving). Not long ago, I was asked to build a 10' Herreshoff yacht tender. That particular model is the subject of a Mystic Seaport pamphlet, and has been considered a superb tender for years. This particular client, however, thought her plain-Jane looks could be improved along with her performance.

His request was to increase her overall length to 12', and to plank down her skeg rather than using the built down one designed. A "built down" skeg is essentially a fin at the after end of the keel, commonly extending from the lowest point of the keel in a straight line to the sternpost. A "planked down skeg", by contrast, is enclosed by hull planking. The profile of the hull remains the same, while–in this case, at least–the volume, and hence the buoyancy of the after sections would be increased. To complete the modifications, the transom was to be faired into the sternpost so that it would be shaped more like a wine glass than a cup.

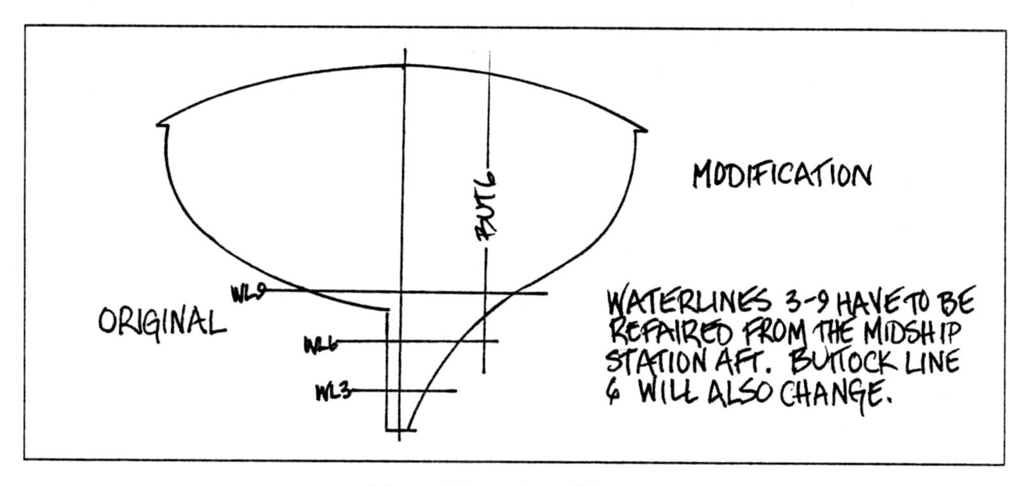

New Tansom Shape

All of these changes were incorporated into a new half model. Carving it gave me the opportunity to fair in the modifications so that they really were aesthetic improvements, and it provided the owner with an accurate representation of the boat that was about to be built. Dimensions for the lofting came from the original table of offsets where possible, and from the half model for all other locations. She worked out aesthetically and afloat, and a very flattering photo of her appeared in the January/February 1990 edition of "Wooden Boat".

Use your model making skills to your advantage. Yes, it takes time to carve a half model accurate enough to use as a builder's model, but your lofting will correct any flaws you may have introduced. If you are particularly parsimonious and already have a model, use the clay overlays. Lacking that–and here is a heresy of the first order–carve a temporary one out of a styrofoam block. Stanley "Surform"™ tools, coarse files, and even 80 grit sandpaper will work on it like chisels and gouges on a wooden model. To coin a phrase, use what works.

Part 3: Lofting

LOFTING PREVIEW

Whether you find yourself working from a half model, a set of plans, or dimensions you have taken from an existing boat, the next step in the sequence of building will be the lofting. Every loftsman began with a "first" lofting. Nearly all of them lived through the experience–hopefully you will too. I remember the frustrations of starting out, so have included this section to provide you with an overview of the entire operation before delving into a detailed discussion of each part.

To a builder, lofting and "laying down the lines" means the same thing–expanding the lines of the plan or half model to the actual size of the boat being built. Our lofting of a trawler yacht, for example covered 57' of shop floor. A completed lofting is a two-dimensional representation of a hull as seen in three views. The front view is known as the profile, the top view the halfbreadths, and the end view the body plan. On a plan the designer has the luxury of separating the three hull views. Space is considerably more limited on a lofting board, so loftsmen have taken to superimposing the three views. As with a half model, only half of the hull needs to be portrayed in the lofting.

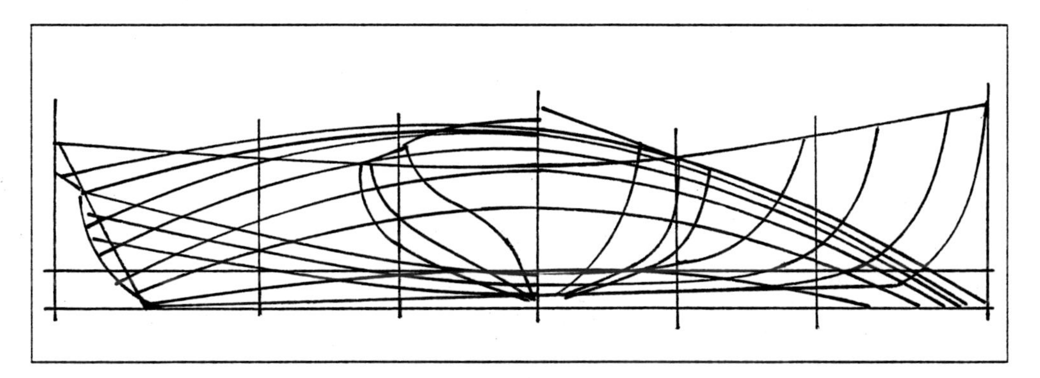

Superimposed Views in a Lofting

I learned how to loft a boat first by reading about it (Chapelle's Boatbuilding), then by being taught by a master boatbuilder, and finally by doing it. Without any first-hand experience, the reading part didn't help me much. Once I began actually lofting, I recalled what I had read, but it didn't foster the necessary understanding on its own.

I'm certain that an understanding of lofting came easily to me because that builder took the time to show me how to loft one boat completely–the 25' Friendship sloop *Pemaquid*. With her raking elliptical transom and pronounced tuck, she's a lofting exercise of the first order. Four weekends of hands-and-knees work drawing her lines also prompted my eventual use of a vertical lofting board. It's not that I don't like crawling about, mind you, it's just that I prefer walking upright (and being able to).

There is no substitute for the apprentice system of learning a skill; the sad fact is that opportunities to learn lofting under the tutelage of a master boatbuilder are indeed rare. Alternatives are the short term courses that are offered at Mystic Seaport, Wooden Boat School, and here in my own shop at Duck Trap, and they are well worth attending should the opportunity arise. The attendance, of course, is limited; I won't presume to speak for the others, but here we generally loft a pair of boats (a 10'-6" yacht tender and a 13' lapstrake canoe) in the course of a week. Like the majority of readers, however, most will have to rely on printed information, such as that contained between these covers.

If you've never attempted lofting, don't hamstring yourself from the beginning by trying to work from a set of plans out of a book or magazine. There are many pitfalls to that, but one important one is that the scale is simply too small to allow accurate work. Get yourself a set of plans of the boat you would like to build and start from there. Things to look for and to look out for are discussed in the section dealing with plans. Another alternative would be to follow through and loft those lines you took off the half model.

If a poll was conducted among those who once considered building a boat, but who failed to begin, I think we would learn that the reason was their inability to comprehend the "lines". Certainly the necessary information can be found in many sources, but lines seem forever to be explained with such a bewildering profusion of detail and advice that the beginner is often confused and frustrated from the very beginning. It's needless. Just as surely as you must walk before you can run, the understanding and interpretation of lines must be arrived as gradually. There definitely is an easier way, and the first step toward working with lines is to learn what they are.

The function of lines is to provide boatbuilders with a two-dimensional portrait of the hull to be built. You know that now because of your knowledge of half models. Despite their appearance, they are much akin to the three-viewed (front, side, and top) mechanical drawings used by engineers. Reduced to simplest terms, the lines that you see in a drawing or on a lofting merely indicate given points along the hull. It is the points themselves that are of primary importance. The faired curves serve mainly to verify the proper alignment of the measured points and project still more in between. That's a useful piece of information, particularly if you are called upon to determine the size and shape of a bulkhead that doesn't happen to land on a station.

Actually, that's a bit of an oversimplification, but it's best to begin with the beginning, even to state the obvious, and leave the finer points until later. A boat is a three-dimensional object, and, as such, it can be measured. The function of "lines" is to allow accurate measurement of the hull form so that it may be drawn to scale or full size (lofted), and ultimately be duplicated.

Lines plans have a way of looking deceptively simple–you'll find them exacting, but your lofting will look the same once completed, albeit to full scale. The table of offsets, if set up in the customary manner, provides all dimensions for heights, half breadths, and possibly diagonals for the hull. The three-number system of entry is to simplify reading, not to confuse you. By convention, the numbers denote feet, inches, and eighths of an inch, in that order. The only other thing to remember is that, should any question arise during the lofting, a dimension noted on the table (or anywhere on any plan) always takes precedence over one you pick off the plan drawing with a scale rule.

Boatbuilders have standardized the use of three systems of planes positioned at 90° to one another. The first is a horizontal plane known as the base, which is parallel to the load waterline but located just beneath the deepest part of the keel. The second is vertical and passes directly through the center of the hull from bow to stern. The third, by convention, has become a series of planes passing transversely through the hull at given locations known as stations.

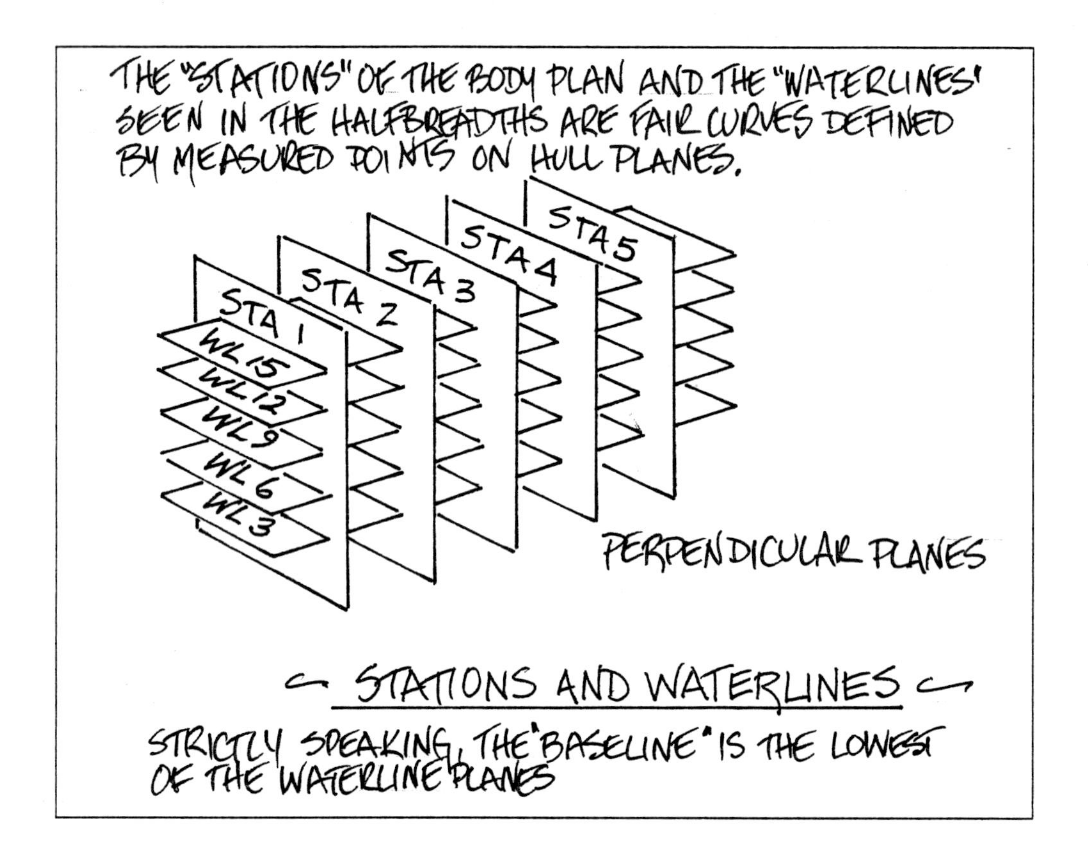

These planes make it possible to locate enough points on the surface of the hull so that it may be reproduced–in the form of a drawing, a half model, a finished boat, or all three. Close inspection of a lines plan will reveal that waterlines are always placed at regular intervals above the base, that buttock lines are always spaced at equal intervals from the centerline, and that stations are set at common intervals along the plan. They are fixed so that their locations cannot vary and their measurement will not be subject to interpretation. Wherever a portion of the hull surface intersects any one of these planes, that particular point can be measured. And each of these measurements is recorded in the table of offsets. Measurements that do not fit neatly into the table are generally recorded elsewhere on the plan–the expanded transom or the profile of the stem would fall into this latter category.

What is termed "the lines" is actually a plan consisting of three distinct portions: the profile, the halfbreadths (the waterlines and sheer as seen from above or below), and the body plan (a combined view from the ends of the hull). Don't be scared off simply because you know that they will be superimposed on the lofting. As soon as you learn to recognize each part for what it is, you will understand their relationships to one another. Understanding the interrelationships is the key to the whole lofting process, because it enables you to recognize inaccuracies in the plan as presented and allows you to make the necessary corrections before the actual work of building begins.

Close inspection of a lines plan will reveal that waterlines are always placed at regular intervals above the base, that buttock lines are always spaced at equal intervals from the centerline, and that stations are set at common intervals along the plan.

If you have previously viewed fair curves as a bothersome nuisance, you have been mistaken in your appraisal–they are a considerable time-saver. The faired curves that you encounter on a lines drawing, or full size on a lofting board, actually serve to simplify matters for the boatbuilder. Without those curves, it would be necessary to measure an infinite number of points in order to determine the entire shape of the hull (in much the same manner that points taken together are used to reproduce photos on a printed page). With curves, on the other hand, only a finite number of points need be measured, with the curves themselves determining all the other unmeasured points in between.

Battens provide the means for connecting the measured points to form a continuous fair curve. A batten, is a tool of the trade, and its correct use requires both understanding and practice. Once you have developed a "builder's eye," you'll recognize battens for the indispensable tool they really are.

I always start with the profile of the boat because it provides an easily recognizable outline–and that seems to help when I begin the lofting of any type with which I am not particularly familiar.

Preliminary work is minimal: strike in a base line with a chalkline or a long straightedge; then erect perpendiculars fore and aft and at each station, and waterlines at the heights indicated. Dimensions for this entire gridwork are noted on the plan. Stations are nearly always evenly spaced, and their distances from the fore and aft perpendiculars are taken directly from the plan and transferred to the lofting board. Similarly, although the profile waterlines may not be drawn in, you will most likely find them ticked off on both perpendiculars–if not, look to the table of offsets. The entries WL3, WL6, and so on, indicate that waterlines are spaced at 3" intervals parallel to and beginning 3" above the base line.

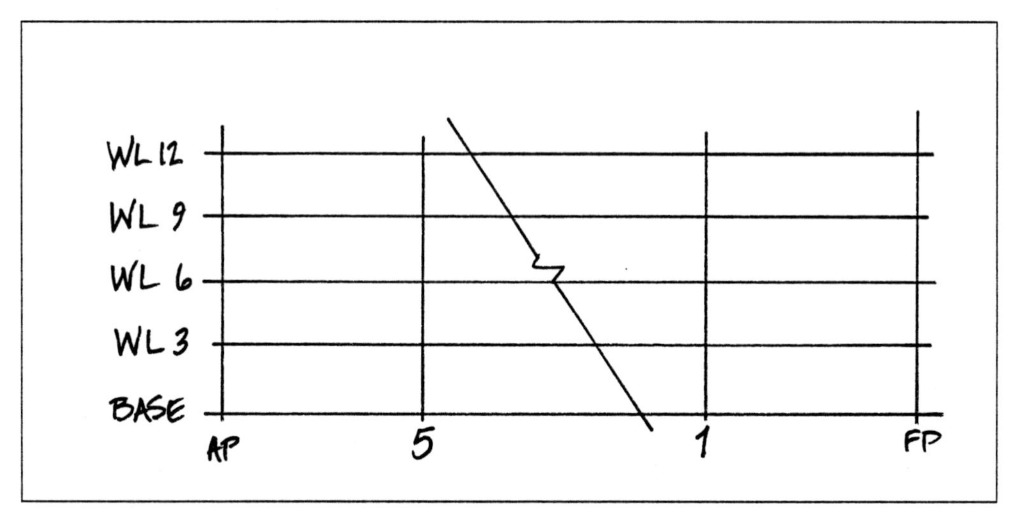

Waterlines and Perpendiculars

Layout of the profile itself, then, becomes simply a matter of transferring dimensions from the plan to the lofting. As I mentioned previously, most of the dimensions required will come directly from the offset table; others are usually indicated right on the plan. If neither is the case, your last resort is your scale rule. The common scale for small boat plans is 1-1/2" to (equals) 1', so even if you don't have a proper scale rule, you can just use your folding rule or tape. Every 1/8" on the plan is equivalent to one full inch on the lofting.

Whatever you do, make certain that you use the same rule all the way through. There can be a substantial difference between measurements taken with a folding rule and a tape even though they are made by the same company. Don't take my word for it–go and check your rules one against another. They are nearly all within tolerable limits as long as you remember that there are differences between them that can affect the lofting. I'm fortunate enough to have a six foot straightedge that belonged to a Sealer of Weights and Measures. It's particularly handy for lofting, because it's accurate and useful for drawing straight lines and for measuring.

Beyond the initial visualization of just what the lines are, the biggest single problem seems to be what to do when the points from the table of offsets don't fall along the fair curve of the batten. As with drawing the profile, you have to know where to begin. We'll discuss the seemingly inevitable problems a bit further along. For the time being, the next step is to lay off the sheer from the body plan. What was the baseline for the profile now also becomes the hull centerline from which the halfbreadths from each station are measured. Don't get carried away and try to loft all of those waterlines right now–chances are that you will have to modify them anyway. Take it a step at a time.

The rationale for this particular procedure is that several points of the entire plan are very nearly inflexible–or at least subject to little error. The profile and the halfbreadth sheer are the first two, and the stations of the body plan is the third. What I do is hedge my bets; I get down those lines that I am certain of, and then fill in the others, using my initial lines to check those following.

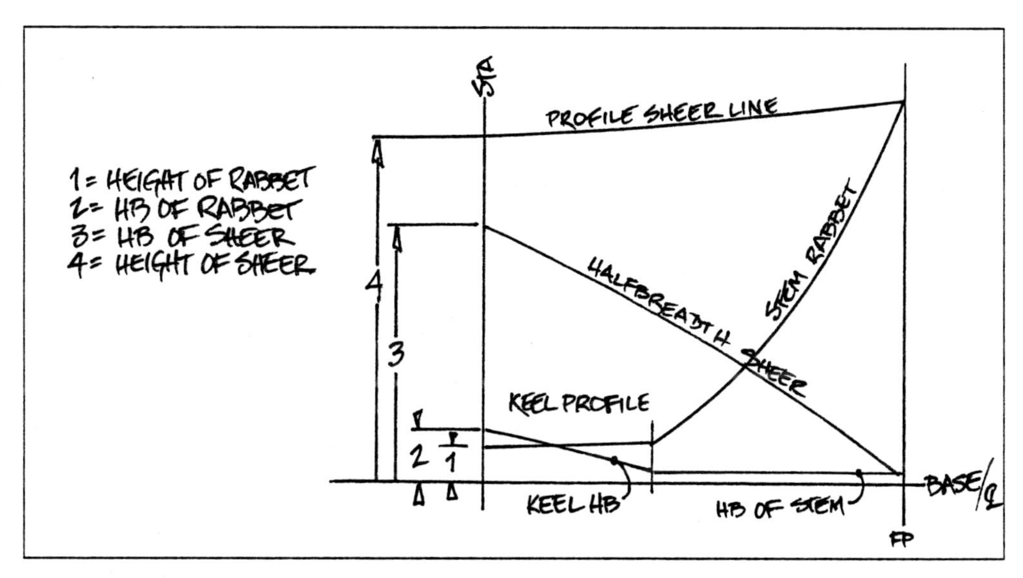

Laying Out Measurements

Having lofted a considerable number of boats over the years, I am now settled on a fixed progression. After the profile is faired in,

I measure and fair in the rabbet and the sheer in the halfbreadth (overhead) view. Both of these lines are essential to positioning the stations which follow. The body plan sections themselves, because of their tight curves, permit only slight modifications–but in order to position them on the lofting board, you must know beforehand where the ends of each will be located. Not until after all of the stations are faired in do I attempt to draw the longer waterline and buttock curves. The lofting of each of them is treated in detail a little further along.

It is at this stage that inaccuracies become most apparent. For any given waterline or buttock line, the dimensions taken from the stations must agree. When they don't lie along fair curves as anticipated, some amount of correction is in order. Corrections should be approached cautiously because each correction will have to be verified in the other views. New builders working from my plans tend to pick up their phones and call me at that point. My wife calls them "good God, what do I do now" calls. So far we have been able to answer their questions.

No two people encounter the same lofting problems, but you will discover even without outside help that gradual correcting is the only prudent course. All of lofting consists of continued verification between views. Professional boatbuilders check several things in addition to the lines themselves: size and condition of battens, their own transferal of measurements, and finally, the feasibility of the dimensions provided in the table of offsets.

The table of offsets is subdivided into heights above base and halfbreadths. Sometimes it includes a section for diagonals as well. Interpretation is straightforward. To lay out the midship station, for example, go to the column in the table with the station number corresponding to the widest station on the plan. For each waterline listed in the opposing row of halfbreadths, you will find a dimension for the distance from the hull centerline at that level. Below that (usual location) in the same column, are the heights above the baseline for each buttock line. By convention, you'll recall, the notation used is a series of three numbers, most tables bearing the legend "Dimensions given in feet, inches, and eighths." The entry 3-10-5 means 3'-10-5/8".

One of the reasons I favor using a half model is for use when some problem arises during the lofting. Models aren't always fair, but even when they are not, it is very easy to locate the unfair portion, sand or carve it away, and continue with your measurements. Lofting from the model provides tangible justification for each and every measurement. When a problem arises, you can check that spot on the model with calipers–if it happens to be a lift model, take that lift out and measure it directly. If the model is indeed fair and your measurements are accurate, then your lofting can't help but follow suit.

Keep working with your battens until all the hull lines are fair. Let me qualify that statement: don't work for an hour or more trying to make a correction that just won't work no matter what you do. At times like that, it is better to leave your lofting board and finish the job later when you can think clearly. What seemed incomprehensible the first time often falls neatly into place after a break and some fresh air.

Lofting isn't terribly difficult, but if you still need reassurance, I strongly suggest that you begin with a half model. It's not a panacea, but at least it is small enough so that when you are sitting in your moaning chair, holding it, you shouldn't feel intimidated. Small consolation, but "better than a poke in the eye with a sharp stick", as my grandfather used to say.

LOFTING BOARDS

Lofting and "laying down the lines", are one and the same thing. It refers to the mechanical, full size rendering of the plan that enables the builder to "pick off" information essential for construction. You can knock together a boat without doing the lofting—many boats have been built just that way–but to do so, the builder would have to guess at the sizes and shapes of the individual hull members, and would have to rely almost totally on fairing battens to make the all important corrections. Lofting is the key to boatbuilding because no matter how carefully a designer draws his plans, there are bound to be flaws that would make the boat difficult to build as drawn.

Lofting eliminates the guesswork, verifying all measurements and curves before you have to make that first cut. It may not always be easy, but you will be rewarded for your pains. In case you wondered, it takes me about a day to loft an open boat up to 20'. With less experience, expect it to take you somewhat longer, but take the time; it will make the building far easier. I would call that a reasonable investment of your time.

In order to begin, you'll need a flat surface large enough to lay down the lines. Assuming that you already have an area large enough to build the boat, that shouldn't be a problem. I know, there are times when the customary lofting is impractical. Recovery from an injury one winter kept me confined to my office when I had planned to be at the lofting board. Since I didn't want the time to be nonproductive, I "lofted" one boat to 3" scale (3"=1'-0") right on my drawing board. It was a modification of a boat that I had lofted and built previously, so it wasn't my first exposure to the lines. The end result was a 1/4 scale lofting that still provided me with the angular information I needed. When I was able to return to the shop, I lofted the body plan and construction details to their actual size, but other than that, my diminutive lofting was successful. I Have to admit, though, that using my adjustable parallel on the drawing board made me wish I had a mock up on my lofting board.

Lofting can be done directly on the building floor, on a raised platform (such as a bench top), or even vertically, on a wall. Suit the location to the condition of your knees and back, but make certain that it is as close to where you will be doing the actual building as possible. One friend went so far as to position his lofting board vertically so that lines could be lofted at the precise height of the boat in her cradle. That arrangement allowed for a direct check of heights between lofting and hull by means of a water level. That was for a 45' Pinky Schooner–small boats require nothing so elaborate, though as an exercise in precision it would be hard to beat.

Your lofting board doesn't have to be fancy, but it does need to be as flat as possible. Additionally, it should be backed sufficiently so that it will remain flat and nails driven in to hold battens in place will stay where you put them. My first lofting surfaces were 4'x 8' sheets of 1/2" Homosote™–a pressed paper product that withstands fluctuating dampness and temperature levels well. It is worth your consideration, not only because it is well suited to lofting, but also because it is made out of recycled paper. Bear in mind that it is flexible, however, so you must work on the floor or a well-backed vertical surface–I used three 1x8 boards down the length, fastened to wall studding.The same cautions apply to 1/2" Celotex™, though it is softer and therefore requires greater care. Even Sheetrock™ would serve, but above all I now prefer 1/4" lauan plywood. It is light, stable and inexpensive.

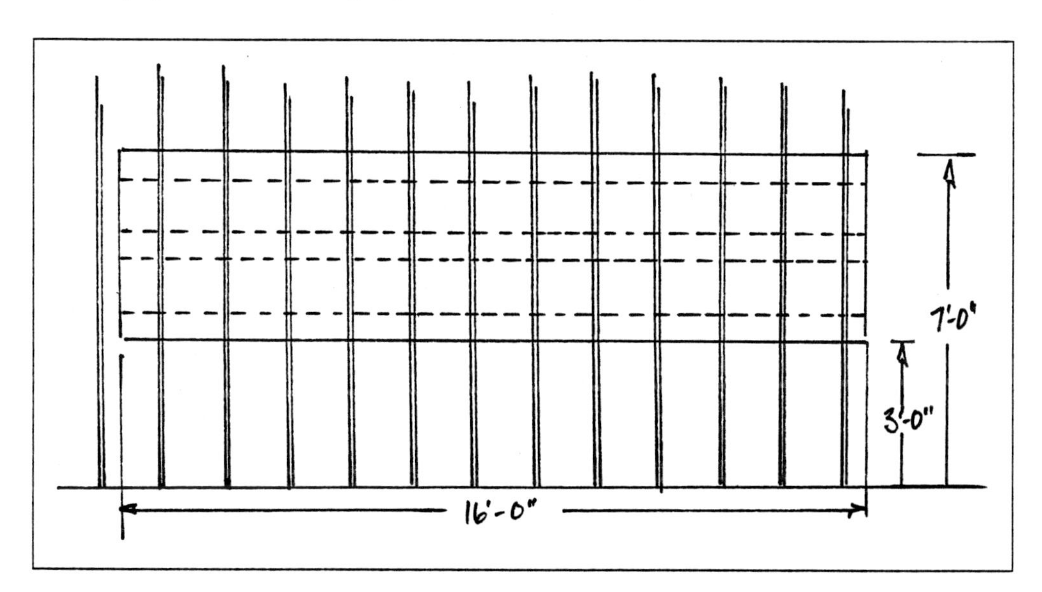

Vertical Lofting Board

All of these materials are available in 4' x 8' sheets. Two sheets placed end to end are sufficient to loft most Wherries, Peapods, and Whitehalls. Lapstrake canoes can be lofted on a single sheet, sawn lengthwise and placed end to end to yield a 2' x 16' surface. Yacht tenders can usually be lofted on a single sheet cut into 3 pieces measuring 32" x 48", arranged into a lofting board measuring 32" x 12'.

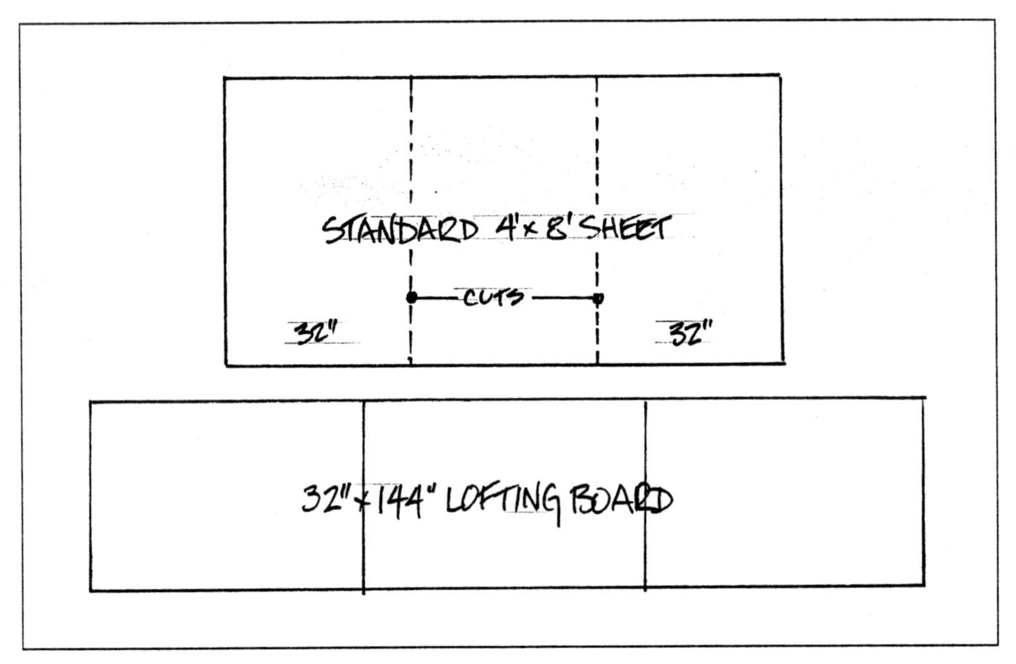

One Sheet Makes a 12' Lofting Board

The lofting surface must either be suitable for drawing or must be overlaid with some material that is suitable. If your work area is in your living quarters where lofting isn't to become a permanent fixture, a sufficiently large sheet of Mylar works well. If you intend to work with pencils, the drafting film has to be frosted on one side. Using pens such as the Staedtler "Lumocolor" line, it can be smooth on both sides. Sheets of paper are not the best choice for the job, because they expand and contract according to climatic conditions. The problem is that they do not necessarily change evenly, rendering the validity of carefully entered lines and dimensions rather haphazard. Drafting film (Mylar™ is one produced by Dupont) is guaranteed to be dimensionally stable, with an expansion coefficient of less than .05%. And it has the added advantage that you can roll it up and store it away for future reference.

TOOLS OF THE TRADE

You won't need a profusion of specialized tools for lofting, and most home shops are already equipped with what is required: a scale rule, a 2-foot steel square, a ruler, a chalkline, straightedge, hammer, some 4d (penny) finish nails, and some battens. There are alternative choices for nearly all of the tools on this list, but I prefer to stick to the basics and tell you what has worked best for me personally, and for those who have attended our lofting workshops.

There are two primary types of scale rule, both are triangular in cross section, and 12" long. The type of graduations differentiate the two. The engineer's scale is divided into graduations of 10, 20, 30, 40, 50, and 60 parts to the inch, while the architectural rule has scales for 3/32, 1/8, 3/16, 1/4, 3/8, 1/2, 3/4, 1, 1-1/2, and 3 inches per foot, plus one standard ruled edge graduated in sixteenths. I have both, but have yet to find a use for the engineer's scale in lofting. If you don't have one, an adequate architect's scale rule can be had for about $6.50, while one of professional quality will cost $15. and up.

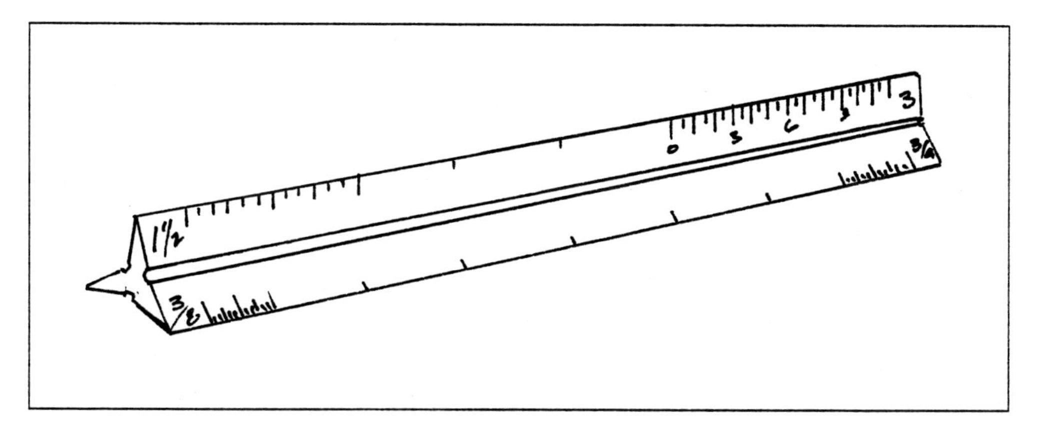

Architect's Scale Rule

The two-foot square is a standard carpenter's rafter square, L-shaped with legs measuring 16 and 24". About the only one of its scales useful in boatbuilding is the diagonal, providing the length of 45° braces. Fixed at 90°, it is useful for erecting short perpendiculars and for projecting information from one view to another. I use trammel points for erecting all but the shortest perpendiculars. With them, any 1/4" x 1-1/2" batten is transformed into a beam compass, and precise perpendiculars of any conceivable height can be constructed using a little basic geometry. One builder I worked with years ago had made himself a 30-60-90 lofting triangle out of 1/4" plywood. If you want to make one of your own, you won't need a protractor to lay it out. The hypotenuse is twice the length of the short side and the other is the short side multiplied by the square root of three (1.732).

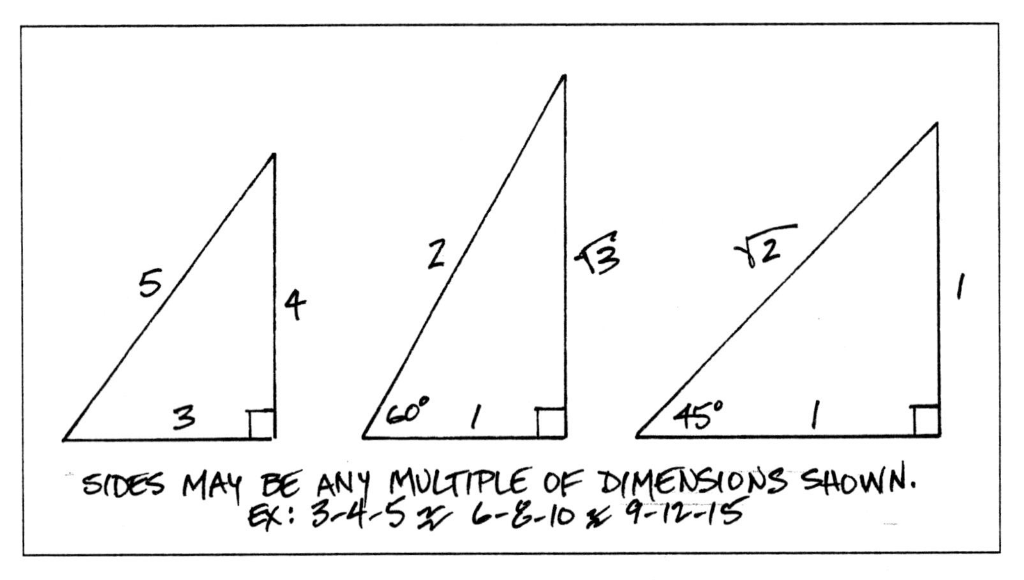

Standard Traingle Layouts
(sides may be any multiple of dimensions shown)

The choice of ruler is up to you, but unless you are certain that they are identical, pick one and stick with that throughout the lofting. Folding rules and steel tapes seldom match precisely, and the ramifications of that should be evident. The ones I use do match and are set aside just for lofting jobs: a Rabone™ 2' folding rule, a Lufkin™ 6' folding rule, and a Stanley™ 25' tape measure. The tape is used primarily for layout of the gridwork; the 2' rule is great for details and because it slides easily into a pocket, and the 6' folding rule handles all of the measurements in between. The tape will handle the offsets as well, but you will end up measuring from the 1" mark (called "cutting the one") and adding it back at the measuring end. That works fine for a while, but once you're tired 1" mistakes begin to appear. That's the voice of experience.

I am using the term "chalkline" generically. Many do use lines that are chalk covered–either done manually, or the self-chalking variety as manufactured by Stanley and Irwin™. They are available in 50 or 100' lengths, and use powdered chalks of different colors (watch out for the red, it makes a terrible mess). Recently, I have set my chalkline aside in favor of my Mackerel fishing reel. It is equipped with a hefty monofilament line, but is still thinner than a chalk line, and I can stretch this tighter. In use, I tick off a few points along its length and then draw in the line using my 6' aluminum straightedge.

The straightedge doesn't have to be fancy, just straight. I often use a 6" strip cut off the edge of a piece if 1/4" or 1/2" plywood. I also use 1/2" pine and cedar, though as a precaution I rejoin the edge with each new lofting. Even the side of a long level will do the trick. The longer the straightedge, the fewer leapfrogging movements will be necessary to pencil in the long grid lines.

My primary shop finish hammer is a 12oz. Stanley with a curved claw and a wooden handle. Standard 16oz. hammers are a bit hefty for driving the 4d and 6d finish nails used to hold the battens in position. The 12oz. model is best for the actual building, where finesse is preferable to brute strength, and if you are thinking of trying one, the lofting is good place to begin (Nova Scotia dimples don't matter on a lofting board).

Brite (as opposed to galvanized) finish nails are best suited to lofting work, and tend to be reused again and again, as their lives aren't terribly stressful. Alan Vaitses, in his book Lofting, advocated the use of awls to secure the battens–and that was the preferred method years ago. Unfortunately, years ago those awls didn't cost $5.00 apiece as they do today. They are pleasant to work with, however, so you might want to try your hand at making your own.

Quick and dirty ones could be contrived of 3/4" dowel sections into which 10d finish nails are driven and then sharpened to a point. Those with more pride of workmanship might elect to turn some hardwood handles and install ferrules to keep the ends of the handles from splitting. Some while ago I found that the metal jackets of spent 12 and 16 gauge shotgun shells make very nice ferrules once the primers are tapped free. Of course they are pretty good sized–the diameter of a 12-gauge shell measures about 13/16"–so would be better suited to larger loftings. Awls that size would make a pretty good mess of a small lofting board.

It seems to me that a lighter-duty alternative would better suit the lofting of traditional small craft where the battens used are seldom more than 1" wide. To that end, I made up a few experimental awls using 6d box nails (brite, not galvanized) and .45 caliber shell casings for ferrules. .45 caliber equates to .45 inches, or approximately 7/16". At 2" long, the 6d nails are long enough to embed in the handle and still leave 1-1/2" exposed on the business end. I bored a 1/2" deep nail-head-sized hole in the handle, set them with the nails pointing upward, and pour the holes full of epoxy. Once that set up, I install the ferrules to keep them from splitting. Finish them off by grinding the tip into a tapering conical point.

By the way, I should mention here that awls aren't intended to be driven into the lofting board. Rather, they are placed using downward pressure and a twisting motion. They are also removed with a bit of a twist to keep from pulling up slivers from the plywood lofting surface with them. Mine worked so well, that one of these days we'll probably add them to our online catalogue.

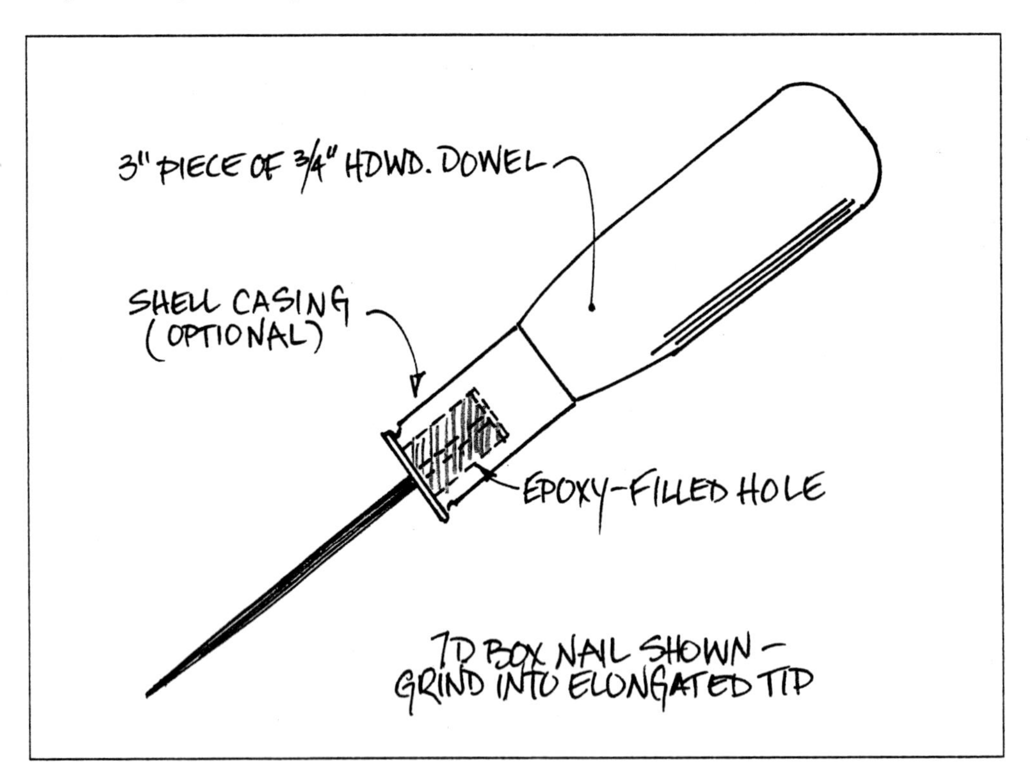

Making Your Own Lofting Awls

We have finally made it to the battens–probably the simplest and least understood of all the tools on the list. Battens, in the most basic definition possible, are strips of wood, metal, or plastic, that enable their handlers to see specific curves. Loftsmen use them to draw the ubiquitous fair curves of the hull and verify measurements given in the table of offsets; boatbuilders use them to predict the run of hull members.

Wooden batten stock should be clear and straight-grained. Pine, cedar, fir, oak, mahogany, and ash, are only a few of the suitable woods. Softwoods are fine for the longest battens where curves will be relatively easy. Hardwoods are better suited to the tighter curves of the buttock lines and stations. For really tight curves, like the expanded profile of a transom, the back edge of a bandsaw blade is just the ticket. Some professional shops even have battens tapered on both ends to facilitate fairing the profile buttock line curves. The size and type of battens needed depends upon the boat being lofted. Typically, you will want one measuring 1/2" x 1" about two feet longer than the boat, another 1/4" x 3/4", boatlength, and the smallest, about 1/8" x 3/4" x 4'.

The easiest way to get battens is to make a trip to your local lumberyard and pick out the clearest piece of select 1"x6"x16' pine you can find, and rip that into the sizes you need. A local cabinet shop probably has a stack of cast-off edgings that you could pick through for suitable battens–chances are that they discard them anyway. If you have difficulty finding pieces long enough, make your own. My longest battens are over 40' long, scarphed together from 16' pieces of clear pine. You can do the same and have them work as well as a natural piece, provided you bear in mind that the scarph joints themselves have to be as long as possible. The glued joint is somewhat more rigid than the non-glued sections, and therefore exhibits different bending characteristics. It stands to reason, then, that the longer the scarph, the more nearly those characteristics will mimic an uninterrupted batten of the same dimension.

Three things not on the list that aren't absolutely essential, but will make your life more pleasant are additional pencils, a bevel, and dividers. The three depictions of the boat that are separated on the plan will be superimposed on your lofting board. Those new to the operation sometimes find the resulting maze of overlapping lines confusing, to say the least. The solution is to loft the views in different colors—waterlines in blue, buttock lines in green, and stations in red, for example. Faber Castell "Col-Erase" and Berol "Prismacolor" are both good lofting pencils, and are even suitable for work on drafting film.

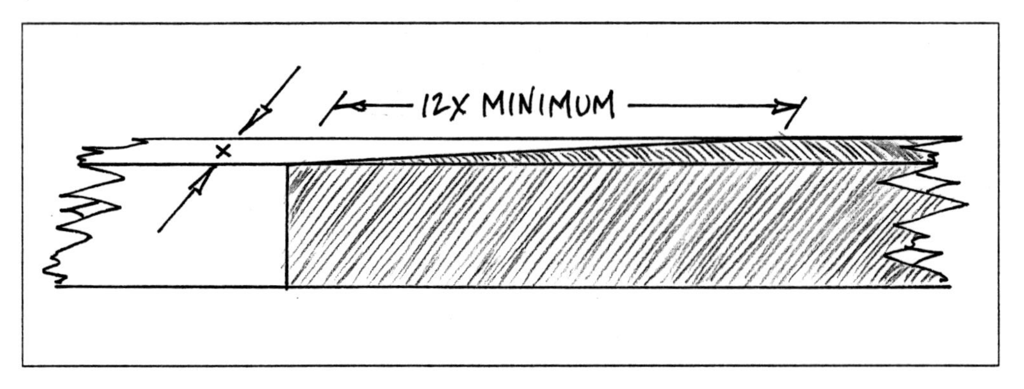

Batten Scarph Joint

3" flat brass bevels can be a real saver too, and I'm not saying that because we make them. You will also find them recommended by Thomas Hill in his Ultralight Boatbuilding and by Robert Stewart in his Boat Repair Manual. I made my first one out of hatch trim to help me while fitting out a sail locker in the eyes of a 70' schooner; one friend saw it and asked for one, then another friend asked, and I have been making them ever since. They are handy throughout the building, but particularly on the plans and lofting because their flat configuration (3/16" total thickness) allows them to lie flat against the drawing surface to pick off angles precisely. Sometimes it is just a quick check; at other times, it is the only way to pick off the information you need. They are particularly nice for dealing with transom bevels during planking, but that is properly beyond the scope of this book.

The dividers are simply another tool for picking accurate measurements off the half model or plan. They needn't be fancy provided their points are sharp and their hinge joint sufficiently stiff that they will hold a dimension for transferal.

GRIDWORK

The gridwork is an array of horizontal, vertical and several diagonal lines you must establish on the drawing surface prior to lofting. Their sole function is to allow you to enter measurements so that a boat can be lofted. Why so many lines? If you were lofting a portion of a building, only two points would be needed to layout each straight line and they could be simply measured. Here, working with curves, at least three points are required for definition, and we will need a number of them–that's where the gridwork is essential. Hull curves on a lofting are defined by points on every grid line they cross.

The gridwork starts with the baseline, an inch or more up from the lower edge of the lofting board, extending from one end to the other. A chalk line is the fastest and most common method used to strike the line, and works well provided it is stretched tightly. For those unaccustomed to using a chalk line, the procedure is to drive a nail at each end of the board, tie off the line, and snap the line from its midpoint. However, when you pinch the line between thumb and forefinger to raise it off the surface prior to snapping, it must be raised perpendicularly–if it isn't, you won't get a straight line, but rather a shallow arc–you'll need the straight line. A surer method is to stretch the line, move to the midpoint, and there carefully press the line against the surface of the board with your thumb; then snap the line to the left and to the right using your other hand. Builders call that "snapping to both sides". The line will still have to be snapped vertically, but you will have halved your margin of error. With the line chalked in, make it more permanent, using a pencil and a straightedge.

Perpendiculars are next. Forward and after perpendiculars (FP and AP) bound the hull forward and aft respectively, and pass through the intersection of the sheer and rabbet lines. The stations, numbered consecutively, are placed at even intervals–they are not necessarily evenly spaced from the fore and after perpendiculars, so be sure to check . Notations on the plan, or your scale rule will give their precise locations. Start with tentative measurements, laying out the station locations, making certain that the midship station (#3 on a five station boat) misses the joint between the two halves of the lofting board.

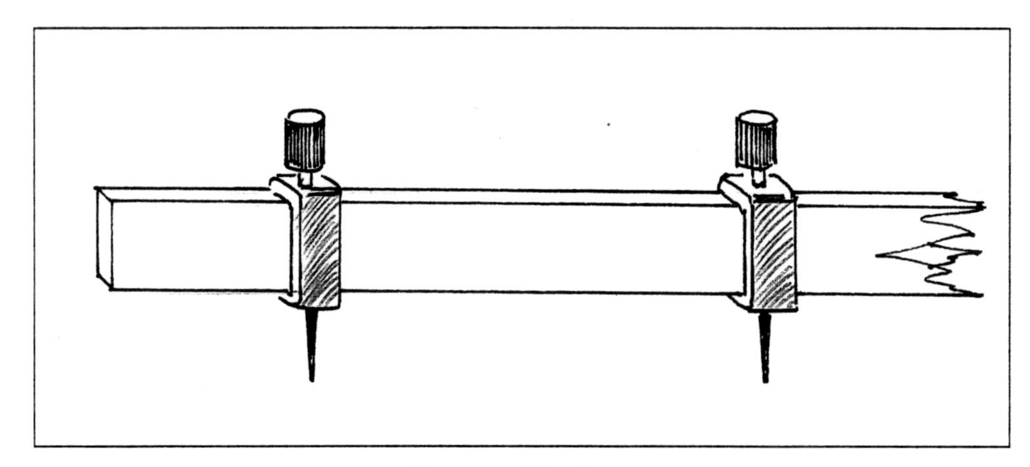

Trammel Points

Once certain of their locations, draw in the stations so that they are oriented at precisely 90° to the baseline. Use a rafter square or erect them geometrically using trammel points. Mine lock on a 1/4" x 1-1/2" batten effectively turning it into a beam compass. It doesn't matter how it is accomplished, so long as they are perpendicular to the baseline and accurate. It's good lofting practice to label every line as you work.

With all perpendiculars in place, layout waterline heights on the end and midship station perpendiculars. Numbers 3,6,9,... on the plan and in the table of offsets refer to their location in inches above the baseline. The chalkline is again used to strike them in full length, using additional height marks on the midship station line as a reference to keep the waterlines straight from end to end. Pencil in the lines. The gridwork already established is sufficient for lofting the profile, the buttock lines, and the waterlines. If the plan you are working from incorporates diagonals (not all plans do) those and some additional grid lines will be required, but not until the time comes to loft the body plan. We'll discuss that when we get there. That's it; nothing fancy, just an exercise in draftsmanship that will work for you through the balance of the lofting.

It should go without saying that the surface of the lofting board should be light enough so that pencil lines will show. The surface of homosote is smooth and medium gray. Pencil marks will show, but they are more readily seen if the surface is given a coat of white paint. Celotex™ comes either plain (a medium brown) or with a painted white surface. Plywood can be used as is, or can be painted. Mylar needs no special surface preparation, though colored surface. Any paint can be used. I prefer an oil based paint such as Interlux™ #242 Flat White, or Interlux #4279 Pre-Coat (white), with a coat of semi-gloss over that. One coat is sufficient, but flat paints are much more abrasive that glosses, and so wear down pencil points much faster. Latex paints work well too.

The overriding concerns are that your lofting board be flat and stable, and that the surface you plan to use for the lofting is light enough that your line work will be easy to read. Taking a little extra time in preparation always seems to make the work go easier, and most who get into this business of boatbuilding–even recreationaly–find that their lofting board gets painted over to be used again.

LOFTING THE PROFILE

I've always found it helpful to loft the profile before anything else. It is a view that will be familiar even to those who have never seen a lofting previously, and it encloses all of the other lines that will follow. If your lofting board is too small, this is the time you will find out. Hopefully, you will have scaled the lines before determining the materials needed for the lofting board.

Those unaccustomed to using scale rules tend to become sorcerer's apprentices once they have mastered it, scaling the plan to derive every needed dimension. The temptation should be resisted: resort to the scale rule only when the dimension needed isn't entered in the table of offsets, or written in directly on the plan. Either dimension takes precedence over a scaled dimension–those noted on the plan are those that would not otherwise be tabulated along with the other offsets. The scale is the last resort, and if you should discover a discrepancy between the offsets and a scaled dimension, it is wise to trust the offsets. The tables are compiled directly from the plan lofted during the designing of the boat. The 3-digit table entries refer to feet, inches, and eighths of an inch. The designer does his best to draw the scaled plan to those offsets, but mistakes do happen. Since the offsets were compiled before the plan was even drawn, it would follow that accuracy would favor the table rather than the lines plan.

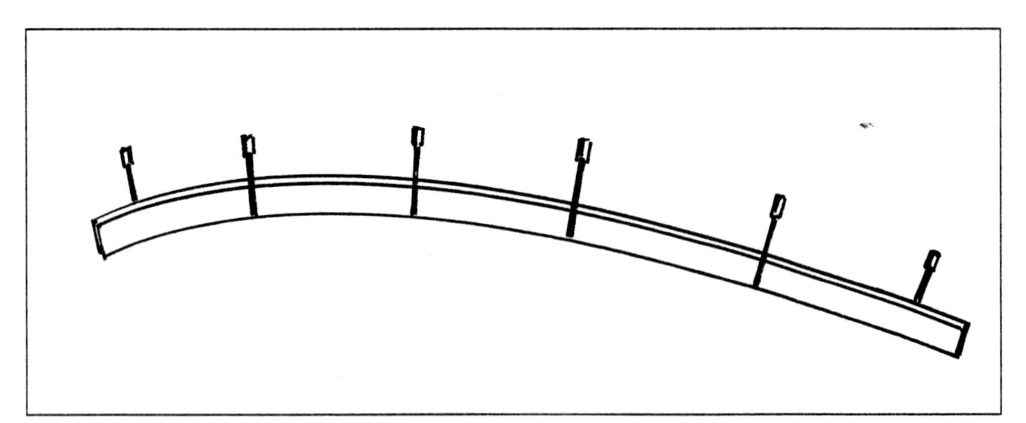

Nailing a Batten
(note that the nails go along the sides of the batten)

Start with the profile sheer. Lay off the heights above base for the fore and aft perpendiculars, and for each station in between, and connect those points using the largest of your battens. Stand the batten on edge, move it up to the height mark at each station, and drive a 4-penny finish nail alongside. Be sure to drive the nails immediately adjacent to the measured points so that they aren't obliterated in the process. The nail holds the batten on the mark, and allows the batten to be bent upward to the next station in line. The ends on the perpendiculars want to be double nailed–one nail on each side of the batten. Otherwise, use only single nails to hold the batten.

The idea is to get the batten to connect the points in a fair curve, not to crowd it into place with so many nails that it is prevented from assuming a fair and continuous curve from one end to the other. You don't wants humps and bumps in the sheer of your boat, so don't allow any to remain in the lofted sheer line. An additional nail to hold the batten beyond the fore and aft perpendiculars will insure a continuation of the fair curve, and make certain that there are no flat spots between the perpendiculars and the end stations. After the batten has been bent to the marks, step back and sight along it from both ends. It's all but impossible to describe a fair curve concisely, but your eye will be drawn to any inconsistencies just as readily as it is drawn to a picture hanging out of level on your living room wall.

Next I prefer to loft the rabbet, as that combined with the sheer already lofted, gives the upper and lower confines of the profile. The rabbet is about the flattest curve on the entire lofting, and is in fact, sometimes straight. Dimensions, with the exception of the end termination points, come directly from the table of offsets, listed as "heights above base" for each station. The point forward where the rabbet ends and the stem begins shows as the intersection of two fair curves (the stem and the rabbet), or a curve and a straight line in some boats, and is nearly always marked on the plan with height as well as fore and aft dimensions. If it isn't, you will have to scale those dimensions for yourself. Being flatter than other curves, but nearly boat length, the longest batten is needed, and it is helpful to use it on the flat rather than on edge. The batten is less flexible layed flat and will help fair in the curve of the rabbet more readily. Might as well make the best use of the tool.

Most of the time, bow and stern profile measurements are given for each waterline, and marked directly on the waterline, between the perpendicular and the stem. Even in double enders they aren't necessarily the same fore and aft, so each stem must be layed out separately. If the dimensions aren't given, scale them from the plan. Measure from the perpendicular to locate points on each of the waterlines. The lower termination point forward is known as the forefoot, and is usually located somewhere above the baseline, between the perpendicular and the end station. Locate the point by scaling the distance from the base and the FP. You can fair in the stem profile with a softwood batten, but a thin hardwood batten is better suited to making tight curves without breaking. If it hasn't already been done for you on the plan, extend the profile of the transom so that it intersects the AP and the base. Scale those distances from the point where the AP and base cross, and transfer them to the lofting so you can draw in the transom face. With the stem and transom faired in, the basic profile of the boat is completed, and should have taken on a recognizable form.

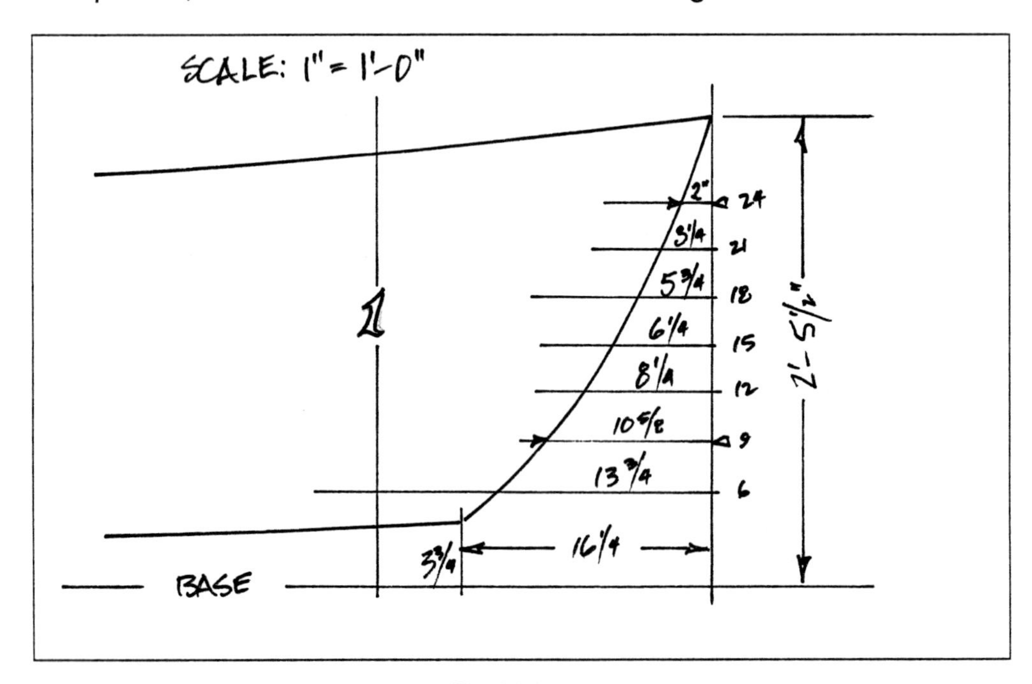

Bow Profile Measurements

As a general rule of thumb, use battens on the flat whenever possible because the increased stiffness works to your advantage. When the curves are more pronounced, as they will be when drawing the halfbreadth waterlines, use the batten on edge. Remember to double nail at the ends of the batten and to place the additional nails beyond the measured endpoints to make certain that the curve is fair overall. Resist the temptation to nail through the batten–use nails on either side only as needed. Nailing a batten to the lofting board restricts its springing tendency and usually traps it in an unnatural position–that defeats its function. It is an important point, because when you finally get to the hull member depicted by that line, you will find that it will spring to a fair curve on its own–only forcing it would cause it to do otherwise. Unless the curves you draw are fair and accurate, they won't show you the actual run of the hull member.

Temporarily, it's time to leave the profile plan and begin the halfbreadth lofting–the view from directly above or below the floating boat. The views are interdependent. The lines plan shows the halfbreadths as a series of quasiconcentric curves, located apart from and usually directly above the profile. Those curves are the various waterlines. On the lofting, the same gridwork is used for both views, though the nomenclature changes. This time, what was the baseline will serve as the centerline, and some of the waterlines will serve as halfbreadth buttock lines. It isn't difficult.

In the profile plan or view, waterlines are spaced at equal intervals above the baseline. In the halfbreadth plan, the buttock lines are evenly spaced out from the centerline. Since the baseline of the profile plan and the centerline of the halfbreadth plan are superimposed, it follows that buttock lines of the one plan will be superimposed over the waterlines of the other. Commonly, waterlines are spaced at 3" intervals, and the buttock lines are spaced 6" apart. Following that one step further, profile WL 6 and halfbreadth BUT 6 are the same line as is the case with WL 12 and BUT 12, and so on. The grid lines are drawn in with a common lead pencil and should be labeled. From here on, you may find it helpful to layout waterline curves in blue and buttock curves in red.

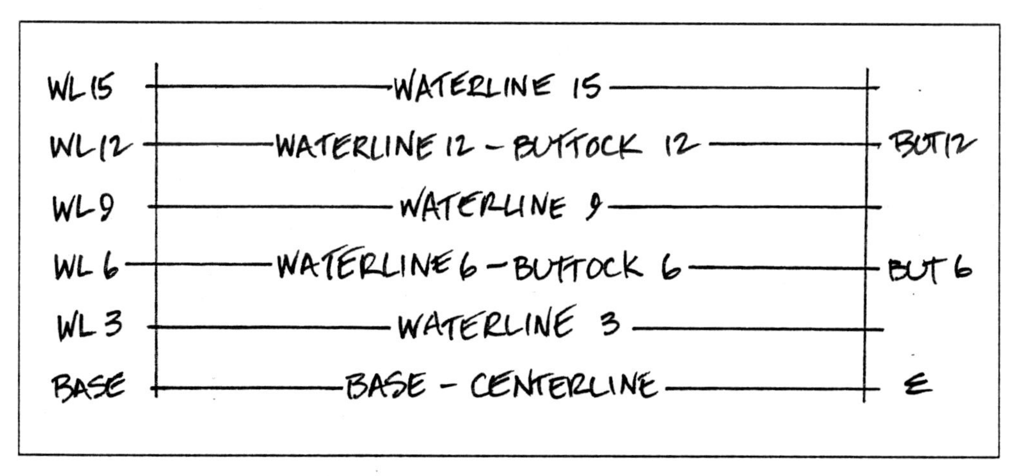

Superimposed Grid Lines

The halfbreadth view of the stems is the place to start. Since we are working to one side of the centerline (hence the term halfbreadth), lay off the half siding of the stem. In the case of many small craft, that would be a line parallel to the centerline, 3/4" away because 1-1/2" thick stems are common. The line would begin at the perpendicular FP, and terminate at the knuckle formed by the intersection of stem profile and rabbet. This is where the superimposed views begin to work to your advantage.

The point needn't be measured over again. Instead, use a two-foot square, its base aligned with the centerline, to project the location of the knuckle to the half siding of the stem. Following the stem, layout and loft the halfbreadth rabbet line. Vertical keeled craft, such as most Whitehalls and peapods, have a keel that matches the thickness of the stems. For them and their kin, the rabbet line in halfbreadth appears as a continuation of the stem rabbet (3/4" from the centerline, as explained above) all the way to the transom. In plank keel types, notably wherries and lapstrake canoes, rabbet halfbreadths are found in the table of offsets. For them, the rabbet is a shallow curve and is drawn in using the long batten on the flat to fair from stem to stern. Halfbreadth waterlines follow in turn, the dimensions, again, coming from the table of offsets. Depending on the model, there could be forty or more waterline dimensions given. With that many measurements, mistakes can creep in, so you have to make yourself work methodically, taking one station or waterline at a time. It's a good idea to label each one before going on to the next station. We will discuss the halfbreadth lofting in more detail in the next section.

This is where beginners encounter their first real problem. The intersections of the waterlines and stations are known, but where do those waterlines end? Obviously, they terminate somewhere on the stem and transom. The question is where? Your two foot steel square will show you, but the answer depends on whether your boat has a rabbeted stem or a stem with a cutwater. In boats with rabbeted stems, the rabbet line is an inch or more aft of the profile of the stem's leading edge, with the inner rabbet and bearding line still further aft.

Wherries, dories, and lapstrake canoes are just a few of the types that make use of stem/cutwater construction. In those craft, the rabbet and inner rabbet lines are superimposed in the profile view.

They have no right-angle rabbet cut in the side of their stem. The rabbet that exists is somewhat less than a 90° angle, and isn't formed until after the cutwater is installed following completion of the planking. Up until that time, the side of the stem is simply beveled away until the individual planks run in a fair curve to the inner rabbet line drawn on the leading edge of the stem.

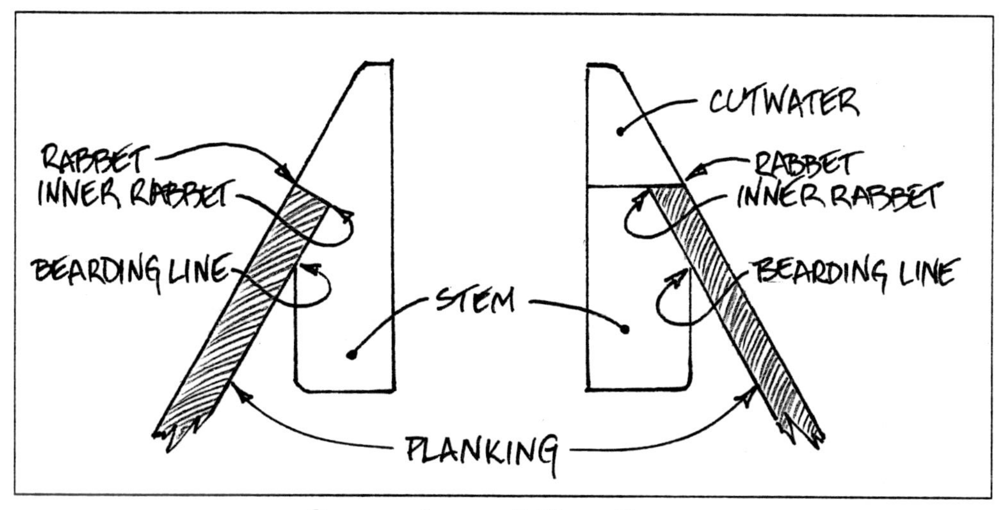

Comparison of Stem Types

The bearding line, by definition, is where the inside of the planking and the backbone meet. As we discussed, lines of nearly all small craft are drawn to the inside of the planking, hence points on that stem bearding line are also points where the forward end of the waterline curves terminate. Aft, the curves terminate on the outboard surface of the transom (assuming there isn't a notation to the contrary near the Table of Offsets).

The procedure is the same as the one already used to project the position of the forefoot from the profile to the halfbreadth view. Align the two-foot square with the baseline, and with the intersection of the waterline and stem profile above, and project the line along the side of the square until it intersects the halfbreadth stem. That point of intersection (done for every waterline), locates the rabbet in the halfbreadth view. To find the location of the bearding line that you want, you will have to deduct the plank thickness, and for that you will need your long batten.

Some people have difficulty understanding the relationship between one plan and another. I've found that nearly all of them are making it more complicated than it is. It is the same boat as seen from two different angles, as if you stood, rooted to one spot, looking first at the side of the boat, watching it rotate on a spit until you were looking right down on top of it. If you think of a hull plank instead of a theoretical line, it is readily apparent that it ends in the same spot regardless of your angle of view. Waterlines do precisely the same thing. Perpendiculars are included on a lofting for reference, and every fore and aft line in a lofting ends at a precise distance from a perpendicular whether in profile or halfbreadth view.

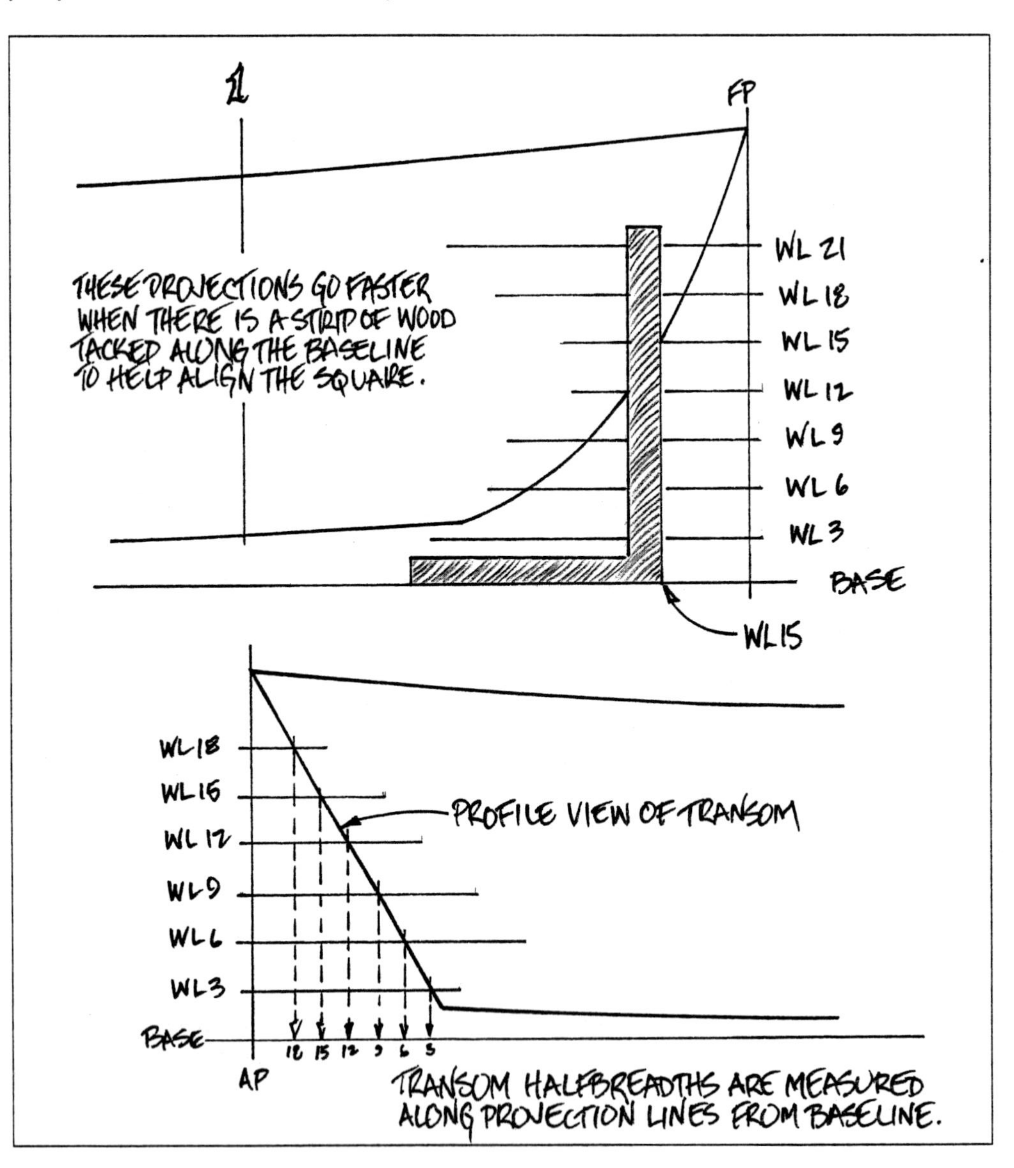

Waterline Projections from Profile to Halfbreadths

Now to pick up those waterline termination points, and through them, the derivation of the profile bearding line. Start with the lowest waterline, positioning the lofting batten with nails at every station. Place the batten so that the pencil line will be drawn on the concave side of the batten. With one hand, pull the batten downward until its inner edge intersects the projected position of the rabbet on the stem. The waterline doesn't end there because by definition, the rabbet, is located at the outboard surface of the planking.

Make a plank gauge out of scrap stock. It should match the thickness of the planking, be square ended, and 6 or 8" long. Hold the gauge against the inside of the fairing batten, and its inside edge will cross the stem line where the planking will meet the stem. Mark that point of intersection, move the gauge out of the way, and fair in the waterline to the new intersection point.

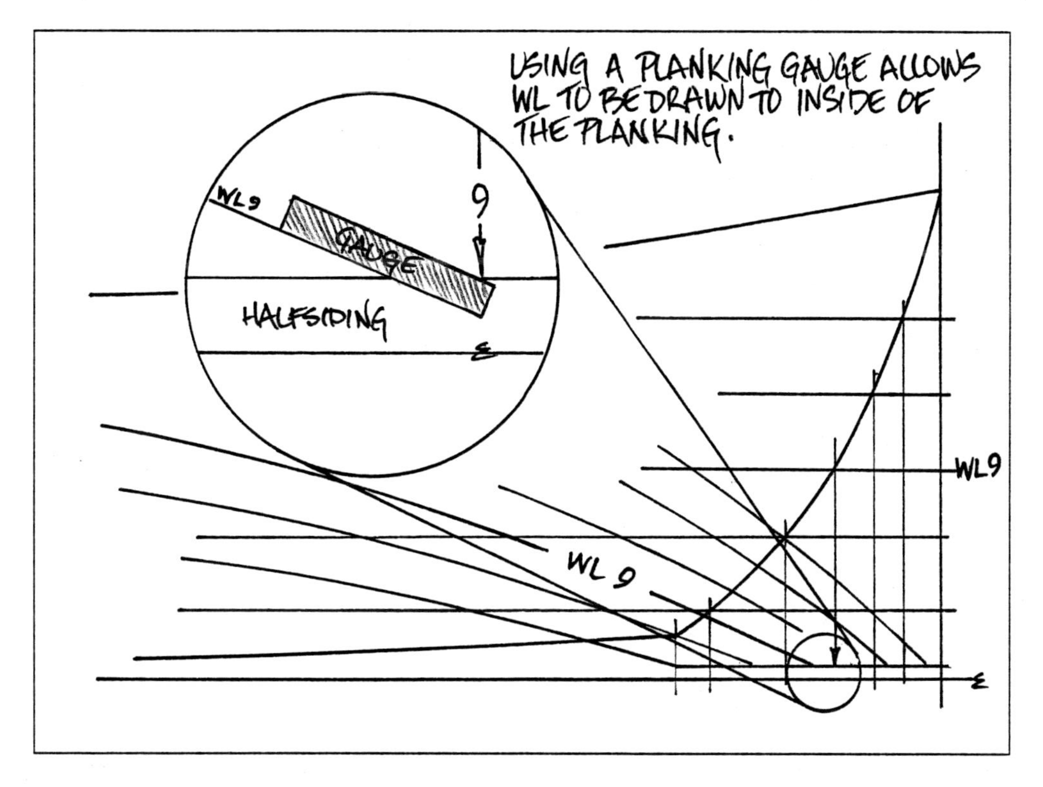

Deducting Plank Thickness

An alternate approach is to use a batten of the same thickness as the planking. Bend it around the station guide nails as before, and at the stem hold it so that its outboard side falls on the intersection of the rabbet and the side of the stem. In that position, the batten mimics the run of the planking, and a line drawn against its inboard side will be drawn to the inside of the planking–just what we want.

If your boat is a double ender–or double ended, like a lapstrake canoe–the procedure will be the same for all waterlines at both ends of the boat. If your boat has a transom, look to the profile for the intersection of the straight profile waterlines and the outboard surface of the transom. Square those points with the halfbreadth centerline, and using the table of offsets, measure off the transom halfbreadths along each of those waterline projections. Those will be your after termination points.

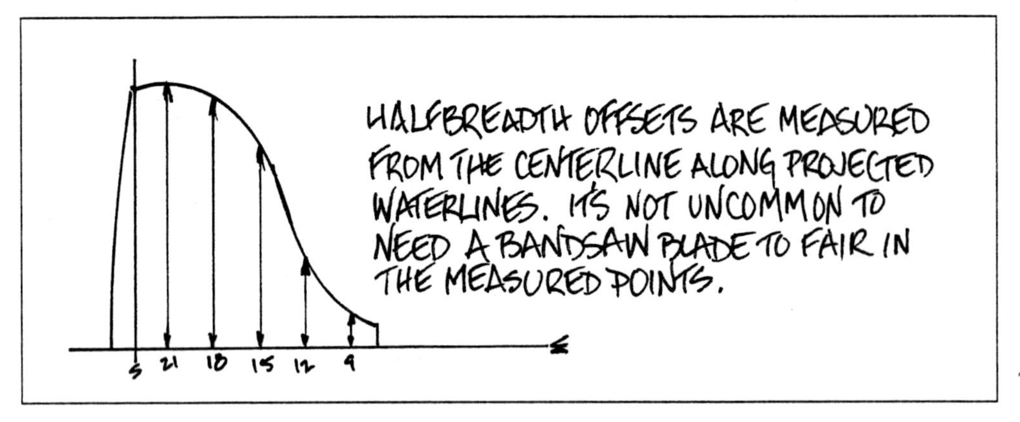

Transom Layout in Halfbreadth View

By convention, the offsets for small craft seldom include waterlines higher than the last continuous waterline. Those above are interrupted by the run of the profile sheer line. If you need to loft some of them–to pick off transom bevels, for example–you will have to project the intersection of that waterline with the sheer as well as waterlines and rabbet. They would fair in as short curves restricted to the ends of the boat, in the halfbreadth view, corresponding to the length of the profile waterline that was the basis of the projection (see Lofting the Waterlines).

Once you have drawn in the waterlines, a two-foot square once again helps project profile waterline/stem rabbet intersections into the halfbreadth view so that the waterline termination points can be located. Since waterlines are then drawn to the inside of the planking, their intersections with the side of the stem are points on the bearding line of the stem. Use the square to project those intersections back to their corresponding waterlines to derive bearding line points in the profile view. Once faired, they will show the run of the bearding line from keel to stemhead. So why does that matter? Because that is the aft extent of beveling on a stem fitted with a cutwater, and the after edge of the right-angle rabbet on a rabbeted stem. There is a method to this madness.

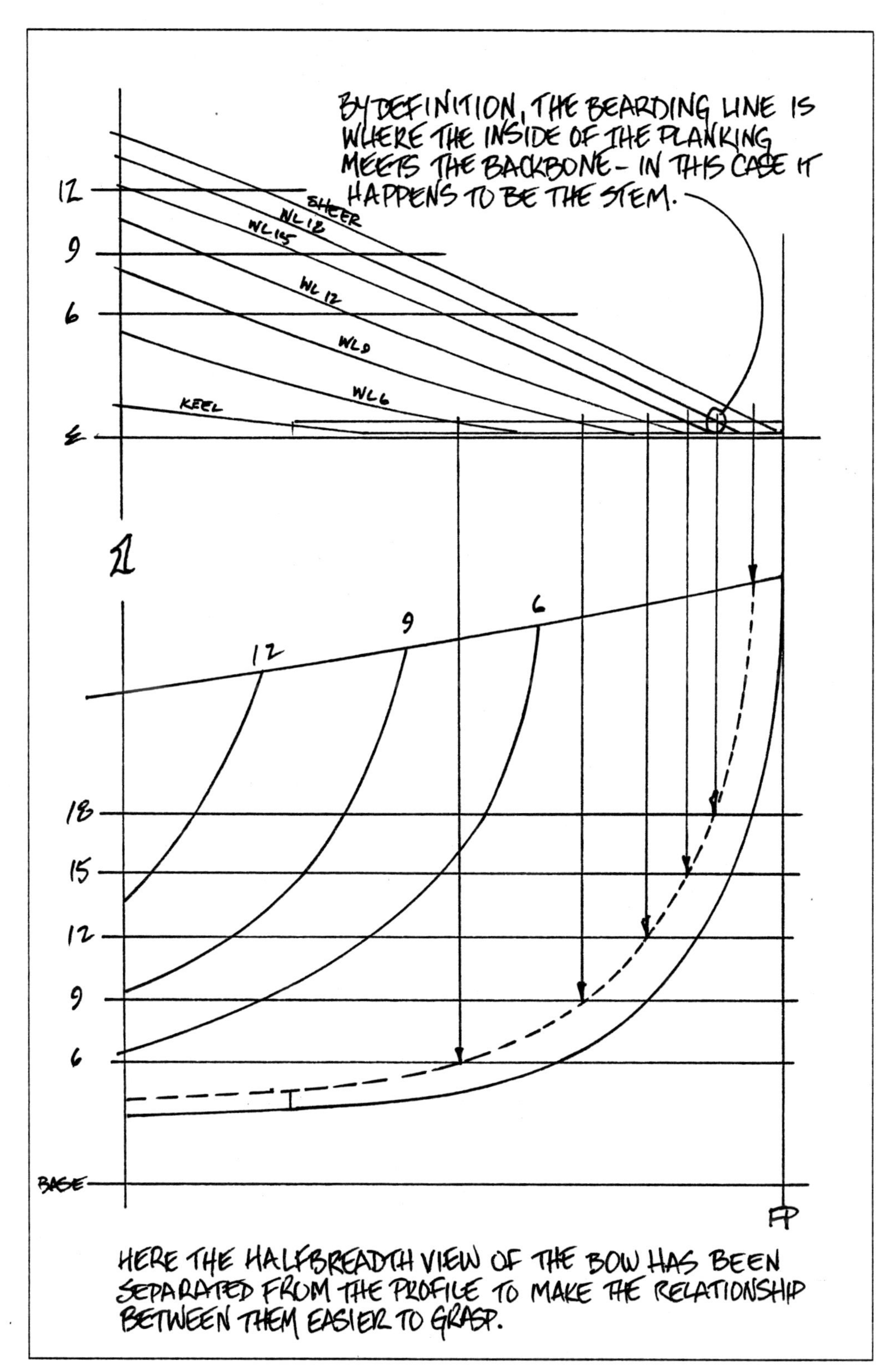

Bearding Line on the Stem Profile

LOFTING THE WATERLINES

Temporarily it's time to leave the profile plan and begin the halfbreadth lofting–the view from directly above or below the floating boat. The lines plan shows the halfbreadths as a series of roughly concentric curves, located apart from and above the profile. The curves depict the waterlines that connect the halfbreadth measurements at each design level. On the lofting, the same gridwork will be reused, though this time, what was the baseline will also serve as the centerline, and some of the waterlines will serve as halfbreadth buttock lines.

Don't let the change in nomenclature confuse you; it isn't difficult. In the profile plan or view of the hull, waterlines are spaced at equal intervals above the baseline. In the halfbreadth plan, the buttock lines are evenly spaced from the centerline. Since the profile baseline and the halfbreadth centerline are now superimposed, it follows that buttock lines of one plan will also be superimposed over the waterlines of the other.

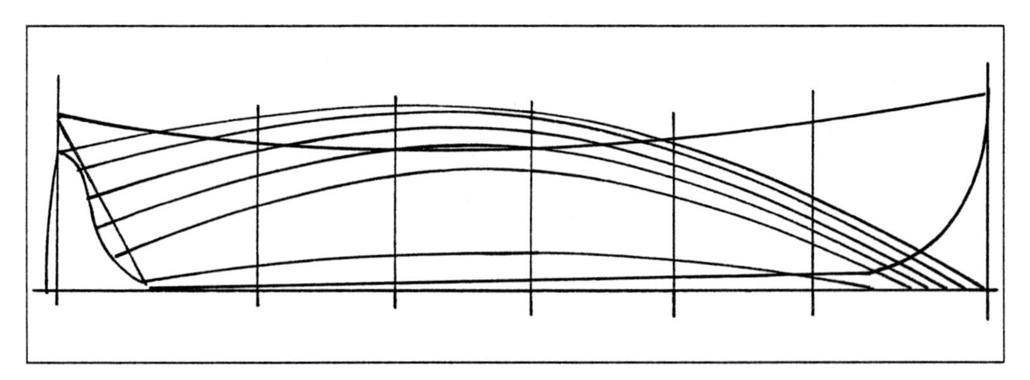

Profile with Halfbreadth Waterlines Added

Commonly, waterlines are spaced at 3" intervals, while the buttock lines are spaced 6" apart. Following that one step further, WL6 and BUT6 are the same line, as is the case with WL12 and BUT12, and so on. From here on, you will find those colored pencils helpful, but whether you use them or not, be sure to label your work.

The halfbreadth lofting begins at the ends of the boat. Since we are working to just one side of the centerline (hence the term halfbreadth), first lay off the half-siding of the stem. That appears as a straight line, parallel to the centerline, and separated from it by 3/4" (assuming a 1-1/2" stem). Double enders, wherries, yacht tenders and other similar craft usually have stems sided 1-1/2 to 2". The line begins at the forward perpendicular (FP), and terminates at the bottom of the stem.

You're right, that's a little nebulous. This is where superimposition of plans begins to work to your advantage. Look to your plan construction details to see the stem configuration. For our purposes at this moment, the terminus of the stem is the point at which the stem and keel rabbets meet. Enter that point on the profile lofting, and using a square aligned with the centerline, project a line from there to where it intersects the stem's half-siding line. That fixes the end of the stem in halfbreadth view.

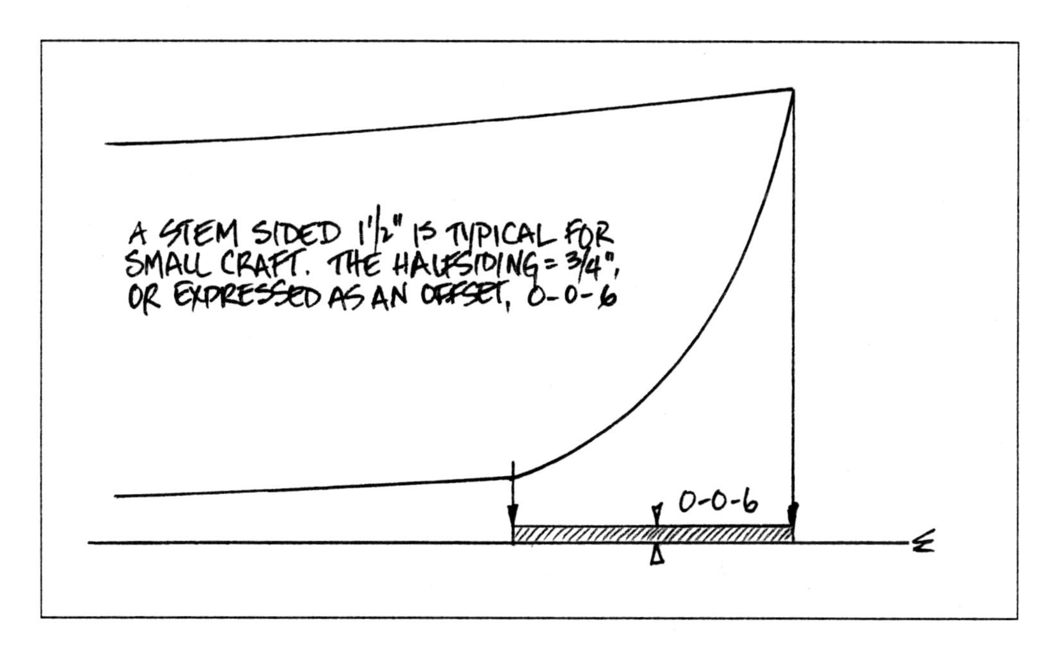

Halfbreadth View of the Stem

Aft, it's more of the same. There, look to the construction profile and the intersection point of keel and transom (outboard). As before, mark that point on the profile lofting, and project it into the halfbreadth view. This time, however, we are working with a transom, so you won't be projecting it to a parallel line; you will be using the projected line itself. Consult the plans, find the halfbreadth offset for the transom at the keel, and lay that off on the projected line to fix the after termination point. It is a halfbreadth measurement, so it is measured outward from the centerline/ baseline.

Lofting of the keel rabbet depends on the keel configuration. For boats with a vertical keel, construction details and the table of offsets will likely tell you that the keel and the stem are the same thickness. When that is the case, the halfbreadth view of the keel rabbet appears as a continuation of the stem rabbet, going all the way to the transom. Simple as that. Boats with plank keels (wherry types, mainly), or flat bottom panels (dory types) will have keel or bottom offsets listed in the table for each station they cross and usually for stem and transom as well. When you loft a plank keel, lay off the points on the lofting board and fair them in with a batten–connecting them with the termination points you have just produced.

Here's where you might need a little reassurance that you aren't losing your mind. When you lay out the rabbet for a plank keel–which in this case is the same as saying its outboard surface–don't expect to see a simple curve. You won't. The plank keel of a wherry has edges that describe a simple curve inboard as well as outboard (after the planking is trimmed off), but before the planking is installed, that outboard surface is pinched inward amidships, much like one half of an elongated hourglass. It is a compound rather than a simple fair curve, owing its existence to the rolling bevel of the keel, and is one of the idiosyncrasies of the type. The same feature is exhibited by the plank keels of some lapstrake canoes, and for the same reason.

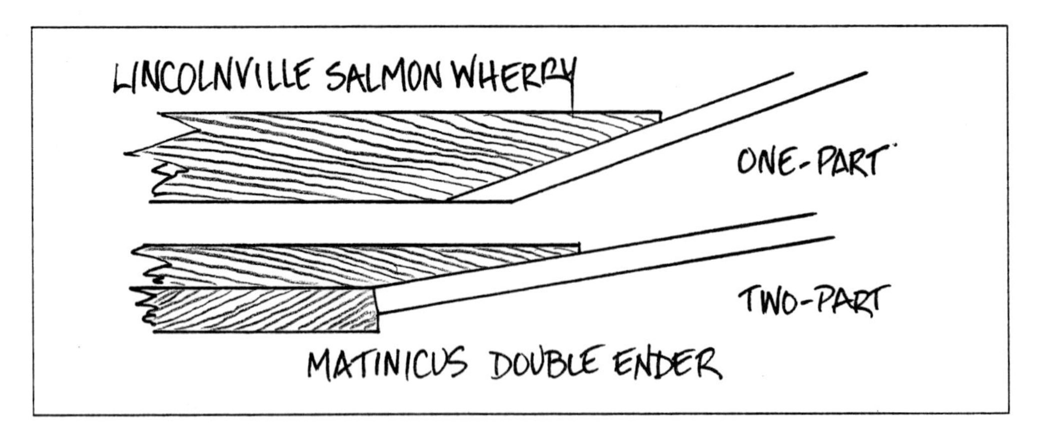

Plank Keel Cross Sections

In order to loft the halfbreadth waterline curves, you will need to locate their termination points fore and aft. Look to stem rabbet already faired in the profile view, and note the intersections of waterlines and stem rabbet. Project those points to the halfbreadth stem using a two-foot square aligned with the base/centerline. There's a hitch here, because those are not the ends of the halfbreadth waterlines. The rabbet intersections you projected are, by definition, points where the *outside* of the planking contacts the outboard surface of the stem. We're lofting lines to the *inside* of the planking, you'll recall, so planking thickness will have to be deducted. In order to do that, we will have to know the run of the individual waterlines. Bear with me.

Aft termination points are found similarly. Project the points where transom profile and waterlines intersect using the two-foot square. A transom is wider than a stem, of course, so this time you will be laying off transom halfbreadths on each of those projected waterlines. Those are the after termination points for the halfbreadth waterlines, where the inside of the planking and the outboard surface of the transom meet.

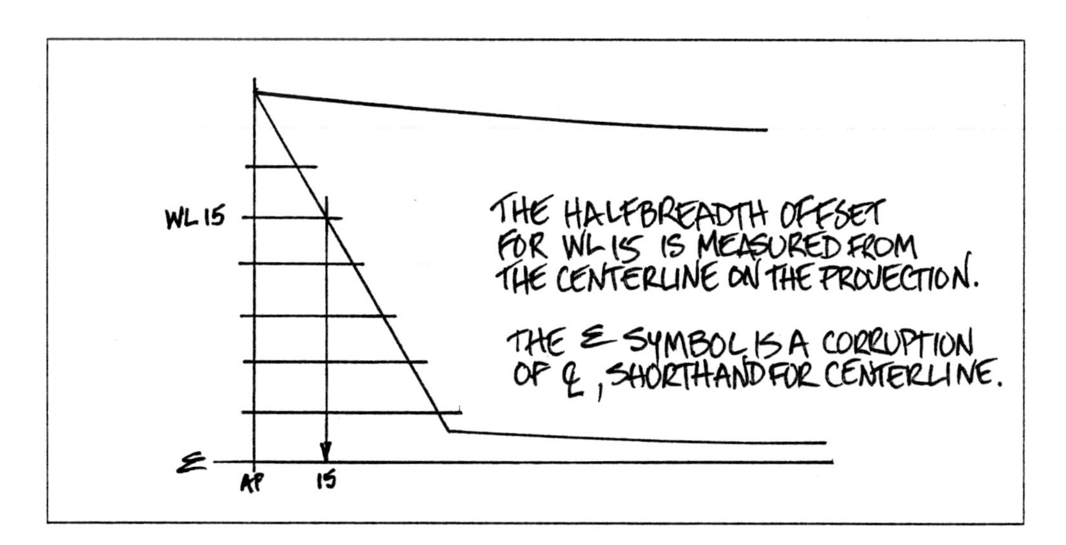

Ends of Waterlines at the Transom

The next step is to lay off the halfbreadth offsets on the stations. There is an abundance of entries to be read from the table of offsets and measured so it helps inhibit errors if you work methodically. Work a waterline at a time or a station at a time. It is much faster if you can have someone read the offset measurements to you while you lay them off on the lofting board.

Now for the final forward termination points. Starting with the lowest waterline curve, bend your batten around the measured station points, positioning it so that your pencil line can be drawn along the inboard (concave) side of the batten. With one hand, draw the batten downward toward the centerline until its inner edge meets the projected position of the rabbet on the stem for that waterline. With a plank gauge matching the thickness of the planking you will be using, deduct plank thickness. Held against the inside of the batten, a line traced along its inboard surface shows where the inside of the planking–and thus the waterline–will meet the stem. Mark the new point of intersection, move the gauge out of the way, and fair in the waterline curve through that point. The sequence of events is the same for every successive waterline.

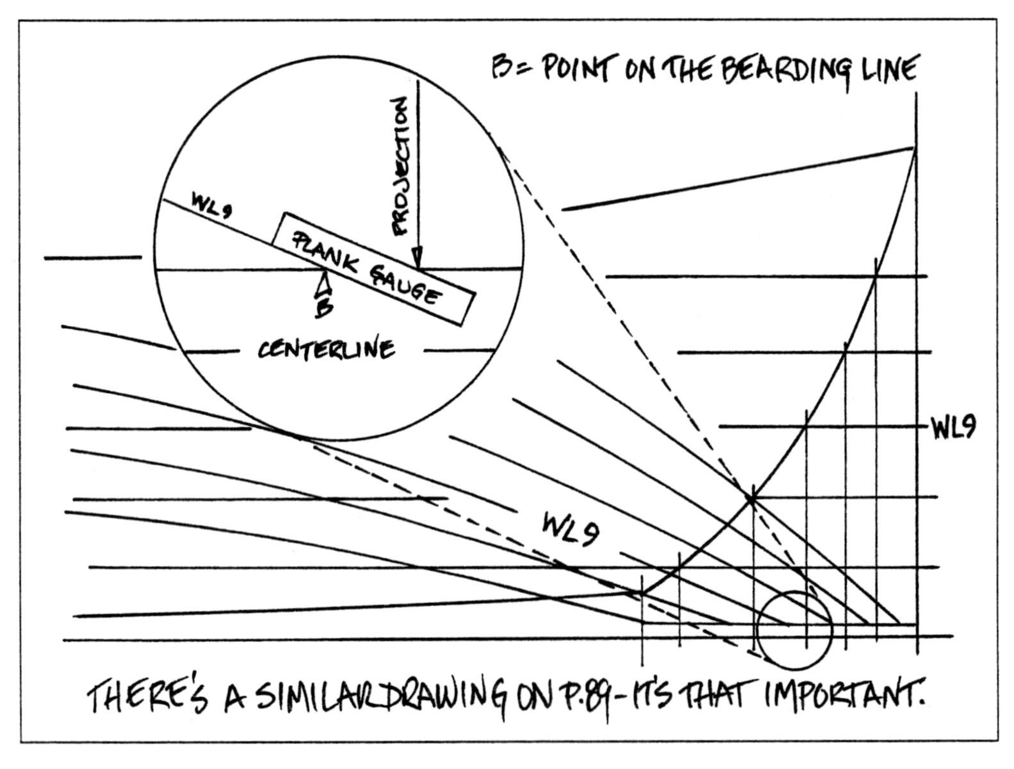

Deducting Plank Thickness

Please note that I said *through* rather than *to* that point; it was intentional. The battens used to fair in waterlines and all other curves should be held in a continuation of the fair curve well beyond the last measured points. To do that, double nail at the termination points (one nail on each side of the batten), and then add another some distance beyond, extending the fair curve. The consequence of failure to do so will be an unfair curve, flattened off between the endpoint and the adjacent station. That wouldn't seem to be much of a problem at this point in the lofting, and you might not even notice it, but I assure you it will be when you try to loft the profile buttock lines.

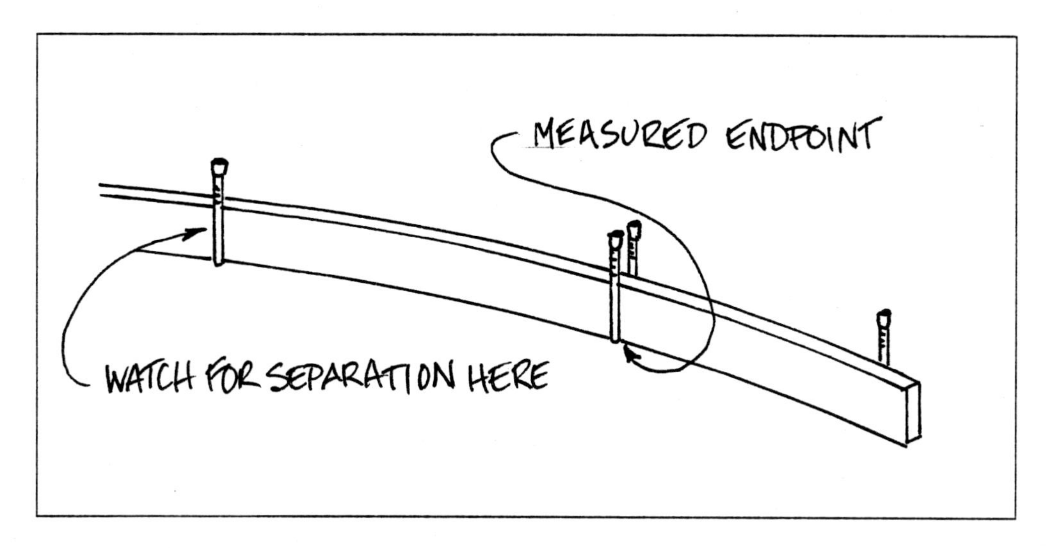

Nailing Beyond the Endpoint

Unless there is a need for further information, plans for small craft call infrequently for lofting non-continuous waterlines (those that are cut by the run of the sheer in the profile view). When there is a need to loft a higher waterline to document the shape of a transom closer to the sheer, for example, begin by projecting the intersection of the profile sheer and that waterline to the halfbreadth sheer. That's one end of the short waterline; the other is on a line projected across the face of the transom at that level. If there is no offset available for that waterline at the transom, you could pick it off the body plan view of the transom (most accurate) which has yet to be completed, or for now scale it off your plan (least accurate, and should be considered tentative). When you fair in the curve, run the batten along the halfbreadth sheer until you reach the forward endpoint, and from there to the transom. The only other alternative would be to establish another station to cross the short waterline, and after that is added to the body plan, pick off the halfbreadth measurement needed.

At first, some I've taught have had a mental block when it comes to superimposed views of the hull; every one made it much more difficult than it is, yet it didn't take long for any of them to master the concept. Usually I walk them over to one of the boats in the shop for the explanation. There, anyone can stand opposite a hull a see that a plank ends a given distance forward of another hull member. Turning that same boat on her side doesn't change the distance of that hood end from the other hull member; the measurements are the same as before. The only change has been the angle of view. Lofted waterlines may well be an abstraction, but the inside surfaces of the planking they trace should be tangible enough for anyone.

LOFTING THE BODY PLAN

It's time to loft the sections of the body plan from which the moulds will ultimately be made. On the lines plan, the hull sections are usually separated from the profile and halfbreadths for the sake of clarity. Owing to the full scale dimension of the lofting, these can also be superimposed without causing undue confusion. If you happen to be working on a vertical lofting board, however, you will save time by lofting the body plan on a separate piece of plywood. The reason is that the moulds are made directly from the body plan, and that's most easily accomplished on a horizontal surface.

By convention, the midship perpendicular (station) serves as the centerline for the body plan, and the profile baseline and waterlines are the same ones you have been using all along. You will have to add buttock lines and diagonals (if any are indicated) to the gridwork. Since the body plan consists of sections through the hull as viewed from the ends, buttocks in the body plan are perpendicular to the baseline and parallel to the body plan centerline. The intervals are given in the table of offsets: BUT6 is expressed as lines port and starboard, spaced 6" from the centerline–BUT12 will be 12" away, and so on.

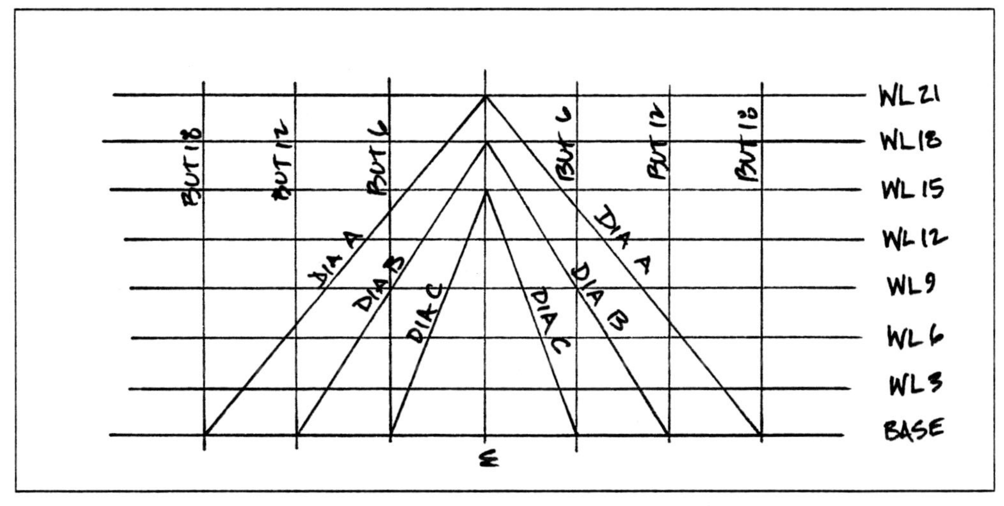

Body Plan Gridwork

You can never have too much information while you're lofting, so if your plan shows diagonals, add the diagonal grid lines so that you will be able to lay off diagonal measurements right along with the heights and halfbreadths, as intended. They are discussed in detail in their own section. For now, complete the body plan gridwork using the diagonal grid endpoints as stated on the plan.

Another convention is that the individual stations are layed out with the forward stations and the stem on the right side of the centerline and the after stations and the transom on the left. The midship station appears on both sides of the centerline, presumably so that the builder will be able to see the entire shape and dimension of the midship station at a glance.

After the gridwork has been established, the sequence of events follows along much the same as before. Work one station at a time, labeling the points as they are entered. Take dimensions from the table of offsets when necessary, otherwise it is better to work from the long waterlines already faired in the halfbreadth lofting. Not only is it counterproductive to consult the table a second time, taking dimensions from the faired lines incorporates any slight corrections you may have made while lofting those curves.

By the same token, a ruler is no longer required–at least not when transferring measurements from the halfbreadth lofting to the body plan. Why take a chance on misreading a ruler when two marks on the side of a batten are goof-proof?

Working from one view to another at the drawing board is facilitated by the full-length adjustable parallel. On the lofting board, a measuring stick is every bit as handy, and because fewer steps are required than with a ruler, there is less chance of making a mistake. This is one of those times when using a ruler could create more problems than it solves. Boatbuilders use this "tick strip" in much the same way that housebuilders use a storey pole. Regardless of its name, the principle is to record the measurements on a batten and carry that to where the measurements are needed, rather than to measure and remeasure. In this particular case, measurements from the centerline to the waterline curves will be carried to the body plan grid for transferal from the plan centerline along each waterline.

First, lay off the halfsiding of the stem on the right side of the plan centerline. Its termination points are the sheer line on top and the forefoot or end of the keel below. Continue by laying off the halfbreadths with the tick strip. You will have to get the buttock measurements (heights above base) and the diagonals directly from the table of offsets.

The transom is layed off to the left of the body plan centerline along with all of the stations from the midship station aft. Remembering that this is a view of the hull as seen from directly aft, the portrayal of the transom will necessarily be foreshortened. Assuming that this transom has a flat face, widths will appear accurately, as will heights above base, but because the transom's face is raked, the only true view will come from the expansion. This foreshortened view does provide pertinent information, however, so it shouldn't be overlooked or ignored altogether.

A word of warning: the lower termination point of the stations is *not* the rabbet that has already been lofted in profile. Remember finding the forward termination points for the waterline curves? This rabbet, like any other, is where the outside of the planking and the backbone meet. All of these lines, you will recall, are drawn to the *inside* of the planking. One reason they are, is that the body plan will be used to make the moulds–the cross-sectional templates around which the planking will be bent during construction.

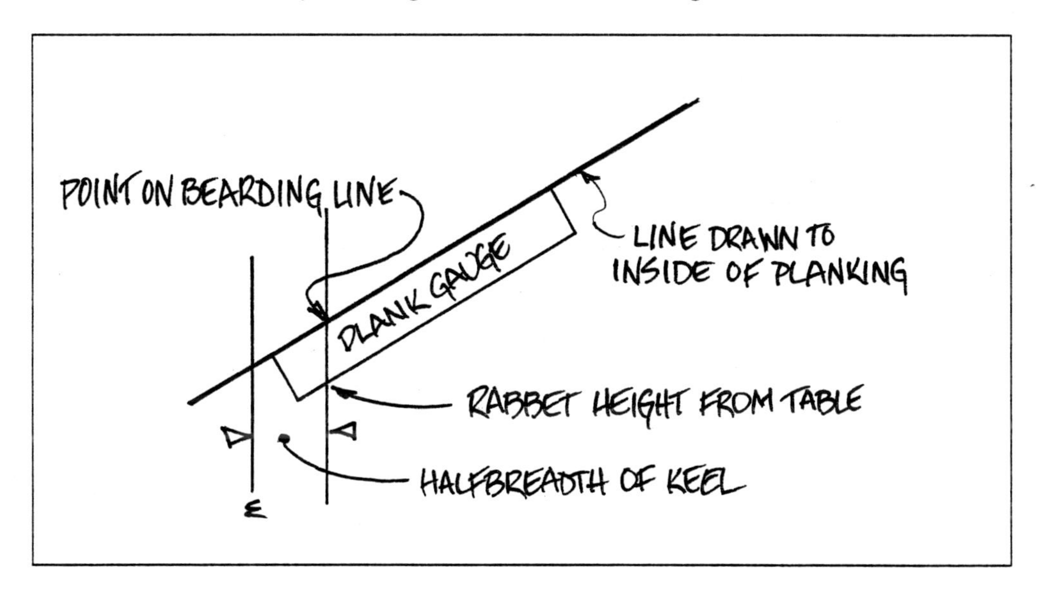

Using a Plank Gauge in the Body Plan

As before, plank thickness must be deducted in order to locate the inboard surface of the planking, and along with it the bearding and inner rabbet points. To deduct the plank thickness, you have to know the run of the station curve, and that is found by fairing in the measured halfbreadth, buttock, and diagonal points for each station. Starting at the sheer, bend the batten around the nails, positioning it so that your pencil line will be drawn on the outboard side of the batten. At the keel, hold the plank gauge against the batten drawing both upward and inward until the outboard face of the gauge intersects the rabbet point. Slide the gauge out of the way and mark along the outside of the batten where it intersects the keel. After that is accomplished, you can take your time to fair in the station curve, secure the batten, and trace its corrected shape.

A fact that may have evaded you is that because the body plan is an endview of the hull the rabbet, inner rabbet, and bearding line at each station appear as individual points defining the actual right-angle mortise boatbuilders know as a "rabbet". The precise location of those points is essential, not only for completion of the lofting–because this is a means to an end–but for the actual getting out of the keel. It is so important, in fact, that I urge you to loft the keel sections for each station on individual pieces of paper.

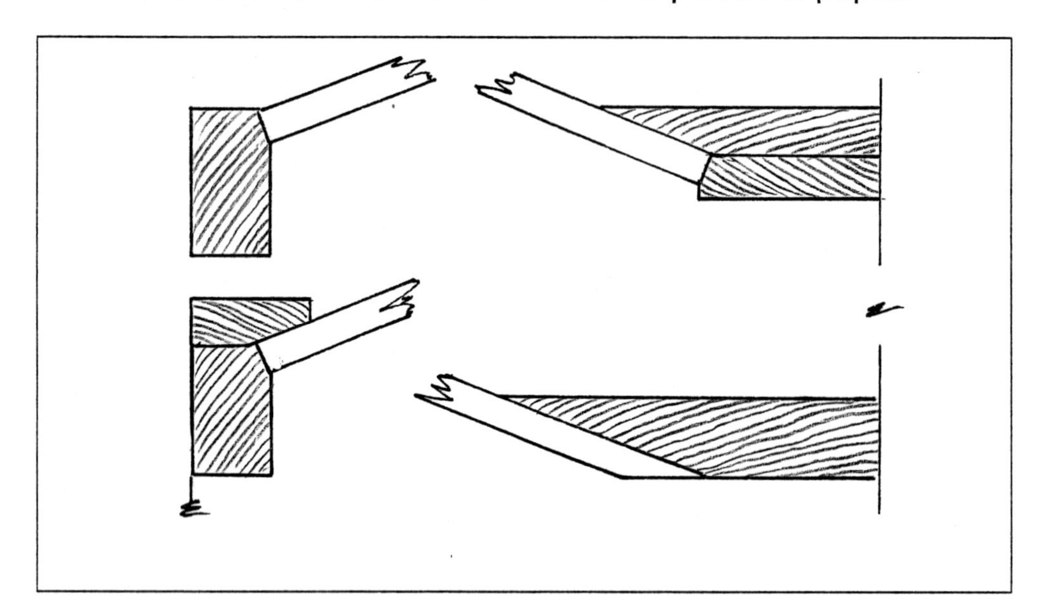

Vertical Keels (left) and Plank Keels (right)

It is absolutely essential that you know the actual keel configuration in order to complete this part of the lofting intelligently. In craft with a straight, vertical keel, rabbet points for all the stations in the body plan would fall right on top of one another. They would all fall on the line denoting the halfsiding of the keel. If the boat has a vertical keel that happens to be deeper aft, the rabbet points will still fall on the halfsiding line but will be one below the other as you work your way aft. Craft with a rockered plank keel, like a Lincolnville Wherry, don't even have a keel rabbet. And those with two-part (inboard and out) member plank keels, display body plan rabbet points that are farther from the centerline and closer to the baseline amidships than at the ends. When you know what you are looking for, your search is easier.

The best approach is to actually "construct" keel sections at each station during the lofting, and then fairing in the station curve. Single 8-1/2"x 11" pieces of paper can be positioned on the board, held there with masking tape, and the centerline and baseline transferred for reference as well as future realignment. Since the object of this approach is to avoid confusion, use a separate sheet for each station. When the time comes, each can be repositioned so that the lines can be taken off for making the moulds, and then the pages can be taken to the bench to help get out the keel.

Those three points–rabbet, inner rabbet, and bearding–are critical. Don't confuse any of them with the term "back rabbet". The back rabbet is bearing surface of the keel or stem rabbet, and is bounded by points on the inner rabbet and bearding lines. As such, it is a term whose usefulness is generally confined to construction rather than lofting. Unfortunately, the term keeps cropping up to cloud the issue.

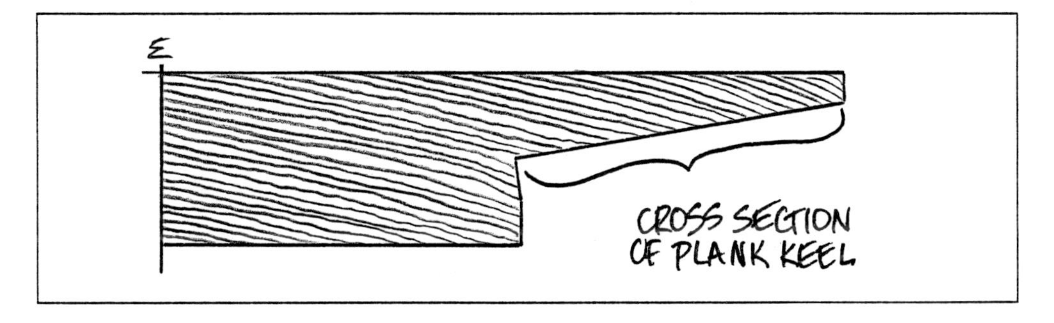

Back Rabbet

The rabbet line position is derived from the table of offsets, and is verified in both profile and halfbreadth views. These stations of the body plan are cross-sectional views of the hull, and at each of these locations, planking buries into the keel. The lowermost edge of the garboard is joined to 90° prior to installation, and the "rabbet" or mortise into which it fits is also a right-angle cut. You have already used your plank gauge to determine the location of the inboard surface of the planking. If your gauge has a square end to imitate the lower edge of the planking, you can also use it to draw in the rabbet. Hold the gauge so that its inboard surface aligns with the station curve, and slide it toward the keel until its lower outboard corner touches the side of the keel. There, it matches the position of the installed garboard, and its innermost corner lands on the inner rabbet, while the intersection of inboard surface and keel is a point on the bearding line.

That description applies to all vertical-keeled boats as well as to those plank-keeled watercraft with inner and outer members (keel and keelson, keel and shoe, etc.). Single member wherry-type keels and flat bottom panels differ. They have no keel rabbet; rather, the side of the keel is beveled off to match the run of the planking. It is a *rolling bevel*, as is that of a typical rabbet, but there is no mortise, as such, to receive the planking. Construction details for those boats call for the protruding lower corner of the planking to be browsed off, with its lower edge eventually shielded by a wear shoe or skid that covers the edge of the garboard and covers the garboard/keel joint at the same time. The offsets would indicate the points along the outboard surface of the keel (usually in the "keel" row of the table of offsets), and no deduction for plank thickness is necessary. The intersection of keel and innermost point of the planking is analogous to the inner rabbet, and the intersection of the side of the keel and the inside of the planking is a point on the bearding line. There is no rabbet.

The last operation in lofting the body plan is to fair in the sheer and inner rabbet curves. There should be no mystery here, other than that engendered because the curves might not be what you anticipate. It wouldn't make much sense for me to cite the various possibilities, when it's easier for you to look at the body plan on your plans.

Your lofted sheer line and the designers' should have similar characteristics. The sheer curve for the forward stations is relatively gentle–in a few plans it is even a straight line–and runs from the sheer of the midship station to the sheer on the line denoting the halfsiding of the stem. For the after sections, the curve is nearly always a compound (taking the shape of the top of the transom into consideration). When the lowest point of the sheer is aft of the midship station in profile, the body plan sheer dips sharply from the midship station to the next one aft, and then climbs immediately to the next, finally curving toward the centerline until it reaches the sheer at the transom. The top of the transom doesn't necessarily fair in with the sheer curve from the stations.

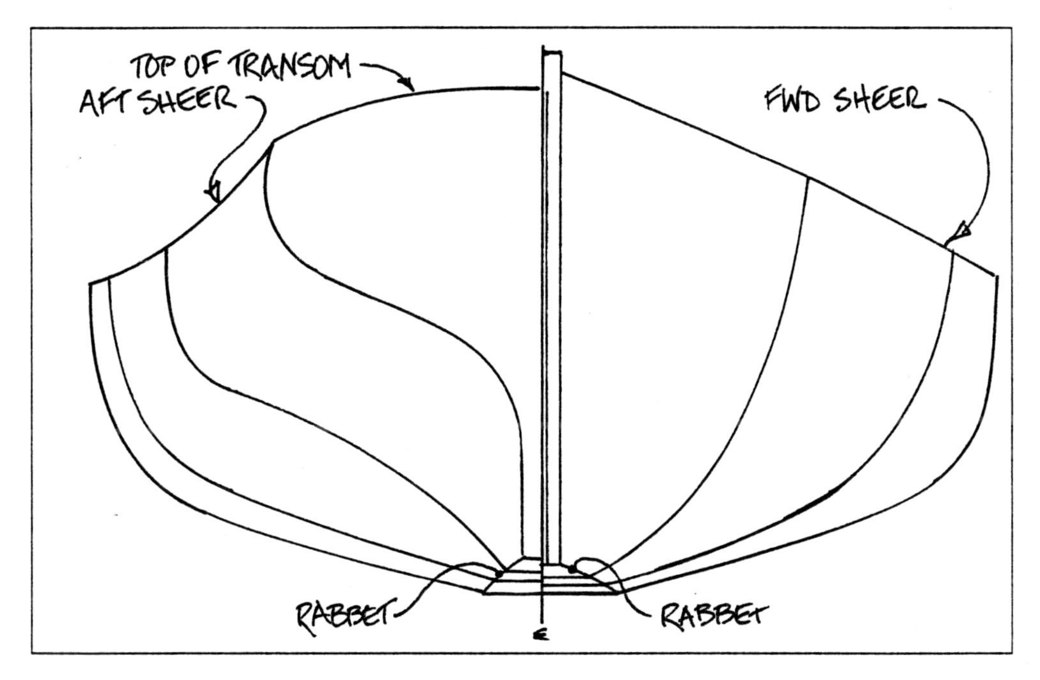

Sheer and Rabbet Curves in the Body Plan

Before you leave the body plan lofting, it is a good idea to add corresponding inner rabbet and sheer marks for each station. That will make it easier when it comes time to assemble the moulds. If the sheer point for STA1, for example, happens to be 3-0-0 above base with a halfbreadth of 1-6-0, that point should appear on both sides of the centerline. That way, when the halves of the mould are separated, you will already have the mark needed to align the port side.

LOFTING BUTTOCK LINES

I still don't understand why buttock lines are such a mystery to so many people. If you think of a centerline plane, analogous to the back of a half model, its outline is the profile of the boat. The outlines of planes parallel to the centerline plane are buttock lines–buttock line curves, to be specific. There are several, usually spaced 6" apart on small craft, that when added to the profile lofting, are roughly concentric. There they appear as lines with little curvature amidships, sweeping upward to terminate along the sheer and edge of the transom.

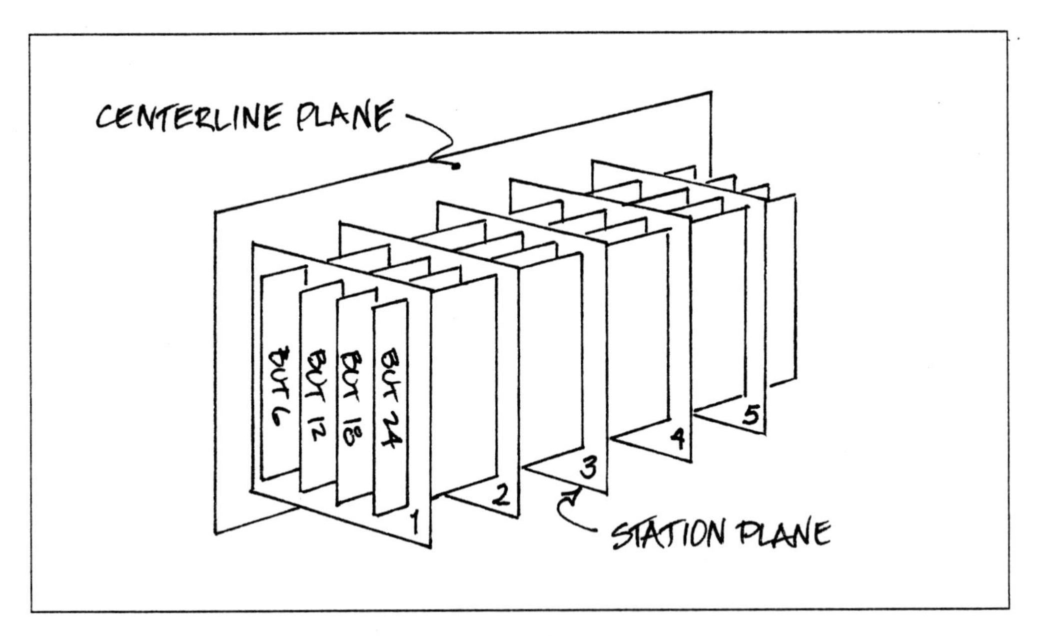

Buttock Planes

The heights needed for the buttocks came originally from the table of offsets, and have already been used during the lofting of the body plan. As discussed earlier, it is to your advantage to take the measurements you need from the lofted station curves. In the body plan, you'll recall, the buttock lines are parallel to the plan centerline and evenly spaced on either side. The measurements needed are the vertical distances from the baseline along each buttock grid line to the station curves. And as before, transferring those measurements from the body plan to the profile is handiest using a tick strip.

To fair in the designated points along the curve, you will need to locate their endpoints. The halfbreadth lofting provides the necessary information. In that view of the hull, the buttock lines are superimposed over the waterline gridwork, so are straight. All you need to do is locate the points where they intersect the sheer and the top of the transom, and using a two-foot square, project those points to the profile sheer and transom.

In point of fact, each buttock line that hits the transom does so in two places–along its outboard edge as well as along its top. Think back to a buttock plane slicing through a hull. The buttock curve describes the profile of the entire hull a given distance out from the centerline. In outlining the profile, it will encompass the gradual 'midship portion of the curve, the upsweep at the ends of the boat, a line along the deck, and a straight line right up the surface of the transom, connecting the deck and planking parts of the curve. All those segments are integral parts of the buttock line, despite the fact that the deck and transom portions will not show from the profile viewpoint because one is coincident with the sheer curve and the other with the transom profile. The latter segment will appear in the body plan and the halfbreadths as well as in the transom expansion.

With the buttock points fore and aft and at the stations, the curves could conceivably be faired, but it wouldn't quite give you the complete picture nor the check of the waterline curves that they are intended to provide. For that, intermediate checkpoints are required. The information is already there on the lofting, all you have to do is make use of it.

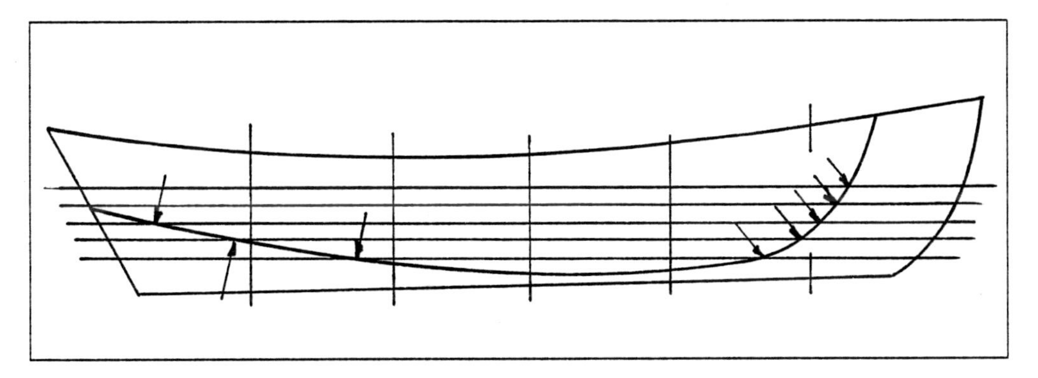

Intermediate Points on the Buttock Lines

The key, as before, are the intersection points. The correlation between views provides additional points along the buttock line curves between the stations that will help define the tight ends of the curves. In order to do that, information will be picked off of the halfbreadth view and projected into the profile.

Note where the straight buttock lines intersect the waterline curves. The salient point is one we have already discussed:every point on a hull or a lofting has a specific fore and aft location regardless of the angle of view. If that happens to be 10" abaft of the stem on the sheer, it will still be there whether it is viewed from the side or from above. That's one of the central themes of the lofting process, and it appears again and again.

As an example, find where curving WL12 and straight BUT6 cross in the halfbreadth view. With the square aligned with the baseline, project that point of intersection until it crosses WL12 in the profile view, and you will have found the location of BUT6 on WL12. Most buttock lines will show intermediate points at both ends of the boat on the same waterline. If the two lines cross in one view, they will do so in the other.

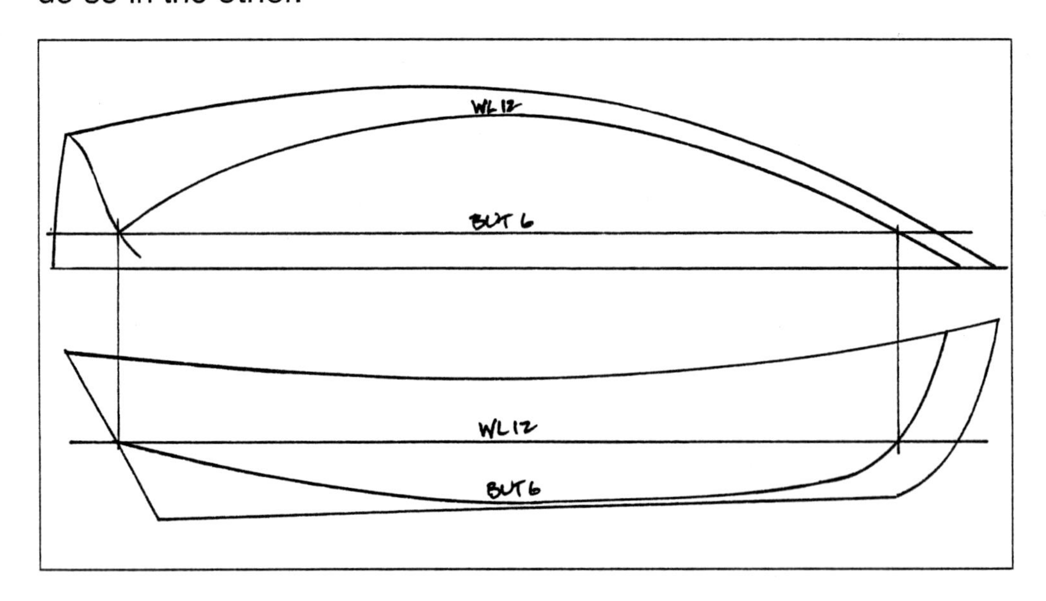

Buttock Projections (Views separated to make it easier to see.)

Old-timers talked of using double tapered battens for fairing in profile buttock lines, but to tell the truth, I have never used one or even seen one used. It would be a logical tool, but is readily imitated with more available battens. For nearly all small craft I use a 1/4"x 1" ash batten, which, because it handles tight curves so well, allows me to draw the curve in one clean sweep. But I realize that is a bit of a specialty item too (as well as one that wouldn't be used in a non-professional shop very often), so I suggest using a combination of battens.

The middle of the curve could be faired with a 1/2" x 1" one, while the ends could be handled with the same batten you used to draw the station curves of the body plan. The overall result will be a fair curve, provided you take the time to fair one curve into the other. Working that way, I draw the flatter portion of the curve first, and then the tighter ends. Fairing in is a little easier if you let the initial curve run past the last station points so that the short curve fairs into a line rather than into an isolated point.

The skeptics among you should be thinking that I have just described the lofting of the buttock curves without so much as a hint of a complication. It worked for me just once, on my 16' Duck Trap Wherry, and I have been in this business too long to consider that anything other than coincidental. The fact of the matter is that the long waterlines as well as the station curves have to mesh perfectly for the buttock curves to fair in precisely across all measured and projected points. Except for that one time, there is always some juggling to be performed.

The basic tenet is that tighter curves are more difficult to modify than gentle ones, owing to the proportionality of change. A repositioning of 1/8" might be all you could hope to achieve on a station curve (and even that would affect adjacent halfbreadths), while some intersections on a waterline curve could conceivably be shifted 1/2" and still give you a point on a fair waterline curve. The trick of correcting, is to do as little damage as possible–don't shift any point very far if it can be avoided, because each move has ramifications that reach into the other views.

There is a separate section that deals with corrections, so here, suffice it to say that modifications required are usually slight. If the intersections don't cooperate and provide the point you need on the buttock curve, chances are that a slight shift in the profile waterline curve will solve the dilemma.

LOFTING DIAGONALS

I have left discussing diagonals until near the end because they aren't frequently used for the lofting of small craft, even though they are common in the lofting of larger sailing vessels. Generally, they are employed when the standard gridwork of waterlines and buttocks is too open to accurately describe important sectional curves. Also in general, diagonals pass through the sections at nearly 90°, corresponding loosely to actual load waterlines with the hull at particular attitudes of heel. Suffice it to say that they serve as a further check of dimensions already lofted. If they are included on the plan it is safe to assume that they are needed; few designers would include them unless they were. Pete Culler was one builder/designer who seemed particularly fond of diagonals, and his expertise would seem to indicate that we should all pay close attention.

To reiterate, all lines are drawn over a gridwork which serves to locate the various points being measured. In the body plan, the gridwork consists of horizontals (baseline and waterlines), and verticals (centerline and buttock lines). The common, though by no means standard, interval for waterlines is 3", and for buttock lines, a multiple of the waterline spacing. A boat with a beam of 58", and a depth amidships of 20", for example will have a midship section that spans a goodly number of gridwork verification lines–intentionally so, as these dimensions are quite common for rowing and sailing craft of up to 20' overall. Because the lofted or scaled sections of such a craft do cross so many lines, it is probable that no additional verification of that shape is necessary in order to loft the section with a considerable degree of certainty. In such cases, diagonals would probably be superfluous.

When the hull sections of a lapstrake canoe are lofted for example, a problem becomes evident because the sections of canoes are smaller than those of the more common pulling boats. Not only are the sections smaller, but in proportion, they change shape more rapidly, exhibiting turns of tighter radius. When this happens, the 3" gridwork commonly used is no longer sufficiently detailed for lofting and building purposes. Lesser intervals are sometimes added, but more commonly, designers add diagonals to the gridwork. Their function is simply to provide measured points along the fair curves of the sections, so that they can be lofted as surely as the sections for any other small craft.

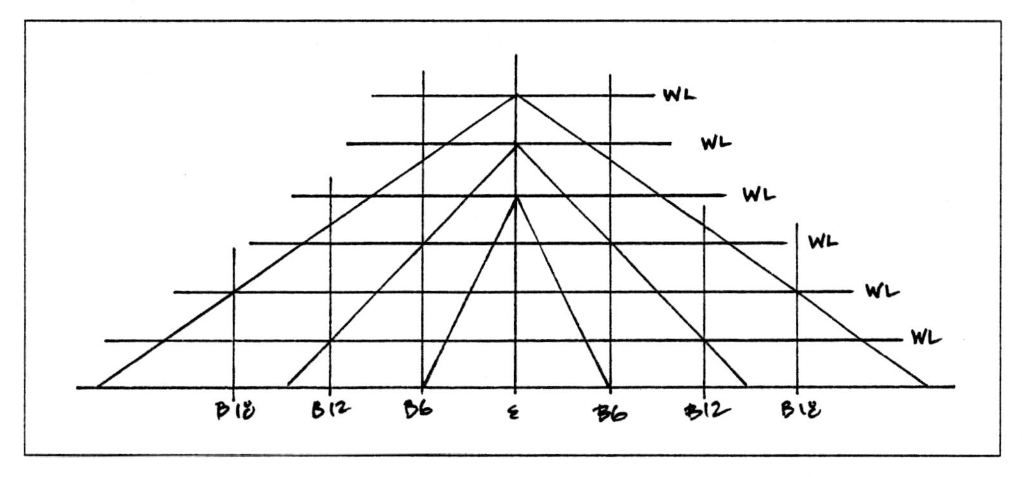

Body Plan Diagonals

Diagonals are the lines of the body plan gridwork that originate at the centerline and terminate at either the baseline or at some readily definable point above the baseline. On the centerline, it is usually quite obvious that they begin at a waterline intersection point. On the baseline, they terminate where baseline and a buttock intersect. Often their termination points are noted in the legend below the Table of Offsets. Since diagonals are commonly placed so that they emerge from the "hull" where the waterline would be under various attitudes of heel, it isn't always possible to have them terminate on the baseline. (They would, of course, if the baseline was sufficiently extended; but that wouldn't be practical.) Another way of saying the same thing is that the diagonals are positioned so as to be nearly square to the hull sections as possible. Choose whatever definition you wish, as long as the picture is formed in your mind.

You will find diagonal dimensions listed in the Table of Offsets, apart from the heights above base and the halfbreadths, for they are neither. Headings in the table appear as DIA A, DIA B, and so on, keying the dimensions to the labeled diagonals in the body plan of the scale drawing. The offsets themselves refer to the distance from the centerline to the particular station as measured along that diagonal–as the name implies, they are diagonal measurements. As I mentioned, in the body plan their top and bottom points are invariably at convenient points of intersection, that by this time, you have already layed out on the lofting board: the intersection of the centerline and a waterline, and the intersection of a buttock and the baseline. The lower ones (originating closest to the baseline) always terminate at a base/buttock line junction. Those higher up terminate at some shown juncture, usually a buttock and a waterline. If you look closely, often a carrat mark on the plan will indicate the termination points.

Measurements for all plan and lofting grid lines are layed down or picked off in exactly the same manner and diagonals are no exception. Halfbreadths are measured along the waterlines from the centerline. Heights are measured along the buttock lines, upward from the baseline. Diagonals are measured along the diagonal grid out and down from the centerline.

On the stations, you should have little difficulty locating the position of each diagonal. Layout the diagonals on the body plan gridwork in the center of the lofting as indicated on the scale drawing. Pick the distance from centerline to station off the body plan, and transfer that distance right along with the heights and halfbreadths station used for the profile and halfbreadth plan. As with previous layout work, it pays to label the measured points.

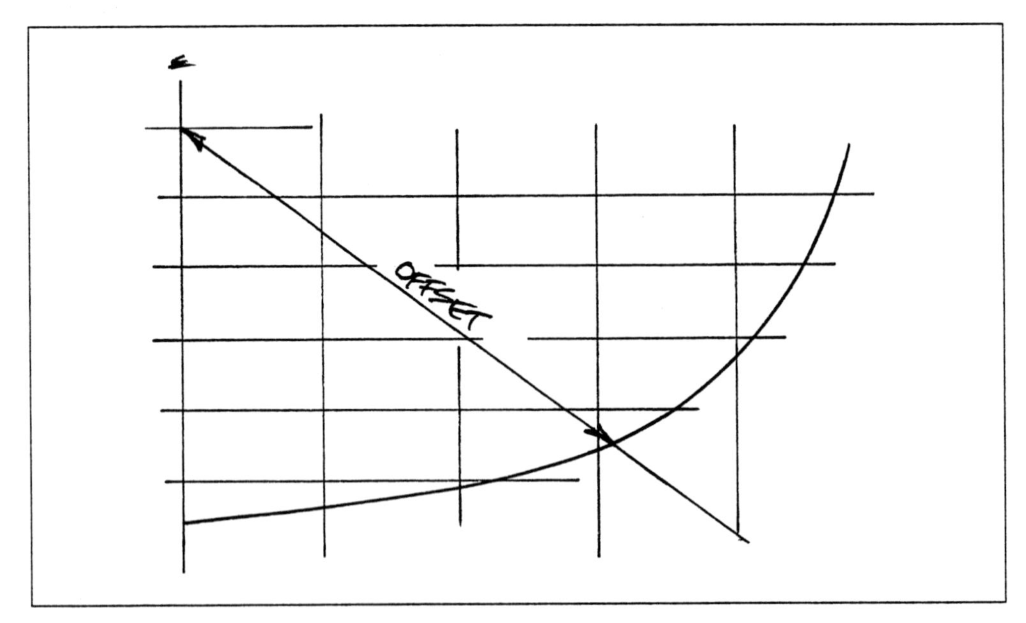

Measuring a Diagonal

A thorough job of lofting would indicate that the long diagonals be lofted after the lofting of the stations has been completed–to make certain that they fair in as well. To be frank, I seldom loft the long diagonal unless I have encountered some problem I am unable to resolve otherwise. That, however, doesn't relieve me of the responsibility of explaining the process here so you will be equipped to draw your own conclusions.

The main portion of the plan, which consists of the profile and the halfbreadth plan, shows the run of the diagonals along the inboard surface of the hull. That's assuming, of course, that the lines are drawn "to the inside of the planking". Being neither fish nor fowl, so to speak, diagonals are drawn somewhat apart from the other two plan parts, commonly just below the profile. The station lines are seldom extended to cross them, though their position is indicated by carrat marks at each point of intersection. When long diagonals are shown on the plan, they most often appear as quasiconcentric curves, concave to and located beneath the baseline.

The lofting board allows for no such separation, so I would advise drawing them with a pencil of a different lead color. Measurements can be made from the centerline (as on the body plan), but the resulting diagonal curves could be confused with the waterlines of the halfbreadth portion of the lofting. On the scale drawing, they are roughly parallel to the buttock lines, but that is because they are being measured in the opposite direction from the centerline. I'm inclined to use the uppermost profile waterline as the centerline for the diagonal lofting, measuring in the direction of the baseline, so that the resulting curves are plotted opposite to the halfbreadth waterlines. Regardless of your approach, diagonals are layed off at each station, and faired in on the drawing board just as they would have to be done on the lofting.

Locating the fore and aft termination points have caused a good many prospective builders to throw up their hands in despair. It is really no more that an extension of the logic used to interpret the diagonals thus far. The information needed is mostly on the body plan, with the rest coming from the profile. For any small craft, it is quite obvious where the diagonals are located on the centerline when you look at the body plan. In addition to the centerline location, note where they cross the halfbreadth of the stem.

Measure the vertical distance from base to the point of intersection on the centerline forward and on the transom aft, and transfer that height to the stem and the transom on the profile. Using your square, project a line from the points of intersection across the centerline you are using for the diagonals, working at 90° to the base. Treat all diagonals similarly. That will fix the fore and aft extent of the diagonals. In the body plan, measure the distance from the centerline to the half-siding of the stem and to the edge of the transom along each diagonal and transfer those measurements to the projected lines to derive the termination points. That's the hard part, now lay out dimensions at each of the stations. The final step is to fair in diagonals with your longest batten.

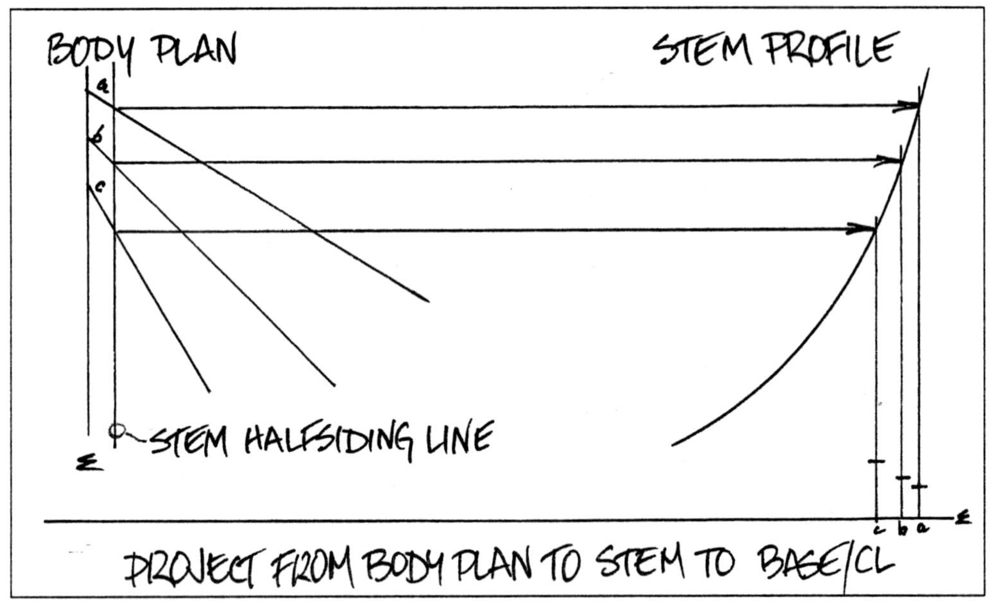

Diagonal Endpoints

In basic terms, diagonals provide another approach to the problem of reproducing hull sections accurately. There are instances, however, where you will find them used to the exclusion of the common gridwork, so it's a good idea to know how to handle them. Pete Culler's plans for his 13' lapstrake canoe *Butternut* are a good illustration. For all intents and purposes, the typical gridwork is absent. Centerline and baseline are there, along with the design load waterline of the canoe. Other than that, all you will see are his three diagonals. Since they are strategically placed, no other lines are necessary. Set up in that way, the plan appears unconventional to the point of being haphazard, when in fact, nothing is further from the truth. Pete was a master in this business, and his Yankee ingenuity led him to concentrate on the essential and to spurn the superfluous. He was a practical man who used what worked best for him.

MAKING CORRECTIONS

I realize that my explanations read as if nothing ever goes wrong during lofting, but now that you know how the process is intended to work, we can deal with the imperfections in the world of lofting. Measurements don't always land nicely along a fair curve. Whenever you are working from plans, you are attempting to make your measurements and the resulting curves match those of the designer. Whether you happen to be working on a boat or any other construction project, you can't assume that things will always work out right away. And when they don't, the troubleshooting sequence that works best is: first, double check your measurements; second, check your batten; and finally, make corrections.

Double checking your measurements should be self-explanatory, but there are some helps that you might not have considered. For one, use a different tick strip to retransfer the questionable measurements. Reusing the original one might result in your inadvertently picking off an incorrect dimension a second time. If that doesn't work, try having a friend recheck the measurement. It is akin to proofreading where you can bypass a mistake simply because, in your mind, you read what you had intended to write in the first place rather than what you actually wrote. Someone else looks at it from a fresh perspective, and as a result often spots the error right away. I have often found the problem to be caused by using the same tick strip over and over without erasing all the marks each time. That's just asking for trouble, but I'll understand if you do, because I still find myself doing the same thing.

No two battens are identical, so the chances of yours matching the characteristics of the designer's batten are remote at best. Fortunately, like using a single ruler throughout, as long as your batten is true, the overall lofting will be successful. Do the best you can to make the batten land along the measured points at every station and give you a fair curve. Sight the batten from both ends to be certain. If the curve is still unfair despite your best efforts, some changes are in order.

There are times when it is the batten itself that is the cause of the problem, and the measured points are just fine. Sometimes all it takes is turning the batten end for end, because the ends bend differently. At other times, all it takes is sliding the batten one way or the other through the nails. Keep at it until you are satisfied with the curve and its run through the measured points.

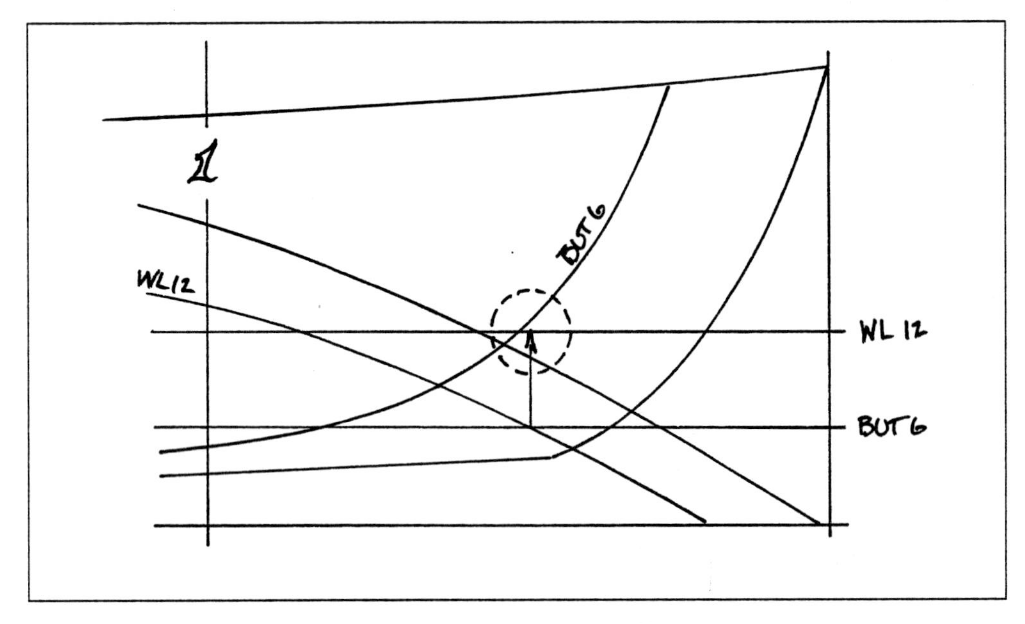

When Views Don't Jibe

In boatbuilding, it is vital that the curves be smooth, even if correcting causes an 1/8" divergence from a plan dimension. Fair curve by batten should be your abiding concern. More often than not, when a curve has an odd characteristic, you will find that a single nail is crowding the batten. When that is the case, pull the offending nail–usually the batten will spring a sixteenth or so, giving you the desired curve. Battens are self-fairing when you give them the chance, but they do have their idiosyncrasies.

That brings up what is always fodder for an argument–the question of allowable tolerances. It would be comforting to have every dimension check precisely, but things just don't work that way. I can't tell you that a divergence of plus or minus 1/8" is nearly always all right. It isn't. On the other hand, there are instances when a curve can be as much as 1/4" off of the measured point and still be fair and check with the other views. Allowable tolerance is a relative term at best, depending more on the situation than on your personal perfectionism. Trying to squeeze out every last sixteenth of an inch rapidly becomes an exercise in diminishing returns.

Station curves should check right on the nose, and intermediate points on buttock line curves are nearly as critical. In small craft, long waterlines and diagonals aren't quite so critical.

We have already cited the body plan as a manifestation of this problem. The station curves that constitute the body plan are much tighter than the halfbreadth waterline curves, and so are much less subject to interpretation. A discrepancy of 1/8" can readily disappear over three stations in a 12' waterline curve and still allow the curve to be faired in nicely without disturbing the adjacent stations, but that same 1/8" on a 2' body plan curve can be an insurmountable obstacle. Actually, it wouldn't be as much insurmountable as it would be terribly messy to correct. If the point was moved that far on the body plan, it would affect points above and below on at least three other waterlines–and then you would have to carry those corrected points over and refair the long waterline curves. For that reason, the initial waterline curves lofted should be considered tentative, to be finalized using the curves of the body plan.

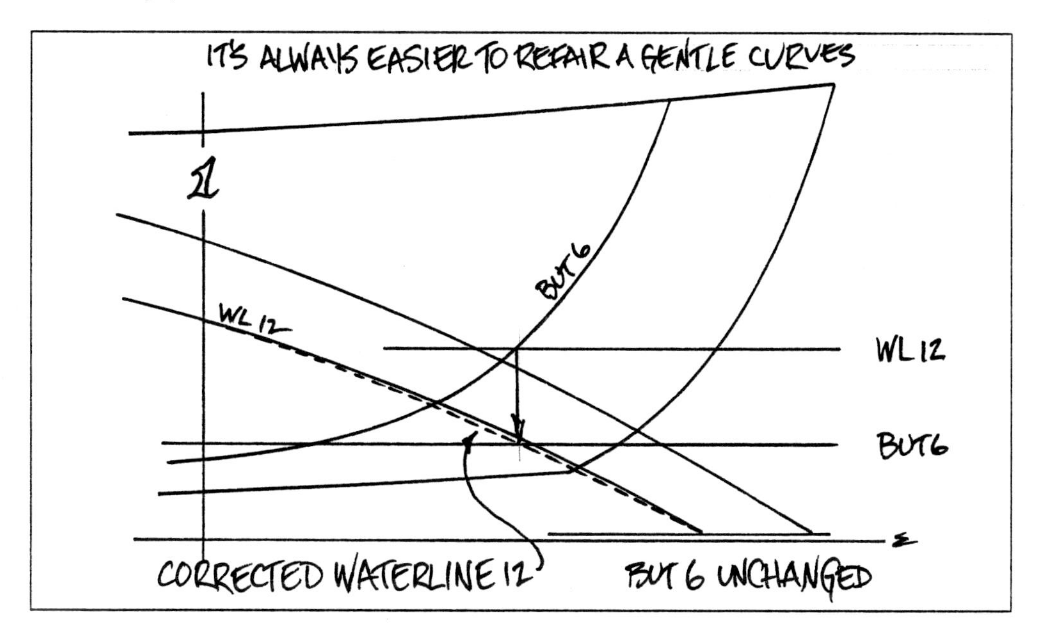

Making a Correction

The profile buttock line curves are another source of complications. Usually the intermediate portion of the curves, being relatively gentle, fair in well–the problems most frequently become evident at the ends where projected intermediate points along the waterlines fix the run of the tight end curve. There, it is a matter of working back and forth between the halfbreadth and profile until the intersections jibe and allow for fair curves in both views. Each situation is a bit different, but your guiding principle should be that *several minor corrections are preferable to a large one*. It isn't difficult to alter the location of a few points 1/8" or even 1/4", because the resulting change in the long waterline curve will be slight. Moving one of those points on the end of the buttock curve 3/8" or more, however, will have repercussions that will ripple through not only the halfbreadth waterlines, but through the body plan as well.

When all is said and done, it's unlikely that I can anticipate every problem you might encounter. I can tell you, however, that nearly all of them are caused by the loftsman rather than by the plan. I have had new builders send me their entire lofting in a mailing tube when they had completely given up. One was so completely frustrated that inside the tube was a blank check and a note that said "HELP, PLEASE !" Nearly all the curves were well drawn; he had fouled up the initial gridwork–the stations weren't spaced evenly along the baseline. A simple mistake. I learned a long time ago to look for the obvious first, as in, "when the light doesn't work, check the bulb before rewiring the fixture".

In all fairness, I am compelled to add that sometimes the plan really is at fault. If nothing else, the law of averages would dictate that every so often the designer is apt to goof, and that goof can find its way onto the finished plan. Your only defense is your understanding of the checking processes involved in lofting. The views must correspond to one another and the curves must be fair. It is safest to consider correcting the plan a last resort while recognizing that it is definitely necessary from time to time.

EXPANDING THE TRANSOM

You are about to discover that this is the most technical and involved portion of this book, not to mention the longest. It will be difficult to simply read through and understand. It will require study, patience, attention to detail, and persistence. Some working boatbuilders still don't know how to expand a transom properly–and yet they build good boats. There is little excuse for you not to know how the job is done after studying these pages. The necessary information is contained here, but as a hypothetical apprentice, you will have to practice in order to comprehend the process of transom expansion. If I learned how, you surely can.

The main problem with explaining the expansion of a transom in print is that the process is a largely visual one, and most easily explained while standing in front of a lofting board. In basic terms, the expansion is a mechanical projection of a sloping hull member–nothing more. The explanation becomes lengthy because of the need to identify verbally each line considered. The illustrations are designed to help, but they will not unless you take the time to examine each one carefully. The best approach is to go ahead and loft a transom and then expand it on your own–using what is detailed here as your guide. Your persistence will see you through. And after you have expanded a transom, you will understand that it really isn't such a mystery.

When you look at a transom from astern, what you really see is a foreshortened version of the real thing. Reduced to line form, its shape is the one lofted in the body plan. It is *a* representation of that particular part of the hull, but alone insufficient for a builder's purposes. The halfbreadth view of the transom is even more severely compressed. What a builder needs to see is a version of the transom stretched out to its actual height, and that's what is called an "expansion". That is why there is also a lines view of the transom on the building plan that is designated "expansion". It requires a bit of imagination, but the expanded version is what you would see from directly aft of the transom with your line of sight perpendicular to its rake. This view alone shows the full height and shape of the outboard face.

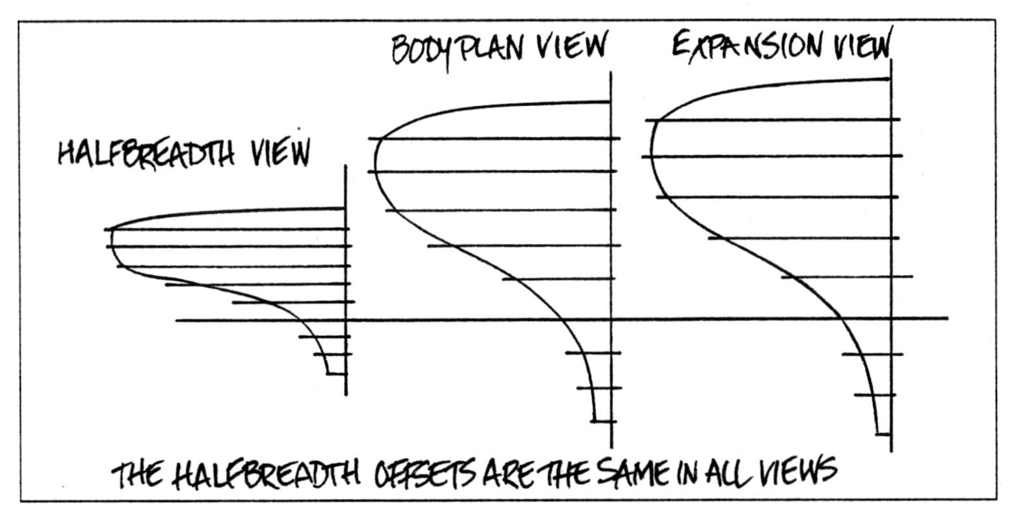

Transom Views

Working from a half model simplifies matters greatly the first time through. Even if you don't have a model, you will find it helpful to at least visualize one to grasp the all-important relationship between hull profile waterlines and expanded transom waterlines. One derives from the other. A lift model provides a ready explanation of expanded waterlines because the transom end of each lift is an expanded waterline. Solid models are useful too, though with them waterlines should be extended from the back side of the model across the transom face. If your model doesn't have them, draw them in using a combination square as your guide so that they are parallel to the LWL and perpendicular to the centerline plane of the hull. Measurements between one expanded waterline and the next can be scaled right off the transom face of the model. Because it is raked out of plumb and therefore crosses the profile waterlines at an angle, the distance between the expanded waterlines will be greater than that between the profile waterlines, and the greater the rake, the further apart the expansion waterlines.

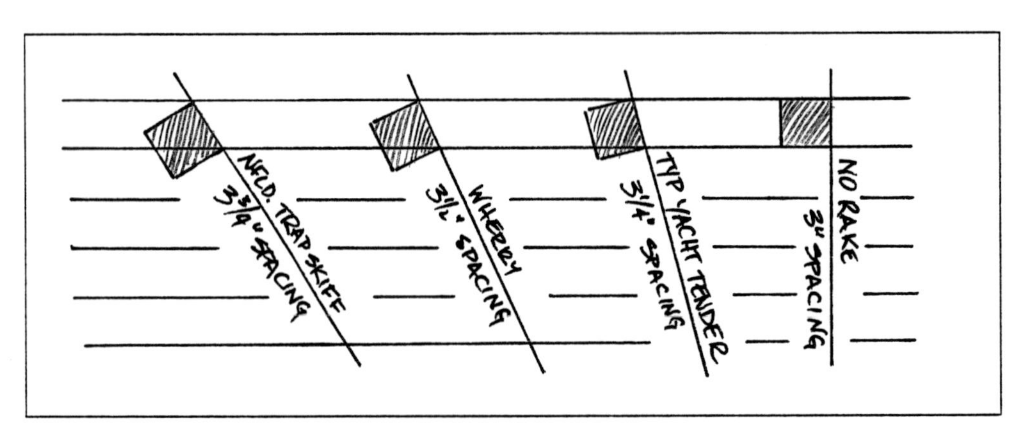

Expansion Waterlines

Note that I said that measurements *can* be taken directly from the model. In practice, you would only do so if you were going to build a boat without benefit of lofting. I phrased it in terms of half models to help you visualize the concept. The information you need for the entire expansion is already included in what has been lofted to this point. To lay out expanded waterlines on the lofting, use a 2' square and project lines aft from the transom profile, using the intersections of profile waterlines and transom as points of origin. The line that denotes the transom profile will serve as the centerline for the transom expansion.

The expansion gridwork consists of the expanded baseline, expanded waterlines, buttock lines, and diagonals (if applicable). To draw the expanded baseline, extend the profile transom line until it crosses the profile baseline; there, project the baseline aft with the square as was done for the waterlines. If the buttock lines were 6"apart on the body plan, they remain 6" apart in the expanded view. Diagonals are drawn in using the same endpoints as before.

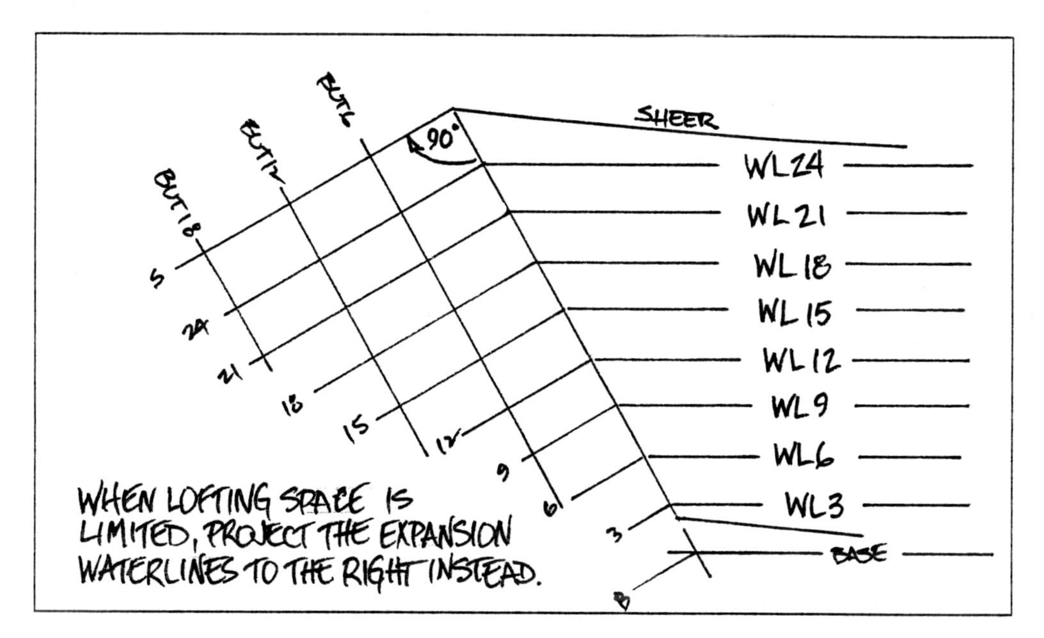

Expansion Gridwork

The halfbreadths are commonly picked off the body plan and transferred to the corresponding waterlines with a tick strip, and the heights can be transferred directly to the buttock lines in the expansion. Without explanation for the moment, I'll add that it lends continuity to the whole process if halfbreadths for the expansion are picked off the halfbreadth view in the lofting, there measuring across the face of the transom. The only thing that has changed from the earlier lofting is the distance between the waterlines.

Complete the lofting of the outboard expansion by fairing in the measured points. Since the curves are less severe than those on either the halfbreadth view or the body plan, the batten used to fair in the station curves will likely handle the job. Look to the plan for fairing in the top of the transom above the sheer. Often, that curve is purely decorative, but not always. Since the function of the lofting is to verify plan information, there is no reason to omit this part. One of the easiest ways to duplicate the curve is to extend the buttock lines on the plan until they intersect the top of the expanded transom, scale the heights above the sheer, and transfer that to the lofting. Sometimes the plan will simply bear the notation "3-inch crown", in which case the top of the transom on the centerline is meant to be 3" above the level of the sheer, and a true arc (section of a circle) connects it to the sheer at the edge of the transom.

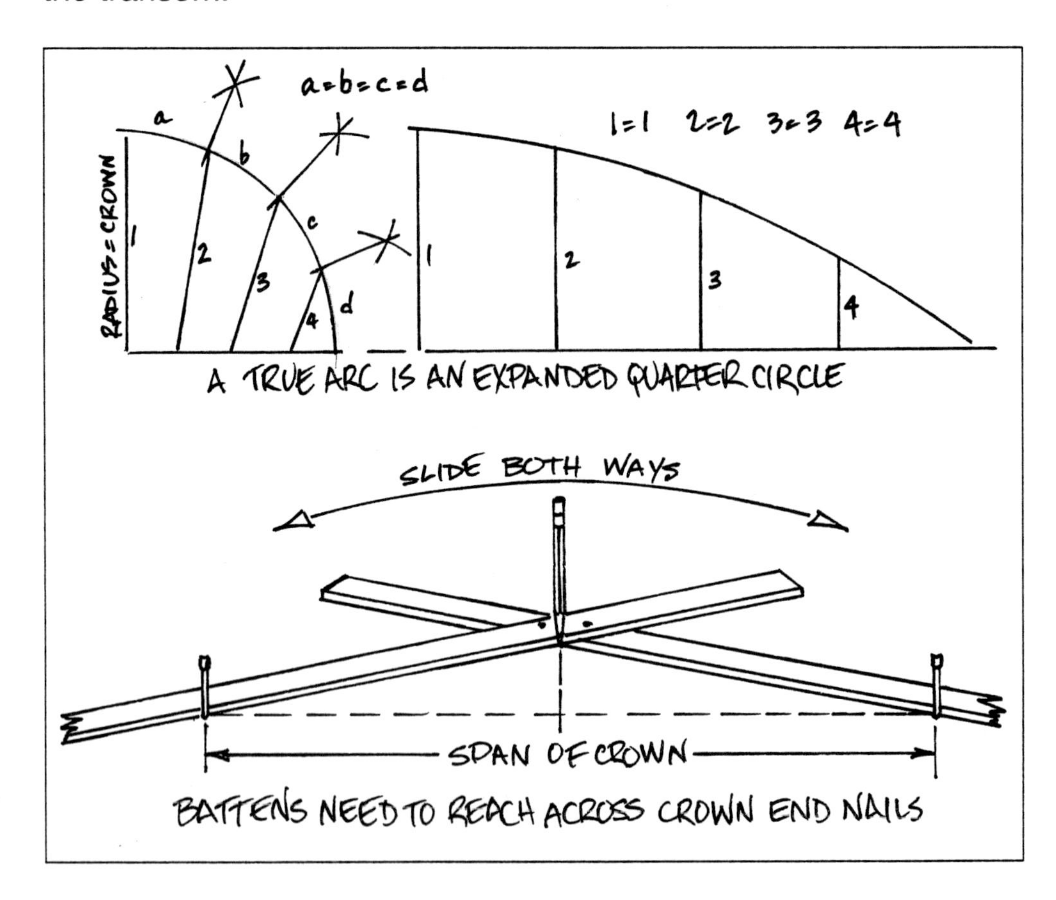

Two Ways to Layout an Arc

Many feel that a half model affords considerably less chance for misinterpretation because it can be measured directly. Waterline spacing, halfbreadths, and heights can all be picked off directly with a scale rule or a pair of dividers. If you prefer, the model can be traced against a piece of paper and the gridwork of waterlines and buttocks overlaid and then measured. I find it less tedious just to work from the model, though to do a complete job you must do one and then the other. As I see it, any unnecessary intermediate steps between half model and lofting should be eliminated. They only provide a possible source of error in repeated measurement or transcription and require additional time to boot.

The sole justification for the work required in expanding a transom is that it provides the builder with the true shape of the transom, and the angular information needed to bevel it accurately before it becomes an integral part of the backbone. What angular information you ask? It is already on the halfbreadth lofting and will become a part of the expansion before long. For now, look at the intersection of the waterline curves and the edge of the transom in the halfbreadth view. Each of those transom halfbreadths was measured along a waterline projected square to the centerline. The angle of the transom edge at that waterline can be picked off with a bevel measuring the curved waterline's angular approach to the same waterline on the transom. That isn't a particularly handy piece of information, you will discover, but it is available should you need it, provided you know where to look.

To complicate your life, I want to call your attention to the fact that the inboard surface of the transom is larger than its outboard face–and it is also of a slightly different shape, just to keep things interesting. From here on, a half model is of limited usefulness; only the lofting will yield accurate enough results. This is the part where we witness the eyes of students glazing over, so pay attention. It's not really all that difficult, but this really isn't an operation to tackle at the end of a long day.

An expansion carried through this far consists of a moderate number of lines. Since we are about to double that number, doubtless you will find it less confusing to use a different color pencil to help distinguish between the two gridworks and expansion profiles. Some even elect to overlay the expansion with a sheet of drafting film so that once completed the two parts can be completely separated. Use what works best for you.

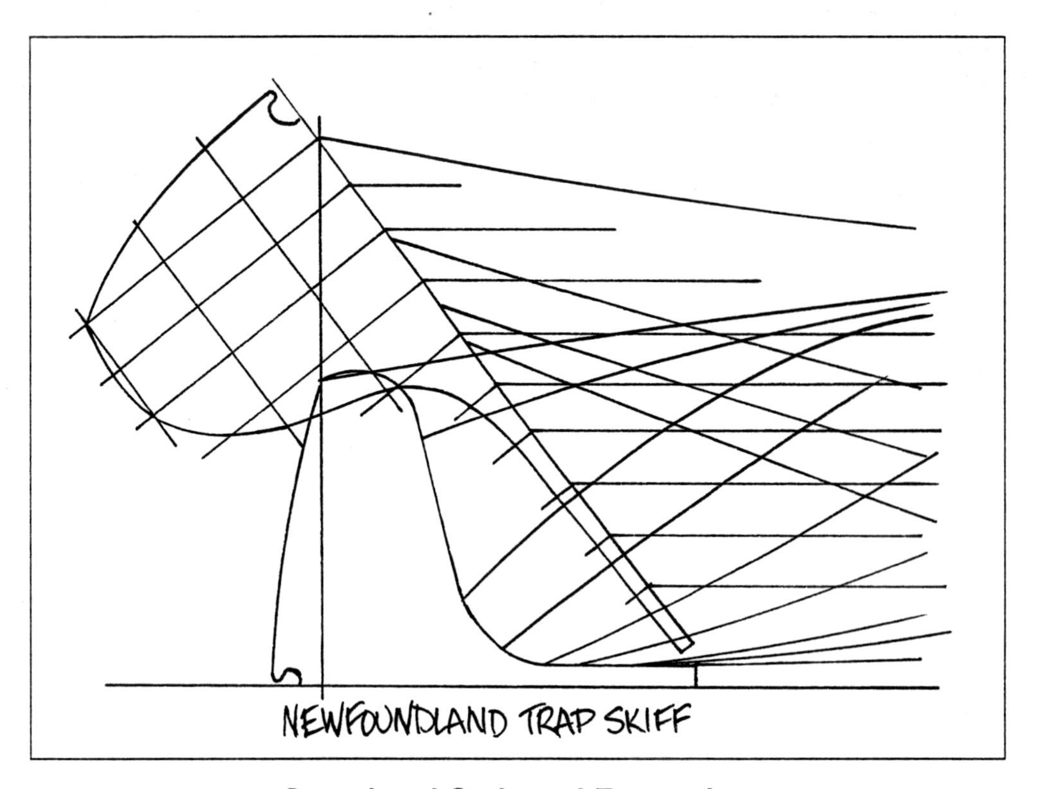

Completed Outboard Expansion

First, lay off the exact transom thickness on the profile view of the hull in the lofting. (See illustration on page 126.) Second, lay off the gridwork for the inboard expansion, including the sheer, waterlines, and base line, beginning in each instance where those lines from the profile plan intersect the inboard transom line just drawn. It is a little tedious, but not at all difficult. Buttocks aren't commonly included for the inboard expansions for small boats, but they are helpful when the waterlines alone bypass an important shape change. If you are doubtful, it would be better to include them, though remember to lay them out by measuring from the outboard transom face when you do. That, of course, makes them coincident with the outboard grid lines already in place. *The transom face from the profile lofting remains the expansion centerline, because inboard and outboard transom centerlines are necessarily in line with one another.* Buttock planes, being parallel to the hull centerline plane are unaffected by the rake of the transom, so heights are simply measured from the expansion baseline.

This part of the lofting requires concentration because you will have to work with profile, halfbreadth, and expansion plans simultaneously. It is worth your effort, as it will greatly increase your familiarity with the lofting as a whole while providing the necessary building information. With this additional gridwork in position, extend perpendicular lines from the intersection of profile waterlines and inboard transom profile to the same waterlines in the halfbreadth plan, and beyond to the centerline. You will find it helpful to work the expansion one line at a time. Trace the projected line, and pick off the distance between the halfbreadth centerline and the waterline curve. If that projection is from profile WL24, then the point that you are interested in is the intersection on halfbreadth WL24. Pick off the dimension and transfer it to that inboard expansion waterline–completing each in sequence (from sheer to base) greatly simplifies matters.

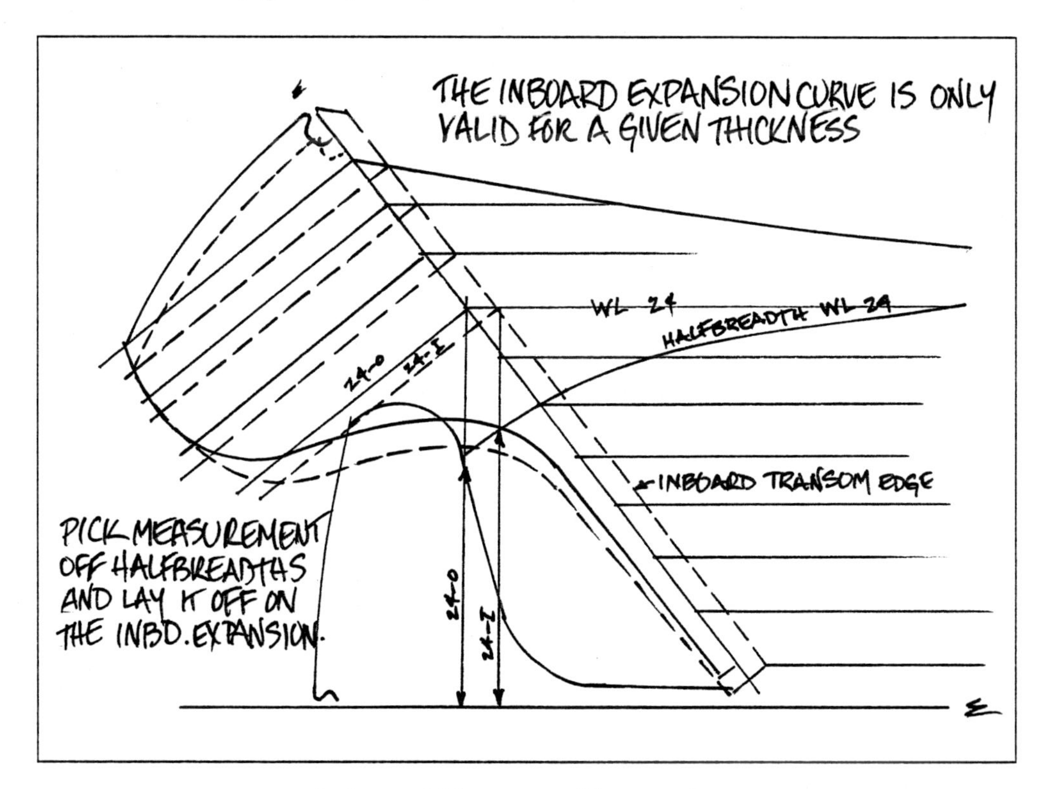

Inboard Transom Expansion

Halfbreadth measurements needed for this expansion come from the halfbreadth lofting, just as they do for the outboard expansion just completed. The dimensions are picked off the perpendicular dropped from the intersection of each waterline and the line denoting the inboard profile of the transom.

Expressed in another way, extending perpendiculars from one plan to the other (profile to halfbreadth) indicates precisely where the waterlines cross the inboard transom face. Since those are the halfbreadths sought, simply measure their distance from the halfbreadth plan centerline and transfer those measurements to the expansion waterlines of the transom. It's really no more difficult than that. Remember though, that the line denoting the profile of the transom is the expansion centerline for inboard as well as outboard.

If this seems incomprehensible, recall for a moment the basics of lines work. The stations are represented by lines that are perpendicular to the base line and cross the profile waterlines. They also cross the halfbreadth waterlines. On the lofting board, the halfbreadth at any station is measured from the centerline (coincident with the lofted base line), along that station to the intersection with the waterline curve in question. The location of the station is fixed by the boat's plan or by your model, but the important point is that it could be located anywhere along the centerline/base line and be treated similarly. (Using that information, you could add a station of your own to move a mould away from an interfering backbone member.)

In lines work, the primary difference between a station and a transom is that the transom is inclined and crosses the waterlines at some angle other than 90°. Should that really cause undue problems? Think about it. The rules don't change, and at this point you have already expanded the outboard transom face. Repeat the process. Forget the outboard expansion entirely for now. Using a different color pencil will help too.

Having explained this over and over again, I know that it is the slope of the transom faces coupled with the resulting network of expansion gridwork lines that causes the confusion. On occasion I have had to resort to four separate mylar pages, one each for profile, halfbreadths, outboard expansion, and inboard expansion. Overlaying them shows graphically how each segment relates to the complete expansion. You shouldn't have to resort to such extreme measures provided you take it a step at a time.

If all else fails to get through, just ask yourself how you would expand the outboard transom face if the hull was to be shortened by the thickness of the transom. The expansion of the inboard face doesn't amount to much more that. If you imagine the hull terminating at the inboard transom face, then the halfbreadth waterlines would have to terminate there and proceed at 90° to the centerline. As before, the halfbreadth is then measured along that perpendicular to the point of intersection. The sole difference is that you are using the body plan to pick off the halfbreadths for the outboard expansion, and the halfbreadth waterlines for the widths of the inboard expansion–that's why I earlier suggested picking halfbreadths off the halfbreadth view of the transom. I'll leave you to work out the details of that for yourself. What's life without a little challenge now and again?

If the waterlines involve the most concentration, then you ought to welcome the buttock measurements as a respite. Nothing is needed other than what is already right there on the lofting board. Look for the intersection of profile buttock line curves with the outboard profile of the transom. All you have to do is align your square with the expansion centerline and project those points across the face of the transom expansion. The points on the transom curve you are seeking are the intersections of the expansion buttock line and the projected intersection. Where profile BUT6 meets expansion BUT6 is a point on the edge of the outboard transom face. Carry that a step further, project from the intersection with the inboard transom profile, and you will also have a point on the expanded inboard transom profile.

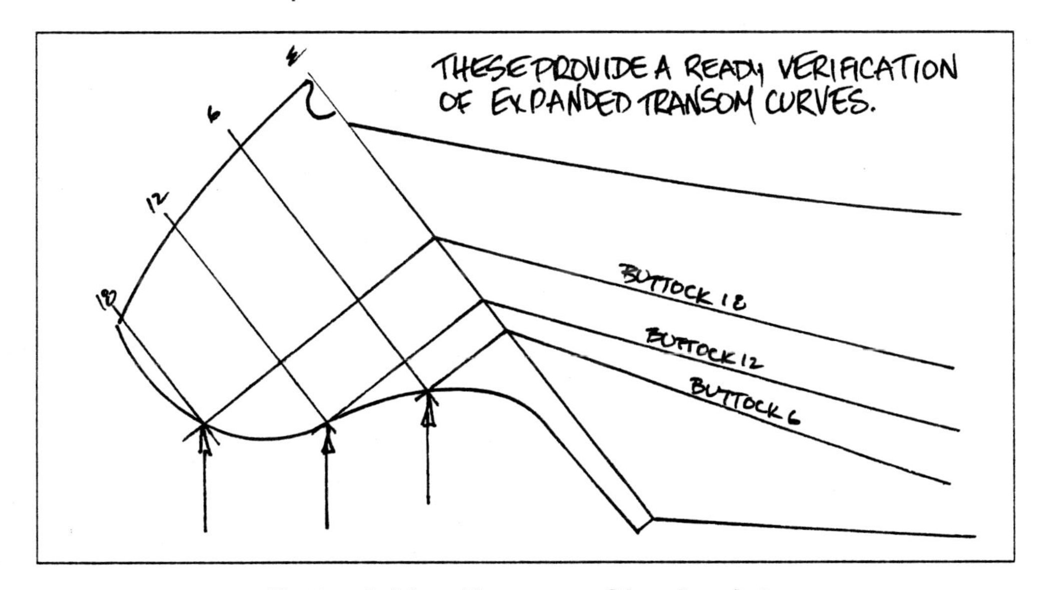

Buttock Line Transom Checkpoints

I did mention previously that it is a good idea to complete the lofting of the transom by fairing in the top edge right along with the inboard and outboard profiles. A second set of buttock figures verifies the configuration of the top and allows measurement of the whole transom at once, the top as well as the underside together. When you get to actually getting out the transom, be sure to allow additional height for the portion above the sheer even though it is already marked. Sawing it to its final dimension before planking is completed is asking for trouble. It is a great place to hang clamps, and tends to get banged up as a result. The extra wood is cheap insurance against damage during the building.

That completes the expansion measurements, but not the entire job. First, fair in the inboard and outboard profiles with a slender rectangular batten. The transom curves tend to be more extreme than elsewhere on the boat, so a hardwood batten, sometimes as slender as 1/8" x 1/2" works best. The hardwood will withstand the bend better than softwood of comparable size. In extreme cases, such as a Duck Trap Wherry, a bandsaw blade can be the best batten of all. It is capable of making the tightest bends, but must be positioned carefully in order to run in a fair curve from one point to the next because it is so flexible.

MAKING USE OF THE EXPANSION

Lofting, of course, is a means to an end, and though actually beyond the scope of this book, a useful adjunct to this discussion would be how to make use of the information just lofted. The object of all this work is to be able to lay out and cut the transom accurately. If this is a one-time operation, utilize all your expanded measurements directly. Tabulate and transfer them to the transom stock, or use a storey pole and transfer them without having to measure and write down each one.

Some builders prefer to continue working from that table of measurements. I'm an inveterate maker of patterns, having become one out of necessity. Making patterns requires additional time for the first boat, but when more than one boat of a type is to be built, they save a considerable amount of remeasuring thereafter. I prefer, too, to make one pattern that incorporates both inboard and outboard measurements so that even realignment is unnecessary after the first time.

The pattern material I like best is Masonite™ hardboard, tempered both sides. The 1/8" thickness is sufficient for all but the largest patterns, none of which I encounter in my work. A less expensive, untempered variety is available, but its softer surface is difficult to write on with a pencil, and it doesn't wear well. It's not unreasonable to expect a pattern made of good stuff to last for as long as you will need it.

A short batten will function well as a storey pole and save you considerable measuring and remeasuring. A square batten provides four writing surfaces before the marks have to be planed away. Hold it in the desired location and tick off the dimensions. Carry that to the pattern stock, or to the transom stock if you disdain patterning, and transfer the ticked measurements.

The relative positions of the inboard and outboard waterlines are critical whether you are patterning or not. Both sets are already there at the outboard profile of the transom, from when you drew the expansion gridwork. Each inboard waterline emerges outboard at the transom face somewhat below their outboard counterparts.

The greater the rake of the transom, the greater the distance between them.

Align the short storey pole with the rake of the transom, and mark at sheer, base, and every waterline (both inboard and outboard) in between. Lay out the heights on the pattern stock, and square each across its face. Before returning to the lofting, be sure to identify every line to avoid certain confusion later.

It is best to transfer the measurements from one part of the expansion at a time and fair it in before going on to the next. One side of the storey pole or tick strip can accommodate all inboard measurements, another all those outboard. The first side has already been used for the expanded heights, and the remaining side will do for the top and bottom buttock measurements.

Fair in both sets of profile marks, and cut the pattern stock to the inboard profile curve and to the outboard above-sheer crown. A series of 1/8" holes bored along the outboard profile line will permit both to be marked at the same time. I usually place the holes at each outboard waterline with enough in between to reproduce the faired line accurately. You will still have to fair in the line again on the transom stock, but that's a small price to pay for the convenience afforded by the pattern.

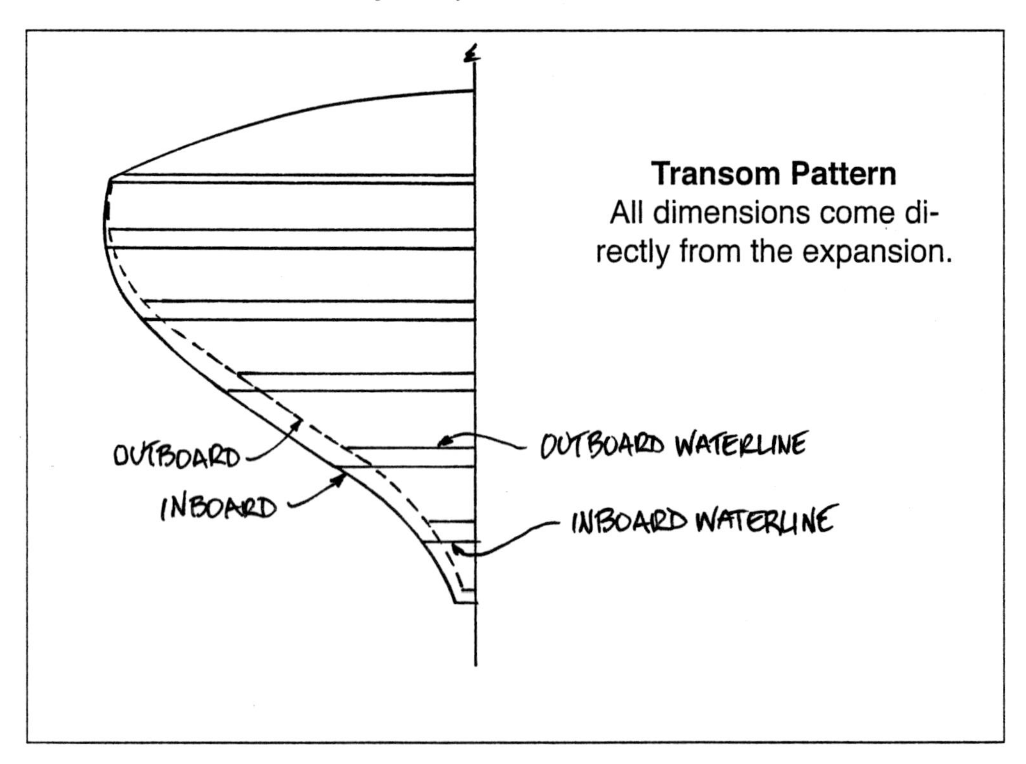

Transom Pattern
All dimensions come directly from the expansion.

Obviously, such a pattern is valid only for the particular transom thickness lofted. That is its one shortcoming. In response, you could use a pattern of the outboard transom face in conjunction with bevels taken at each waterline. Those bevels can be taken only from the halfbreadth plan (or cautiously from a half model), and they will be valid if subsequent transoms vary as much as an inch in thickness. Such an eventuality is not at all hypothetical if the first boat of a type built is to be a proper working boat and others are to be clipper versions. A house carpenter's 6" bevel will do the job, but it is awkward for close work. I much prefer my flat 3" brass bevel. Put the labeled bevels on a piece of stable scrap planking stock (known henceforth as a bevel board), and the angles will be there for future reference.

You will discover that the pattern/bevel system calls for careful measurement when laying out the transom for the final cuts. Those bevels were derived from the halfbreadth plan, so they are actually taken at each waterline. To check them when the transom is fastened to its knee, the bevel square must be held exactly along that waterline–what builders call a "level bevel". Any deviation above or below the actual waterline plane when you are getting out the transom, will result in a distortion of the bevel and with it the inboard shape.

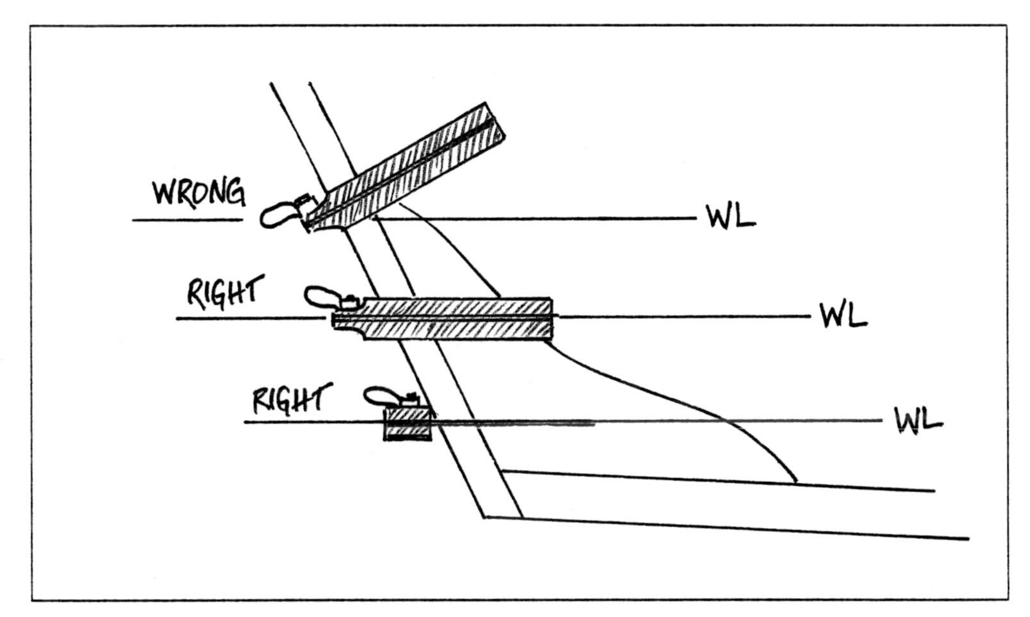

Level Bevel

I use the twofold pattern on the premise that with it the inboard and outboard shapes are accurate and properly aligned, so simply removing the wood between the lines traced inboard and out will automatically result in the proper bevel at all levels. You will find this approach particularly useful when the rake of the transom approaches 45° and there is a pronounced tuck. Wherry types such as the Lincolnville model, and particularly the Newfoundland Trap Skiff, require nearly 2" more wood inboard than out where the planking emerges from the hardest part of the tuck. That is a particularly difficult area to substantiate working with bevels alone.

You can't escape the fact that getting out a transom is a lot of work. It would require considerably fewer words if we could stand in front of a lofting board while the details were discussed. If you haven't grasped all of this after the first reading, take heart. I didn't catch on the first time through either, nor the second. Fortunately, you can expand a transom without a complete understanding of all details. As they say, "when all else fails, follow the directions".

LOFTING A RAKING CURVED TRANSOM

One last small point–not all transoms are flat. The ultimate test of your capabilities will come when you have to expand a transom that is curved as well as raked. Then, it must be expanded vertically (as we have just discussed) as well as horizontally. The horizontal expansion is accomplished by expanding the distance between the buttock lines. In fact, the surface of a curved transom can be visualized as a portion of a cylinder, and you would measure a shape drawn on the surface of a cylinder in the same way that you will on one of these transoms.

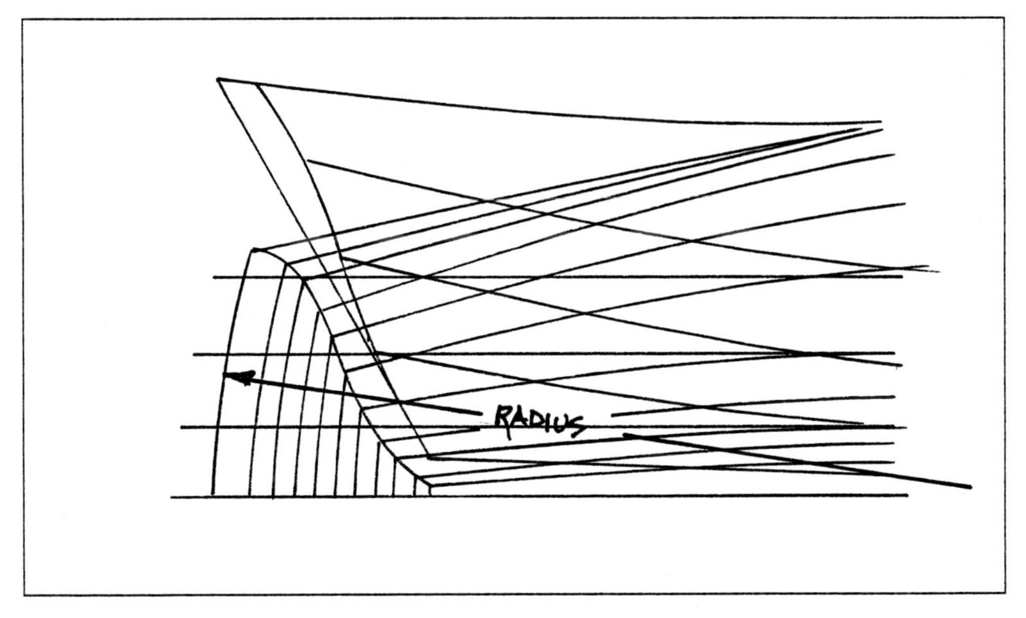

Raking Curved Transom

I learned by lofting the Friendship Sloop *Pemaquid*, with her raking elliptical transom. That's beyond the scope of small boat construction, but the principles are the same regardless of the size of the boat. Just as an aside, it's only fair to add that when I was asked to put a curved transom on a wherry, it was quite sufficient to cooper the individual members and assemble them in order to derive the curvature needed. Friendships, in contrast, are built like much larger craft with multi-layer transoms and planking bent athwartships over a substantial framework. That requires a three-part expansion: inboard and outboard transom faces plus framing. Since we are lofting small craft rather than large ones, I have simplified my explanation of the expansion. It is sufficient for lofting any small boat you are likely to encounter.

Regardless of the ultimate construction method used, the function of the expansion lofting is to lay the rounded surface out as a flat surface. Plans of these craft differ in that the transom is drawn to a specific radius, and that is noted on the plan. That radius is used to draw the halfbreadth waterlines across the surface of the transom. The secret to the expansion, however, is in the buttock lines. Bend a tick strip (here known as a radius rod) around the curve of the transom at sheer level in the halfbreadth lofting. Along it, tick off centerline, sheer, and every buttock line it crosses. (Note that I said at sheer level–not along the top curvature of the transom.) The tick strip picks up the distances between the expanded buttock lines, and between the expansion centerline and the sheer, which can be layed off on the expansion.

As I have explained before, when I encounter a lofting problem I invariably turn to a half model for the answer. In this case, a model provides a ready solution–one far less convoluted than any I have ever read. If you have a half model of the boat with the curved transom, you are halfway home; if not, it will pay to make one here and now, if only of the after half of the boat. A lift model is the easiest to use, but if you make a solid one, your first chore will be to incise the waterlines and buttock lines. Fine v-groove knife cuts will work fine for our purposes.

Since the centerline profile of a raking curved transom is straight, it only curves in one direction and so can be overlaid with a piece of paper. Make a rubbing to pick up the outline as well as the buttock and waterlines. Expanded–in other words, removed from the model and layed flat–you will see that the expanded waterlines are curved. Overlay the lines drawing with your rubbing, and prick through with a sharp point to transfer the shapes and gridwork locations.

The precise curvature of those expansion waterlines has always been a sticking point. Interestingly enough, after repeated experimentation, it appears that the actual initial curvature of those expanded waterlines is a function of the original transom radius and its rake. For purposes of explanation, if the original transom radius happened to be 6'-0", and its profile is raked 1'-6-

1/2" from top to bottom (as measured between perpendiculars on the base line), the radius of the sheer expansion waterline is 7'-6-1/2", the combination of the two. And knowing that, the expanded waterlines could be layed out without using a half model at all. The important point is that a half model (actually several) provided a straightforward answer to a sizable problem.

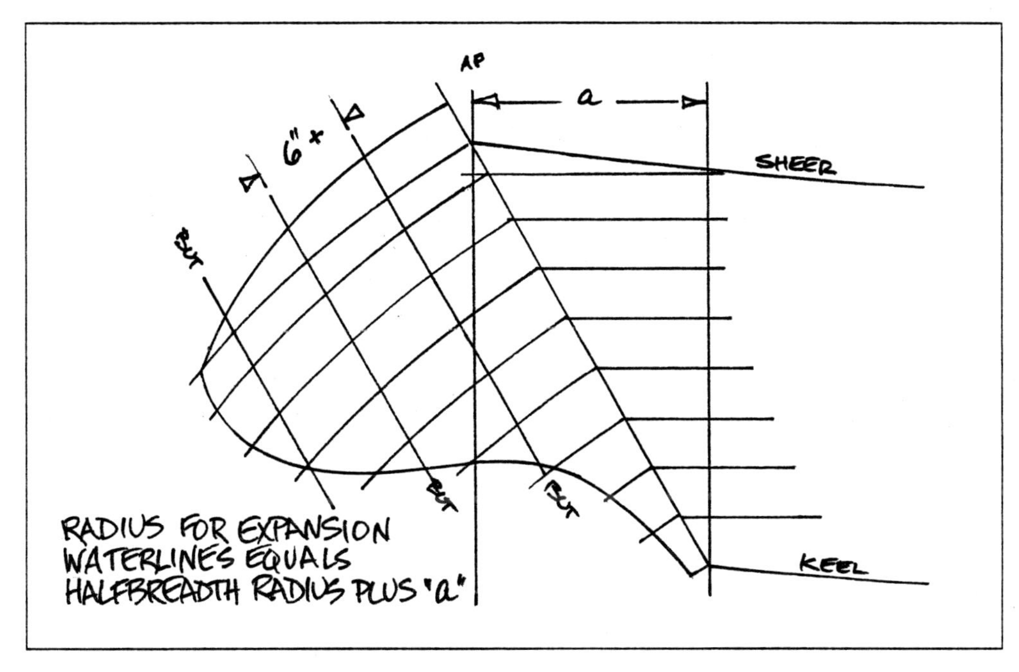

Expanding a Curved Transom

The halfbreadths have to be layed off along those curves. The point of origin for the arcs is on an extension of the expansion centerline, and because the curves are concentric, the point of origin is the same for all. As we have already discussed, use a tick strip to pick dimensions from the halfbreadth waterlines on the surface of the transom, and transfer them to the expansion. To do that, of course, it will have to be bent to the shape of the curved waterlines in both places.

The buttock line checkpoints still work with a raking curved transom as they do with a raking flat transom. Find where the profile buttock line curves cross the profile edge of the transom, and expand those points outward. The projected line crosses its mate in the expansion gridwork at a point on the expanded outline.

There are other approaches, all of them considerably more involved. It took me a while to understand the process, working my way through the traditional explanations, even with Merrill's help. In point of fact, back then I used it so seldom for lofting small craft that even after I did master it, I needed a refresher each time I needed it again. I can't state unequivocally that the half model approach I have just explained will work every time–but I can say that it worked unerringly every time I tried it. The only part that might be subject to conjecture would be the radius of the expanded waterlines, but if there is any discrepancy, I was unable to discern any. To coin a phrase, "it works for me". After reading this far, it shouldn't really surprise you that the half models that have provided boatbuilders with answers for centuries continue to serve their time-honored function.

ADDING CONSTRUCTION DETAILS

At this stage, you have completed the lofting of the lines. If you consult your plans, however, you will likely notice some rather specific construction details. The designer has gone to the extra effort of including them to detail the scantlings, show you how parts of the hull relate to one another, and also to help you past difficult areas. Whatever the reason for their inclusion, you can be assured that they weren't put there solely to spruce up the plan.

This is where your lofting really begins to point you toward the construction. You can apply the line data on the board, and add any number of construction details to help you through the initial stages of setup and construction. One example would be getting out the moulds, another would be getting out the stem, and still another would tell you about backbone fastenings. There are a good many more examples, but nearly all of them relate to getting out the backbone and setting up.

In order to get out the moulds, you need to know the configuration of the keel and/or keelson. In position for planking, the moulds sit on the inboard surface of the keel structure. To build them so that they sit at the right height, you have to know the thickness and the width of the keel and how the rabbet, inner rabbet, and bearding line relate to the inboard surface. If you lofted the body plan as per our discussion, then you already have that information in hand; if not, now is the time to "construct" those keel sections on the lofting board. The new lines will be added to the lofted sections of the body plan.

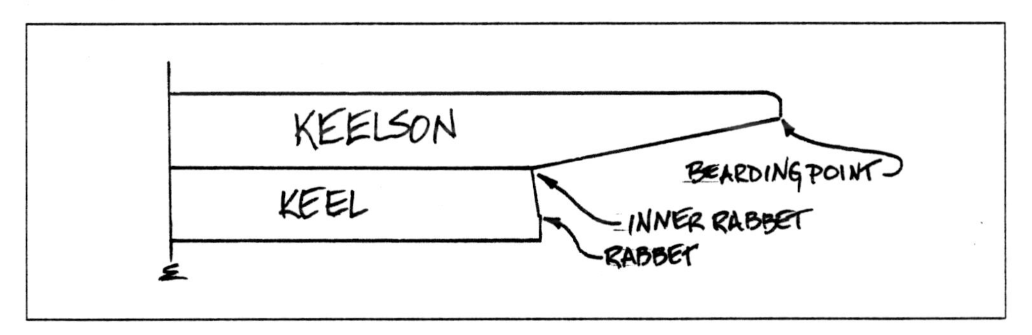

Plank Keel Cross Section

Once the keel sections are completed, the heights above base can be transferred to the profile and the keel members drawn in full size. In the profile, a plank keel would only show as a pair of lines, parallel to one another, with some degree of rocker fore and aft. In the halfbreadth view, it shows as a shallow arch, much like a fine waterline curve. In fact, I usually draw in both the inboard and outboard edges in that view. A simple vertical keel would also show as a pair of parallel lines, perhaps 3" apart, nearly straight overall. A more complicated vertical keel might be straight, but deeper aft, and with a keelson on top to provide solid backing for the garboard planks. All can be added to the lofting so that you can pick off measurements or make patterns, as you wish. Information that isn't already on the lofting can be taken from the construction details or notes of the plan.

Getting out other backbone members also involves knowing their size, shape, and relationships to one another. Add in all of the members individually: the stem and stem knee, apron or cutwater, transom knee or sternpost–even the bedlogs of the centerboard case. All can be drawn to size beforehand to help you grasp the construction of your boat more fully, and to help you purchase the stock that is actually needed for the job. Some of these members aren't as readily picked off as others, and you may have to be a bit resourceful to duplicate the curved surfaces as shown. Those curves by the way, are structural, not simply aesthetic.

One of the niftiest tricks is laying out the backbone fastenings before you even have the backbone made. The bronze carriage bolts often specified don't come cheap, and no one wants to buy more than is needed. Consult the plan for the intended arrangement of the bolts, paying close attention to the angles at which they are installed (a bevel is handy for that). Lay them out on the lofted backbone members, and you will have their exact lengths for each application. Most carriage bolts, regardless of material, have about 1" of cut thread, though you can thread them back further on your own. Knowing that backbone members eventually shrink and that someone is bound to overtighten the bolts sometime in the future, leave them with at least 1/2" of thread inside the wood, with about the same amount protruding above. After the pieces are made, they can be placed on the lofting, and the run of the bolts transferred to them directly.

More than a few new builders have been shocked to see a

centerboard case passing right through one of their stations. Some plans call for at least installing the bedlogs before the planking begins. I don't work that way, myself, but if faced with that problem I would loft my way out of trouble. Whether you were going to install just the bedlogs or the entire case, you could add the cross section to the body plan. Then you are faced with a choice: notch the mould to fit over the case, or move it to avoid it altogether. The first should be self-explanatory; the second takes a little concentration.

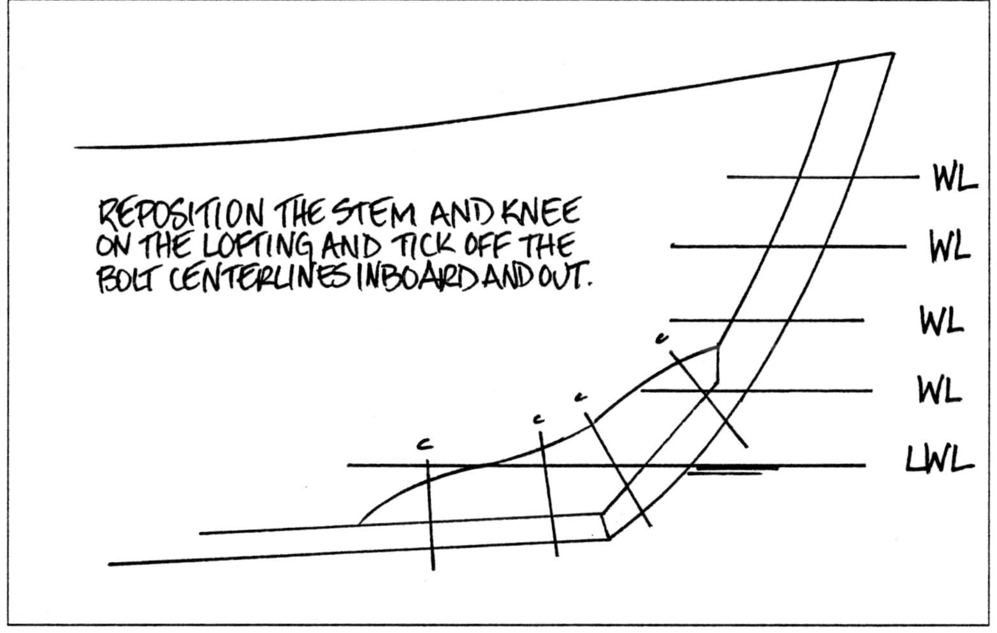

Bolt Layout on a Lofting

First, loft the centerboard case as it will appear in the profile view. It doesn't have to be a work of art, just draw the outline. Using a two-foot square, shift whichever mould has to be moved the least, to a spot immediately adjacent to the case. The vertical line drawn at the new mould position cuts through waterline and buttock curves as well as keel and sheer. Realizing that, all you have to do is pick off the heights and halfbreadths and fair in the mould you have created on the body plan gridwork. You can use the same steps to move a mould clear of any troublesome obstacle. You can also use it to predict the shape of a bulkhead or any other transverse hull member.

Another example would be the location of the stopwaters. For those unfamiliar with the term, these are pieces whose function matches their name–they stop the entry of water via capillary action through backbone joints. They pass through the backbone, athwartships, and one is needed wherever a joint crosses the planking rabbet. Stopwaters are installed by placing the pilot of a 1/2" auger bit on the intersection of the joint and the rabbet, and drilling straight through. The hole is filled with a softwood dowel that is trimmed off flush. After the planking is installed, only a semicircular end will show outboard. Key to our discussion here, however, is that their locations are evident on the lofting, and should be picked off right along with the other pertinent construction details.

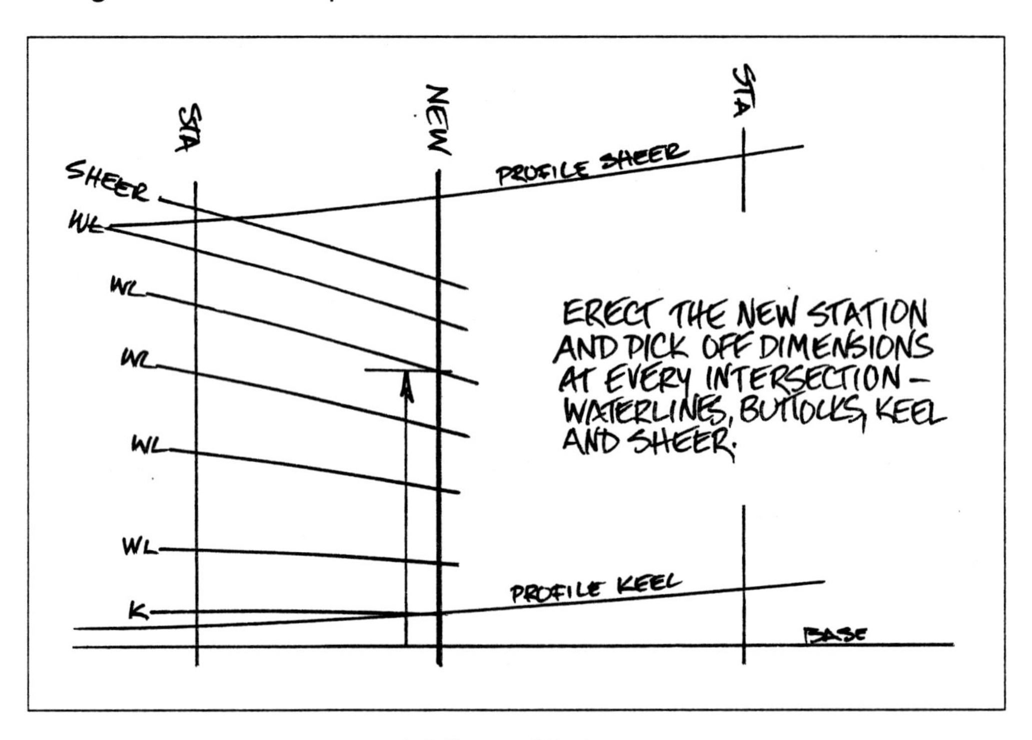

Adding a Station

The possibilities are numerous, and as your familiarity with lofting increases, you will find yourself using it more and more. When a detail doesn't make sense, or you don't know what angle to drill for a bedlog bolt, or how long it needs to be, the lofting is there with the answers. You just have to know where to look. You can add any detail you need, right down to the planking layout at the midship station. What could be handier?

GLOSSARY

Aft Hook The sternmost station of the three used in whole moulding as practiced in parts of Newfoundland. Its configuration derives from a half model and is transferred with rising squares.

AP The abbreviation for after perpendicular; in the profile view, it passes through the intersection of the sheer and transom.

Apron A part of the backbone fitted to the inside of the stem, that spans and reinforces the stem/knee joint.

Back Rabbet The side of the rabbet mortise that is bounded by the bearding line and the inner rabbet line, and provides the bearing surface into which the garboard is fastened.

Backbone Analogous to the same skeletal structure in animals, working your way aft in a small boat it consists of stem, knee, apron (if any), keel structure, transom knee and transom.

Bald-headed A colloquial term for a schooner rigged without topmasts.

Baseline The primary horizontal line of the plan and lofting gridwork from which all heights above base are measured. On a lofting board it serves double duty as the centerline of the halfbreadth view.

Basswood The wood from a linden tree, soft and light yellow in color, particularly well suited to carving half models.

Beam Compass A wing compass consists of two legs joined at one end, like an inverted V, and the size of the arcs it is capable of drawing is limited by the span of the legs. A beam type consists of two points affixed to a batten. Useful for scribing arcs of larger radius because the batten can be of any length.

Bearding Line The line tracing the juncture of the inside of the planking and the backbone. On a stem viewed in profile, the innermost of the lines that limits the inboard extent of the stem rabbet mortise.

Bedlogs The base of a centerboard or daggerboard case to which the top of the case is fastened, and through which the whole case is secured to the keel.

Bevel Board Any piece of flat stock on which angles are recorded for use in construction. Used primarily for keel and transom bevels, though on larger carvel plank boats, they are used to record plank edge bevels as well.

Body Plan The collective end views of the hull in which the forward stations and stem are shown to the right of the centerline and the after stations and transom are on the left.

Boottop On a boat, a strip of antifouling paint several inches wide and immediately above the load waterine. On a solid half model it is usually portrayed by an insert of contrasting wood.

BUT Abbreviation for buttock found in the heights above base section of the table of offsets, in the company of numbers indicating their location–BUT6 is 6" out from the centerline, for example.

Buttock Lines Traces of the periphery of the hull along planking and transom face at given intervals out from the hull centerline.

CAD Program Computer software designed to fair in curves from plotted points, calculate sectional areas and volumes, and send the information to a plotter. There are many different ones ranging in price from several hundred to several thousand dollars.

Carriage Bolts Fastenings typically used to assemble the backbone members of small craft, with a moderately domed head and short square portion to the body immediately under the head to prevent it from turning in the wood while being installed or removed. Commonly available in 1/4, 5/16, 3/8, and 1/2", in lengths to 8", in silicon bronze, stainless steel, or galvanized steel.

Celotex™ A soft and fibrous sheet material, similar in composition to acoustical ceiling tiles and available in 4 x 8' sheets.

Centerboard Case Essentially a watertight box extending from the keel to above the waterline inboard that allows a board to be lowered through the keel and into the water, thereby increasing the boat's hold on the water while sailing.

Crank A colloquialism that means about the same thing when applied to boats as it does when applied to humans. Not a term of endearment.

Cross Battens Short pieces of wood measuring about 1/4" thick x 3/4" wide x 8-10" long, with an offset point on one end. Useful for building station templates when taking the lines off a small boat. Also called pointers.

Cutwater A hull member whose function is implied by its name. Steam bent or laminated and attached to the leading surface of the stem, it shrouds the bitter ends of the planking yet renders the rabbet accessible for future repairs. Typically found on dories, wherries, and most lapstrake canoes.

Deadrise Generally used in subjective context, as is "a wherry has more deadrise than a double ender"; it is actually a measure of the amount of angle between the baseline (or baseline plane) and the station curves, and is readily apparent in the body plan. Essential to a discussion of stability.

Deck Lift The uppermost piece of a lift style half hull model.

DIA Abbreviation for diagonal, usually accompanied by a letter or number for definition.

Diagonal A trace of the water level along the surface of the planking at a given attitude of heel. When present on the plan of a small boat, there are usually three of them, radiating out from the body plan centerline. Offsets for them are measured along the diagonals and so are neither heights nor halfbreadths.

Dory An old workboat type with a flat, rockered bottom panel, and flaired straight sides (usually),favored by trawl fishermen because they were very seaworthy when loaded, nestable, and cheap. In parts of New England, the term is applied to about anything that floats. One chandler's catalogue actually advertized a model of a "Peapod Dory", whatever that is.

Drafting Film The ultimate sheet material for drafting and lofting, due to its dimensional stability. Made of polyester, .002"-.006" thick, it is available in sheets or rolls in widths up to 42". Dupont manufactures one with the tradename Mylar™, and others are made by Dietzgen™, Koh-I-Noor™, and K&E™.

Duck Trap Wherry A 16' clipper version of the much larger Newfoundland Trap Skiff, intended for tandem rowing. Designed by W.J. Simmons in 1984. recently adapted to glued lapstrake construction.

Expansion The mechanical process by which lines are reworked to provide a true view of a hull part as it would appear if flattened. Determining the shapes of transoms and the actual length of and station positions on a rockered plank keel are just two examples.

Expansion Coefficient A decimal by which a dimension of a piece can be multiplied to determine to what extent it will shrink or swell, once the temperature is factored in to the equation.

Fair Curve A line that is not straight and exhibits a smooth run from one point to another. An unobstructed phone wire between poles is a simple fair curve; compound curves can also be fair, and neither can include any flat or hard spots.

Fairing Batten For typical small pulling boats such as Wherries and Double Enders, these are 2-3' longer than the overall length of the boat and measure approximately 1/2" x 1". Their function is to help the loftsman draw the long curves of the profile and halfbreadth views.

Ferrule A metal ring or cap that is designed to fit over the end of a wooden handle to prevent it from splitting. Some, like the ones on jointed double canoe paddles, also form a socket to receive another piece.

Firmer Chisel In general, a chisel with the blade beveled on one side only, the back remaining flat–as opposed to a paring chisel which is beveled on both sides. They are 10-12" long, and have a wooden handle which fits into a conical socket at the top of the blade. My Stanley™ Series 120 is a good example.

Floors In boatbuilding, the transverse pieces that fasten to the keel and support the lower planking between the ribs. Mention of "flat floors" is a comment on the degree of deadrise, as well as on their configuration.

Fore Hook The furthest forward of the threestations of a whole moulding process used in parts of Newfoundland.

Forefoot As used in this text, the juncture of stem and keel. Generally, the part of a hull in that immediate area.

FP Abbreviation for the forward perpendicular on the plans and lofting which commonly passes through the intersection of sheer and stem rabbet.

Frames Transverse hull members that support the planking from keel to sheer. Often used interchangeably with "ribs", the connotation of "frame" is a heavier timber, often sawed to shape, while "rib" connotes a lighter piece of hardwood that is steam bent into position.

Friendship Sloop A pretty little single masted gaff rigged sailing vessel with a clipper bow and raking elliptical transom. Has also been defined as "a sloop built in Friendship (Maine) by Wilbur Morse".

Garboard The lowest plank on a hull; the one that fastens to the keel.

Gridwork A lines system consisting of hori zontals, verticals, and diagonals that allows the loftsman to plot the location of points provided by the table of offsets.

Halfbreadth Years ago, dimensions were of length and breadth--today it's length and width. In boatbuilding, the original terminology stuck, and though archaic, it just means one-half the width. The "halfbreadths" are offset measurements layed out on the stations.

Halfbreadth Lofting The full-size portrayal of half the hull as seen from directly overhead. This is the view that shows the curves of the waterlines.

HB Abbreviation for halfbreadth. In the table of offsets, found with a number specifying its distance from the hull centerline–BUT12, being located parallel to and 12" away.

Half Siding Siding is the thickness of a backbone member. Half that dimension appears in plans and lofting because only half of the boat is being considered.

Heeling The athwartship inclination of a boat.

Homosote™ A pressed paper product, manufactured from recycled paper, that is available in 1/2" x4'x 8' sheets. Suitable for lofting boards because it is largely unaffected by dampness.

Hood Ends The forward ends of individual planks.

Inner Rabbet The point or line at which the planking buries deepest into the stem or keel rabbet mortise. The middle of the three lines that describe the rabbet, with the rabbet line outside and the bearding line inside.

Inwales Inboard fore and aft hull members running along the sheer and fastened to the ribs, terminating forward at the breasthook and aft at the quarterknees.

Keel Lift The bottom piece of a lift style half model.

Keel Rocker Upward curvature of the ends of the keel as seen from the side. It serves to raise the forefoot closer to the surface of the water for maneuverability.

Level Bevel The only accurate bevels of the transom edge once it becomes part of the backbone. In measuring, the bevel square must align with the run of the waterline, which is parallel to the floor and hence level.

Lift Model A half hull model consisting of horizontal pieces corresponding in thickness to waterline spacing, made so that it can be disassembled for tracing and measuring.

Lines The schematic of a hull drawn to scale and consisting of three views and the offsets needed to duplicate or loft them.

Load Waterline The level at which the boat is designed to float in the water--sometimes called the design waterline (DWL).

LWL Abbreviation for load waterline.

Midship Bend The central of the three stations used in a whole moulding process as practiced in Gander, Newfoundland.

Midship Station Properly amidships station, the widest of the stations located in the middle of the boat. It would be #3 in a boat with five stations, and #4 in a boat with seven stations.

Moulds Full size cross sectional building templates around which the hull planking is bent during installation. Their shapes are picked off the station curves of the body plan lofting.

Mylar™ A Dupont tradename that I tend to use generically for all drafting films, not just theirs.

Newfoundland Trap Skiff The largest of the wherries, readily identified by their pronounced sheer, fine lines, and champagne glass shaped transom. A "trap" in Newfoundland is a box-like cod fishing net, and this has always been their name for the fishing boats they use to tend them. A superb rough water boat and sailer as might be expected.

Nova Scotia Dimples Hammer marks; a holdover reference to the often rough construction of fishing dories of years ago. I understand that in Nove Scotia they are called "Newfie Dimples".

Plank Keel Properly a single-member keel set horizontaly. In a wherry, it would measure approximately 1-1/4" thick and could be as much as 12" wide. Advantageous because they allow their boats to stand upright when beached.

Point of Entry An area, actually, where the submerged waterlines converge on the stem. A fine-lined craft would have a rather sharp point of entry while a more burdensome craft would not.

Profile The side view of the lines of a boat that includes not only the profile itself, and the long buttock line curves, but the transom expansion as well.

Profile Sheer The view from the side of a line describing the top edge of the top plank, running from stem to transom.

Pumpkin Pine A particular type of Maine white pine that is noted for its quality and pleasing mellow color that develops as it ages. The full-grown trees are monsters, often more than 3' in diameter and limbing out 30' and more above the ground.

Rabbet A two-fold term meaning either a point or line at which the outside of the planking meets the backbone, or the right-angle mortise into which the planking seats when fitted to stem and keel.

Radius Rod A batten used to pick measurements off the waterlines of a transom with a curved face by bending it to conform to the halfbreadth waterlines, ticking off the distance from centerline to profile, and then transferring them to the transom expansion in the profile lofting.

Rake Of a transom, or mast, refers to the inclination of that member out of plumb. It usually is expressed in inches per foot rather than in degrees.

Rising Square One of a pair of curved measuring devices used in duplicating the station curves during whole moulding a hull.

Rocker The upward curvature of the bottom of a boat or keel as seen in profile.

Rodney Somewhat like a Trap Skiff, though smaller, they are used by fishermen in the Conception Bay area (Newfoundland) as tenders. The story goes that Rodney was the name of one of the early crown fisheries commissioners, and his name has since been applied to anything of limited usefulness.

Rolling Bevel Refers usually to the bevel within a stem or keel rabbet, or along the edge of a plank keel, that changes from one location to the next. On a wherry keel, for example, the bevel is nearly vertical at the forefoot, about 15°amidships, and again vertical at the transom.

Run Refers to the flow of the planking below the turn of the bilge from the midship station to the transom.

Sawn Timbers The transverse framing of large wooden vessels where individual members are sawn to shape and fastened together in layers to form the required curvature at each location from keel to sheer. Analogous to the steam bent ribs of small craft.

Scale Rule A measuring device graduated to allow direct reading of miniaturized lines plans of a vessel. The architect's type is used for boatbuilding applications, with divisions from 3/32"=1' to 3"=1'.

Scantlings A collective term referring to the dimensions of individual hull members such as the ribs and rails.

Scarph Joints A common boatbuilding joint consisting of complementary bevels on two pieces of the same size, used to produce a longer piece. For a 1/2" thick batten, for example, a scarph could be as long as 12". Also used for lengthening rails and hull planks.

Schooner A sailing vessel with two or more masts and a fore and aft gaff rig (as opposed to a square rig where the yardarms are perpendicular to the hull's centerline).

Sheer Line The line that traces the top edge of the uppermost hull plank, whether seen from the side (profile), above (halfbreadth), or the end (body plan).

Ship's Curves An old style set of graduated curves of varying characteristics used by designers to draw lines on a plan. My set includes 15 pieces made of mahogany. Supplanted by French curves, and lately by flexible plastic battens that are adjustable to hold nearly any curve.

Siding Refers to the thickness of a backbone member. A stem with a cross section of 1-1/2"x 3" is said to be sided 1-1/2" and moulded 3".

Sir Marks The index marks on the rising squares used in whole moulding.

Skeg A roughly triangular shaped part of a boat at the after end of the keel that forms a fin to aid in tracking. A built down skeg is a piece of solid wood fastened to the outside of the keel. With a planked down skeg (as in a Wherry or New Jersey Beach Skiff), the triangle is within and enclosed by the hull planking.

Solid Model A half hull model carved from a single block, whether natural or laminated.

Station Form By strict definition this could be a mould; but when taking off lines refers to one of several L-shaped pieces used to hold the cross battens that document the shape of the boat at the stations.

Stations Transverse sections of a hull that are depicted in the body plan and are the line equivalent of the moulds. Also the locations of those sections.

Sternpost In small craft, the vertical backbone member that supports the transom, usually extending from keel to sheer; or as in some yacht tenders, from keel to sheer enclosing the after end of the skeg as well as supporting the transom.

Storey Pole A batten used to record measurements for future reference at another location. An elongated tick strip.

Surform™ Tools An innovative type of rasp made by the Stanley Tool Company. The cutting surface is a perforated metal sheet with the protruding edges of each hole sharpened for one-directional cutting. Once known as "cheese graters" by builders, they are available in several shapes and sizes.

Tick Strip A slender batten on which measurements are recorded for transferal to another part of the lofting.

Trammel Points These are movable metal fixtures that can be attached to a batten (1/4" x 1", commonly) thereby creating a beam compass with a radius limited only by the length of the batten available.

Transom The member that forms the flat, trailing end of a boat, as opposed to the pointy end.

Tuck The concavity of a boat below the turn of the bilge between the midship station and the transom. May be rounded or angular.

Tumblehome A flared section of boat planking leans outboard; a straight section is vertical; and where there is tumblehome, the planks turn inboard. From astern, the sheer plank appears to be tumbling toward the centerline.

Turning Turtle Synonymous with capsize, likely deriving from the look of a hull upsidedown in the water.

Vertical Keel A primary backbone member that in place has greater vertical height than width. Typical of Double Enders, Peapods, and Whitehalls.

Water Level A liquid filled tube that works on the principle that water seeks its own level, i.e., will be of precisely the same height at both ends of the tube, even though run over uneven ground or around the corner of a building.

Waterline Any of a number of horizontal levels on a boat's profile. Seen as straight lines in the profile and body plan views, and as long curves in the halfbreadth view.

Wear Shoe Sacrificial hull members fastened to the outside of a plank keel so that they enclose the lower edge of the trimmed garboards and cover the keel/garboard joint. Made of hardwood for durability, especially beech.

Whole Moulding An older process for transferring the lines from a builder's half model to a pattern or directly to a piece of stock from which a timber is to be cut. The transfer is accomplished with a pair of rising squares. Predates our lofting system, and still very much in use in Newfoundland.

WL Abbreviation for waterline, used in conjuntion with a number denoting its height in inches above the baseline. WL9=9" above the base.

INDEX

Table of Contents from Wherries

Books and CDs from Walter Simmons and Duck Trap Press...

Lapstrake Boatbuilding covers the basics of lapstrake construction from stock selection to steaming and planking. Written because there was no other comprehensive source of information about American lapstrake practice. This book is used in boat schools across the country.

Lapstrake Boatbuilding, Volume 2 delves deeper into lapstrake construction and attendant operations. Centerboard cases, spars, oars, pouring lead, and even some patternmaking are all covered along with tricks of the trade.

Building the 9'-7" Maine Skiff is step-by-step boatbuilding from the plans to the finishing. It is arranged in 40 individual lessons requiring about an hour apiece. Full size 1-1/2" plans are included, in your choice of Maine Skiff, Lobsterman's Skiff, or the Dory Skiff.

Building *Sunshine* is another step-by-step book, detailing the construction of our most popular yacht tender. These boats row and tow beautifully and are in use around the world. Lofting, setup, the backbone, planking, joinerwork, and even making the oars are all covered.

Building Lapstrake Canoes...lovely boats with the maneuverability of a kayak and the stability of a double ender. These are the easiest to build of all lapstrake boats. They are fast, dry, light, and able. A traditionally built 15-footer weighs 56 pounds. Includes a 25% off coupon for any of our canoe plans.

Finishing discusses the finishes to use (and a few to avoid), how to prepare for them, how to apply them, and how to maintain them. Here are the tricks of the trade along with the tools you'll need for painting, oiling, varnishing, and even gold leafing.

Lines, Lofting, & Half Models Called a "must have" addition to every boatbuilding library by reviewers, this is the only lofting book you will ever need. Lines work begins with half models, and so does this book. From half model basics to the easiest way to loft a raking curved transom you will ever read.

Pigeons & Gudgeons Here is a reference that every boatbuilder and armchair sailor should have close at hand. Don't even try looking in a dictionary for "apple bow", "bevel board," blacksmith weld," dumb iron," "gone democratic," or "gin poles," —they aren't there, they're here. Chock full of boatbuilding information, not just terms, but shop tips and rules of thumb to make your life in the shop easier.

Repairs Experience is a great teacher, and this book is the product of 30 years of building and repairing wooden boats. Here's a way to avail yourself of lessons learned without having to learn them the hard (and expensive) way. Chapters include: Things You Need to Know (clamping, steaming,...), Backbone & Framing, Planking (lapstrake, carvel, strip), Inboard Joinerwork, and Finishing Up.

Glued Lap Construction began as a supplement to our Duck Trap Wherry plans and turned out to have wider applications because the information is applicable to other traditional small craft as well. The explanations are concise but specific, and there are large illustrations on every other page.

Basic Decoy Carving So what do you do with all those too-good-to-throw-away boatbuilding leftovers? We turn them into decoys. Here's how it's done. Carving is a great way to keep your hand in between boatbuilding projects.

Wherries Duck Trap was the center of the Atlantic Salmon fishery, and we've been gathering information on the salmon wherries and their builders for nearly four decades. Not only historical information, but carried through to today, it discusses the wherries we're still building. Lots of photos, most in full color.

The Rhodes Wherry With a digital camera close at hand while we built the first Rhodes Wherry in Duck Trap in 106 years, she was thoroughly photographed from making her moulds to rigging her lug sail. Originally a salmon fishing boat, she makes a superb yacht tender. CD and printed versions.

The Littlest Boats details the construction of the Littlest Wherry (cradle), the Littlest Yacht Tender (coffee table) an the Skiff Youth Bed. Sound information and plenty of photos straight from our shop to yours. Also good to have close by if you're building any sort of skiff, because this youth bed goes together just like her floating kin. CD and printed versions.

The Newfoundland Trap Skiff, is our largest wherry. 143 pages with 185 photos, following the construction from setting up the moulds all the way through rigging the sprit/ketch rig and selecting a boat trailer. The planking chapter alone runs more than 40 pages...in a word, it's invaluable. CD and printed versions.

The Duck Trap Wherry sparked the renewal of interest in wherries with her beautiful traditional lines and shapely transom–with good reason. She's an eye catcher. The frosting on the cake is that she's actually the easiest to build of all our wherries, and the way she handles on the water is simply amazing. Her construction is fully documented in 180 pages and 260 photos. CD and printed versions.

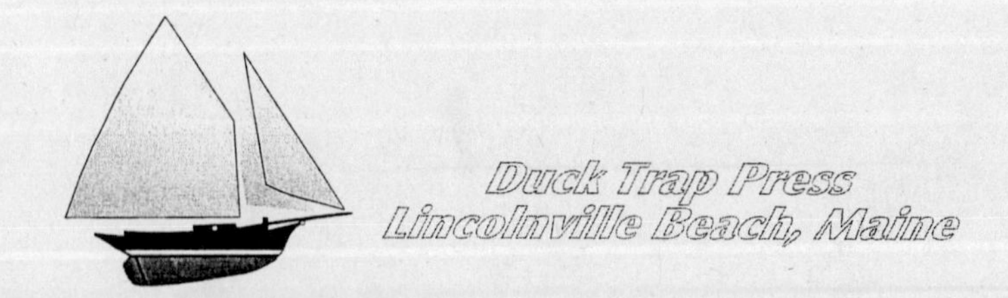

You can read all about these titles by visiting our website at
www.duck-trap.com

Should you have questions, we can be reached at
207-789-5363